FAMILY MEDIATION: COOPERATIVE DIVORCE SETTLEMENT

FAMILY MEDIATION

Cooperative Divorce Settlement

JOAN BLADES

Mediation Center, Walnut Creek, California
Families in Transition, San Francisco

Prentice-Hall, Inc., Englewood Cliffs, New Jersey 07632

Library of Congress Cataloging in Publication Data
BLADES, JOAN.
Family mediation.
Includes index.
1.-Divorce mediation—United States. I.-Title.
KF535.B55-1985 346.7301'66 84-6262
ISBN 0-13-302431-8 347.306166

Editorial/production supervision: Joyce Turner
Cover design: Wanda Lubelska
Manufacturing buyer: John Hall

Printed in the United States of America

10 9 8 7 6 5 4 3 2 1

ISBN 0-13-302431-8 01

Prentice-Hall International, Inc., *London*
Prentice-Hall of Australia Pty. Limited, *Sydney*
Editora Prentice-Hall do Brasil, Ltda., *Rio de Janeiro*
Prentice-Hall Canada Inc., *Toronto*
Prentice-Hall of India Private Limited, *New Delhi*
Prentice-Hall of Japan, Inc., *Tokyo*
Prentice-Hall of Southeast Asia Pte. Ltd., *Singapore*
Whitehall Books Limited, *Wellington, New Zealand*

CONTENTS

PREFACE

Countless attorneys regard divorce work as discouraging, even unsavory, business. When I graduated from law school, I chose family law as my field of interest because this is a field in which the law is developing to better meet the needs of the people using it. The changes taking place in the family reflect some of the most significant and fundamental societal alterations since the Industrial Revolution.

Divorce, and society's attitude toward it—particularly American society's attitude—has changed and is continuing to change greatly. Until recently, divorcing couples had the choice between do-it-yourself and lawyer-assisted divorces. If the do-it-yourself way is impossible (for any number of reasons), or if the couple want to take responsibility for creating their own settlement (rather than having lawyers advise them separately and manage the settlement negotiations or litigation), a third option comes into play: mediation. Through mediation, couples not only get assistance in dealing with their divorce, but they also keep their decision-making powers without sacrificing the professional guidance they want.

This book is written for the divorcing client, the attorney, and the mental health professional. The first section of the book acquaints the reader with the fundamentals of mediation. It provides a comparative look at adversary and non-adversary approaches to divorce as well as an overview of fundamental similarities and differences in mediation styles.

The second portion of the book gives detailed information on five basic models of mediation so that both professionals and couples can choose the mediation style that is best for them. Each chapter discusses the different styles and provides examples of five models, with descriptions of individual mediators practicing within that format. Transcripts of selected mediation sessions furnish the reader with an accurate idea of what mediation is actually like. (Background information about the divorcing couples has been altered to protect the anonymity of the contributors.)

The third section is a compendium of various mediators' forms, brochures, letters, training materials, sample parenting or property settlement agreements, and referral and training resources.

Joan Blades

ACKNOWLEDGMENTS

Many thanks to the many people who helped me write this book . . . my family and friend/editors, in particular David Gerrard, and the mediators who have generously contributed their time and knowledge.

FAMILY MEDIATION:
COOPERATIVE DIVORCE
SETTLEMENT

ONE

INTRODUCTION

Divorce affects us all. Because ending a marriage is a turning point in the lives of the people immediately involved, the most constructive means possible should be used, so that both parties can start their new lives on firm ground. Presently the vast majority of those faced with a divorce seek out lawyers and proceed through the court system—but often this has a very bitter ending. There are other options to the adversarial divorce, one of which is mediation. Under this system husband and wife create and agree to a marital settlement outside of a courtroom, aided by a trained third party whose primary goal is to help them mediate a settlement that both the couple and their family can live with for years to come. Nobody loses. The mediator's role is distinct from that of a lawyer or a mental health professional, though legal skills and/or counseling skills enhance most mediators' abilities. The mediator's function is to facilitate the couple's creative problem-solving efforts, not to decide how the couple should separate their property or to explore the couple's hostilities.

Who can best decide the issues of property division, alimony, custody, visitation, and child support? Who has the most information about what a fair distribution of marital assets and responsibilities might be? Surprisingly, when the couple shoulder the responsibility for resolving these issues, agreements are more satisfying, more flexible, and less subject to the erosive effects of time. After all, it is the couple whom these decisions affect the most and whose cooperation is necessary for creative solutions to these issues.

A mediated divorce settlement, then, is simply one negotiated by the couple themselves, with the help of a professional third party.

When couples who want an uncomplicated divorce understand the uses of mediation early in the divorce process, many unnecessary conflicts are avoided. Regrettably, few people even know what family mediation is, or how they can use it. Divorce mediation allows couples to retain control of their lives. A mediator simply guides the couple through the emotional and technical demands of separation, while the couple cooperatively create their own marital settlement agreement.

This book answers fundamental questions about divorce mediation.

1. What is it?
2. Who can benefit from such mediation?
3. Who is qualified to act as a mediator?
4. What is the best way to find a mediator?
5. Is a mediated settlement as good as a settlement drawn up by two attorneys?
6. Can mediation work if only one party wants to mediate?
7. What is co-mediation?
8. What is the difference between court mediation and private mediation?
9. What is structured mediation?
10. What are the advantages of using an attorney as mediator?
11. What are the advantages of using a mental health professional mediator?

This book's primary focus is on divorce mediation. However, mediation is appropriate for many other family disputes. Child/parent differences, inheritance squabbles, business issues, and family problems can be constructively and economically resolved using mediation.

Divorcing people are vulnerable: hopes and dreams are discarded; the future is uncertain. The beginning of the divorce process is a crucial time. Having a clear head and taking the time to choose the means of divorce that is best for you can make the difference between inviting a destructive experience and creating a sound basis for starting a new life. People often consult family, friends, or counselors in an attempt to keep the marriage together. While such advisors may be able to steer the angry, withdrawn, even grieving spouses to a more constructive divorce, they may also set the stage for disaster. For example, Nancy has been married for ten years. During the last four years, her husband Bruce has been on the road much of the time. Nancy feels out of touch, empty, dissatisfied, and angry; she wants a divorce. If Jane asks her best friend Nancy whether she is planning to mediate her own divorce settlement, Nancy may:

1. Ask what mediation is, if she is unfamiliar with mediation in this context
2. Ask where she should go to find a mediator, if she is interested but unaware of local resources
3. Start considering the possibility of using a mediator, if she is familiar with mediation and local resources

On the other hand, if Jane asks whether Nancy has an attorney, or about who gets the house, or about what will happen to the kids—while at the same time talking about what an inconsiderate husband Nancy has—then Jane may unintentionally be fueling the fire for an expensive and hostile divorce. Of course, in the best of all possible worlds, family and friends would play an informative, helpful, and supportive role.

THE ADVERSARY DIVORCE

Criminal offenses, business conflicts, and claims related to personal injuries are all typically handled by our court system—so are divorces. The system runs on the presumption that presenting the opposing interests of two parties before a judge, governed by rules of law, will result in the best solution possible. Generally, this system does work. However, more and more people are questioning its usefulness in resolving family problems. The following chart shows what often happens when attorneys are unable to negotiate a divorce settlement and the divorce is brought before the bench.

THE ADVERSARY DIVORCE

PROS

Fighting is an outlet for the pain caused by the divorce.

The "winner" may experience some psychological vindication.

The challenge of the battle may provide temporary diversion and excitement.

"Winning" may have economic rewards.

Developing an aversion to the other party may sever lingering bonds of affection that continue to cause emotional pain.

Going to court provides a symbolic end to the marriage.

CONS

The couple often lose sight of their long-term interests in the heat of the fight.

The "loser's" morale is probably crushed.

The "winner's" self-esteem may be diminished because of unsavory tactics utilized in order to "win."

One or both parties will be financially worse off due to the expense of litigation.

Children often emerge from a bitter divorce with severe emotional problems.

Cooperation necessary for continued involvement with the children will probably be impaired.

Future friction is more likely and may cause continuing hostile confrontations in and out of court.

Obligations imposed by the court may not be adhered to in good faith because they were not voluntarily agreed to.

THE MEDIATED DIVORCE

Mediation is founded on the belief that people should retain control of the major decisions that affect their lives. A mediated divorce settlement can only be entered into when both parties agree to it. A mediator is a neutral party who facilitates negotiations. Mediators help to establish an atmosphere of trust and cooperation. They encourage creative problem solving, assist in making issues clear, intervene when emotions hinder the process, and test the feasibility of proposed solutions so that the final agreement will work. A judge can only guess at parties' needs and may or may not gain the parties' commitment to obey the court order. In the final analysis, the couple themselves are the best judge of their own needs and of what solutions might be easiest to live with. The following chart provides an overview of the attitudes fostered when a divorce is mediated.

THE MEDIATED DIVORCE

PROS

Both parties are satisfied with the fairness of the outcome because they both took part in its creation.

The couple learn to cooperate for their mutual benefit. Honest exchange of information is fostered.

Increased self-esteem develops as a result of their ability to take responsibility for the resolution of their own conflicts.

There is less likelihood of future litigation, because of a greater commitment to the settlement and the couple's knowledge of their ability to cooperate.

Less money is spent on attorney fees, court costs, and so on.

Children are far less likely to be traumatized.

The couple avoid a public display.

CONS

Emotions may be too high to allow the couple to work things out rationally.

For those who want a public display or validation as "winner," this method is not satisfying.

If the balance of power between the couple is too disparate, mediation may be impossible.

It would be misleading to imply that mediation is right for all couples getting a divorce. Couples approach divorce from many different standpoints. Some spouses are both knowledgeable and cooperative, not needing any help in deciding how to divide property or parent their children. Other couples are vindictive and deceitful, unable to mediate. Couples vary tremendously in the degrees of guidance, structure, and authority they want and need in order to complete their divorce. Mental health professionals help couples cope with the emotional turmoil of divorce. Attorneys provide legal information, and frequently protection, to divorcing clients. For those couples who want to work cooperatively on their divorce settlement, there are attorneys and mental health professionals who are trained as mediators, offering clients greater control over their divorce. Mental health professionals, attorneys, and mediators all have important roles to play in divorce.

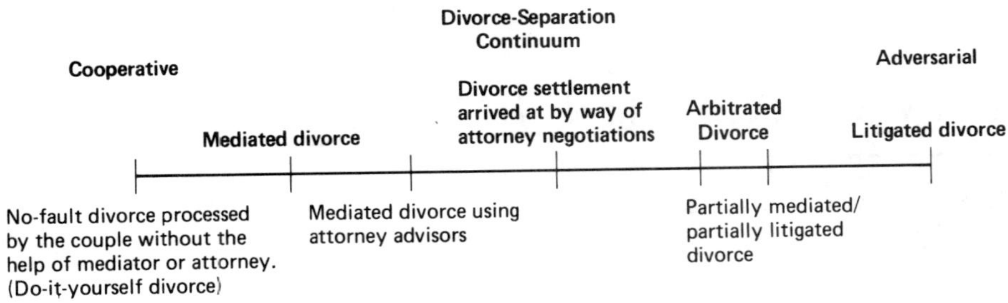

Financial and emotional costs tend to increase as one moves to the right on this spectrum. How would you add to or alter this continuum?

TWO

DIVORCE IN THE SHADOW OF THE LAW

Divorce settlements involve complicated issues, such as distribution of property, alimony, child support, custody, and visitation. It is not easy to decide these issues. There are several choices open to those who want a divorce—from little outside help to a good deal of it, and from cooperative to adversarial proceedings. Some choose do-it-yourself plans and negotiate their own settlements without any outside professional help. Others decide they need some help and opt for a partially or a totally mediated divorce. Still others seek out a lawyer's aid in negotiating a settlement. Finally, there are many who still look to a lawyer for an in-court settlement, that is, litigation.

The first three methods mentioned above occur, in a sense, in the shadow of the in-court, litigated divorce. What does this mean? Let's say Beth wants a divorce. Before hiring a lawyer and taking it to court, she takes a look at the best and the worst possible outcomes of a court decision. She must also think about the cost of the lawyer, how long the proceedings will take, and uncertainty and anxiety associated with the whole procedure. She weighs any negotiated settlement she can make out of court against what might happen if she goes to court. In other words, why should she settle for a negotiated agreement that does not at least measure up to what a court settlement will give her?[1] Many couples want to minimize the costs of a divorce and come out with a fair settlement that is the same as, if not better than, what they can expect in court.

There is no reason for Beth to let her attorney negotiate away her right to the house if she has reason to believe she would be awarded the house were she to litigate the matter. Furthermore, Beth's husband Mark is not going to maintain an unreasonable position when he knows that Beth can simply take him to court and get what she is asking for—at greater expense to both of them. Suppose Beth were to choose mediation: She should first ask herself what advantages there are to this form of divorce. She knows she can always have an attorney negotiate or litigate her divorce if this will be better in the long run. Likewise, if Beth is doing her own divorce and feels overwhelmed at some point by her husband, she may no longer feel that the savings of not hiring a mediator is worth the price of blundering forward without professional help. Each divorce process has its pros and cons. If Mark is extremely angry and wants to fight Beth in every way possible, a less structured, more cooperative means of divorce will be out of the question. Beth will need the protection of an attorney. Understanding the needs and dynamics of a couple as a unit and of each party individually is important in choosing the best possible divorce process for them. Today a couple can choose just how structured they want their divorce to be.

Are attorneys' offices and courtrooms suitable places for the divorcing couples to create a parting contract? An ever-increasing number of people think not. More and more couples are trying to stay out of court and are using attorneys less and less. Family issues do not belong in a courtroom. The legal system was not designed to accommodate the very special needs of families. Most judges and attorneys have no training in child development or in the psychology of family systems. A brief look into the origins of our legal system of divorce will shed some light on its strengths and weaknesses for resolving marital disputes.

EARLY LAW AND DIVORCE

The American legal system is descended from British Common Law. Prior to the reign of Henry the Eighth, it was impossible to get a divorce in England, because English law followed the tenets of the Roman Catholic Church. With divorce today more common and less eventful than ever before, it is hard to imagine the labor Henry the Eighth expended four centuries ago to get legal recognition for his divorce from Catherine of Aragon, aunt of that most Catholic monarch, Phillip II of Spain. Legal recognition was then, and is still today, the most important factor in the entire divorce process.

For Henry, the recognition had to come from Rome, from God's Vicar on earth, the Pope. No recognition of Henry's divorce meant no legal recognition of Henry's heir—if providence should grant him one through Anne Boleyn. Henry's obsession with legal matters led him to break with the Church of Rome and create the Church of England, with himself at the helm. This church, created to carry out a divorce, was most reluctant to grant divorces, a process that was handled exclusively in ecclesiastic (clergy-run) courts. The ecclesiastic courts of England could hardly risk undermining their own authority by granting frequent divorces. While the persevering gentleman of good family and with well-documented charges of marital misbehavior was, at times, able to obtain one, women and men of lesser means remained unable to divorce. This same church had little tolerance for the more conservative groups that eventually left the country in the next century to put down roots in Massachusetts. Divorce, be it in King James's Old World or in Cotton Mather's new one, was nearly impossible to obtain.

Nearly a century after the Constitution of the United States recognized separation of church and state as one of the fundamental principles of that nation, a divorce was still very difficult to obtain in most states. American divorce laws (like those in England) were originally designed to discourage or disallow divorce, except in exceptional circumstances. The principle of church/state separation was, and is, deceptive. The court is certainly not an extension of any religious body, yet the mores of the community are reflected in the divorce statutes of each state. In Underwood versus Underwood (Florida, 1968) the court stated: "It would be aiming a deadly blow at public morals to decree a dissolution of the marriage contract merely because the parties requested it." In most states couples were required to prove adultery, extreme cruelty, insanity, or desertion in order to obtain a divorce. The process was so demeaning, hostility provoking, painful, and expensive that many couples simply parted with no legal end to their marriage, never to marry again—or else they remained unhappily married. Those who endured the divorce process were marked for life by the ordeal and by society. Women in particular were branded as "loose" and were ostracized by "decent" society.

In many states formulas for divorce developed which invited perjury or collusion by the spouses in order to meet basic legal requirements for divorce. For instance, in states such as Florida, where it was illegal for a couple to agree to divorce each other, a couple might surreptitiously decide who would bring an action for divorce, at the same time agreeing that the other spouse would not contest the action. These agreements were regarded as fraud upon the court. At times, when there were insufficient grounds for divorce, couples manufactured grounds. In one colorful New York case, an obliging attorney stood in as the wife's lover in a staged hotel raid designed to prove adultery.

Some couples however, used the legal system to express their rage and satisfy their greed. Blackmail was not uncommon in bitter divorces. A spouse willing to use his or her mate's fear of social ostracism, of embarrassment, or of losing custody of a child frequently coerced the mate into agreeing to unfair out-of-court settlements. Rather than face a public trial where their reputation would be besmirched, or where they might risk losing their children, men and women often chose to give up property or custody rights to which they were entitled.

Fifty years ago divorce was rare and was condemned by society. Divorced persons were regarded as a threat to the social structure. No doubt, some people considered the humiliation and loss required by the divorce process an appropriate punishment for couples who challenged social norms.

About twenty-five years ago, the social climate began to change. The fact that a large number of families are now experiencing divorce—and that many of these families are middle class and "respectable"—and has caused legislators and the public to rethink the policies behind divorce laws. We are examining our old assumptions and current procedures, hoping to find better alternatives. Most people now feel that the trauma of divorce should be minimized so that the reordered family can go on living constructive lives as soon as possible. The idea is not to encourage marital breakups through an easy divorce but rather to bring about as smoothly as possible the dissolution of painful and perhaps unbearable social, emotional, and financial living arrangements between two people.

CHANGES IN DIVORCE LAWS

Gradually state legislators have responded to the need for modification of divorce laws in order to reduce the hostility which has characterized traditional divorce proceedings. Attempts are being made to make divorces less expensive, less complicated, less litigious, and easier on the children. (Some states now use the term *marital dissolution*, as opposed to divorce, because of all the word has come to mean.) Examples of these changes include the following:

1. No-fault divorce is designed to minimize blame and the adversarial incentives in divorce. No-fault statutes allow couples to divorce because of irreconcilable differences rather than requiring one spouse to prove that the other spouse is insane, is diseased, or has engaged in marital misbehavior—probably the most common grounds for divorce prior to the no-fault divorce laws. Adultery is no longer a factor for the court to consider. By 1983 some form of no-fault divorce grounds were available in every state except South Dakota.

   No-fault divorce has affected property division, alimony, child support, and custody decisions in and out of the courtroom. Parties no longer have to identify a "wayward" spouse who must make retribution for his or her inequities. The court's primary legal guidelines are based on what is fair and equitable between the parties. Courts are devising child support and spousal tables to make their rulings more consistent. (These actuarial tables are developed according to income and local cost of living, and should be available at most local courthouses.) No-fault divorce has been a major breakthrough, providing an opportunity to create more straightforward or humane, and effective divorce procedures.

2. Many states have simplified divorce laws so that couples can handle their own divorces without the aid of attorneys. Divorce manuals written for laypeople are available in most of these states. Divorce manuals walk the reader through the process on a step-by-step basis. *How to Do Your Own Divorce in California*, a manual by Nolo Press, has sold 1,200,000 copies in the last ten years.[2]

3. As recently as 1970 joint custody was virtually unheard of. Ten years ago a judge presented with a joint custody agreement might have insisted on a more traditional custody and visitation arrangement, in which one parent has sole custody. This is no longer true. Counselors and courts are beginning to recognize that both parents are important to a child's well-being. Some states still don't recognize joint custody arrangements. More and more, however, both joint legal and joint physical custody are encouraged by judges and court personnel. Judges no longer automatically bear the onerous burden of choosing the more fit parent.

   Though the definitions of joint physical custody and joint legal custody are not clear until the rights and responsibilities of the parents are outlined in an agreement, the intent of these new arrangements is clear. Both parents are encouraged to have maximum involvement with the children. Typically, parents that have joint legal custody both remain involved in major decisions affecting their child, ranging from schooling to medical attention. Parents with joint physical custody share a substantial amount of their child's time as well. This does not mean the child is shuttled from house to house on a strict 50/50 time schedule. The schedule may be 60/40 or 70/30; it is more a question of attitude. Parents who share custody tend to have good cooperative relationships with regard to their children and are flexible as regards the children's needs (for example, weekdays with one parent, weekends with the other, alternating the pattern every year). When neither parent has been disenfranchised, the whole family feels more secure and involved.

4. Some states have created policies whereby custody is awarded to that parent who agrees to the most liberal visitation schedule. This motivates parents to offer each other generous visitation rights. Generosity and willingness to cooperate create a better atmosphere for the entire divorce process.

5. On January 1, 1981, California became the first state to pass a law requiring mediation of child custody disputes prior to any court appearance.

Unfortunately, changes in the laws intended to make divorce less combative have only been partially successful. Old competitive attitudes toward divorce still haunt us. All too often the couple's anger and frustration find an avenue for release in the adversary system. They may even receive encouragement from family or friends. "Look after yourself, he's certainly looked after himself all along." Or "Take the children. You're a good father, and the courts are giving the kids to fathers more and more." While much advice is meant to be sympathetic and supportive, it often results in further stress on the already strained relationship.

Most couples contemplating divorce consult attorneys when they begin the divorce process. More often than not, this escalates hostility. If the couple's attorneys fail to reach an out-of-court settlement, hostilities are inevitable. Custody battles in particular retain the bitterness encouraged by the fault system. Parents parade each other's failings in the courtroom, hoping to appear the more suitable custodial parent. The judge becomes the reluctant arbitrator of these very personal and highly charged decisions.

A large part of the problem involves our attitude toward divorce. Divorce has historically been an adversarial proceeding. It is easy to forget that we are no longer forced to approach it as a battle. Most couples considering a divorce do not know where to turn if not to an attorney. Depending upon how they present the situation, and the attorney's attitude, this may be the first step on a long and painful journey toward separation. A win/lose approach to divorce is self-perpetuating—cooperation becomes less and less likely.

NEGOTIATED SETTLEMENT

In general, the least expensive, most civilized divorce conducted by two attorneys is the negotiated out-of-court settlement. Good divorce lawyers settle the majority of their cases in this way. Why? Because there is a heightened opportunity for parties to cooperate and satisfy each other's needs. When spouses aren't after revenge, there is no reason to waste time and money on legal battling.

There are many instances in which cooperation benefits both spouses. For example:

1. Thoughtful child-care scheduling allows parents to reduce child-care expenses and maximize opportunities for quality parental time.
2. When a family business is involved, the ability to negotiate or mediate a settlement may permit the business to prosper, whereas a contentious separation could force the sale of the business or destroy the business due to conflicts in its management.
3. Adverse tax consequences can be minimized by cooperative tax planning. Depending upon how payments are characterized, deductions can be arranged so that both parties end up with more spendable cash. Alimony is deductible, child support is not. If a parent in a low income bracket is receiving both alimony and child support while the paying parent is in a high tax bracket, both can have more money if they call the payment "family support." This term is a new classification for a combined payment of alimony and child support, and it is wholly deductible.

The advantages of coming to settlement by way of negotiations, as opposed to court order, are similar to the advantages of mediation. There are more opportunities for cooperative problem solving, less time and money is spent fighting, and the parties who must live with the agreement have consented to it.

Taking a case to court is the ultimate threat at the negotiation table, whether stated or not. Even attorneys intent upon negotiating a settlement may be held liable if they do not maintain a favorable position for possible litigation. Their clients must be advised of their chances of winning more or less at trial; and the attorney's prediction of what might happen in court inevitably has an effect on the client's willingness to enter into good-faith negotiations. Though information revealed in settlement negotiations cannot be presented in court (because the courts do want to encourage parties to settle differences out of court), the information gleaned in negotiation may nonetheless be used to plan strategies and to find other admissible evidence. In other words, if wife offers husband her portion of the house in exchange for sole rights to her pension, when negotiations break down, husband can't tell the court what wife offered, even when she argues that she has rights to all of her pension and to the house. However, occasions may arise where information that would speed up negotiations is not shared, for fear that negotiations could break down and damage the lawyer's position at trial. In every settlement proceeding a lawyer must be prepared to go all the way to trial. Considering the expectations and demands of the adversary process, it is to the lawyer's credit that most divorces are settled out of court.

COMMON DIVORCE

The Anglo-American legal system has its origins in the belief that when two opposing sides face off in the judicial arena, each side presenting his or her own version of the facts, the truth will ultimately be revealed and justice will be served. Even outside the legal profession, this adversary-conflict model serves as an important technique in resolving financial or commercial disputes. The problem is that this "face-off" technique is rarely the best way to settle the intricately entwined legal and emotional issues of divorce.

A typical case is that of Mark and Beth, married fifteen years, both professionals in their late thirties, with a five-year-old son, Sheldon. When Mark and Beth decided to divorce, they planned to do it as quickly and painlessly as possible. They agreed that their marriage had been unsatisfactory for years. Mark moved to an apartment, and six months later Beth began seeing another man.

When they went to separate attorneys asking for help with an uncontested divorce, the attorneys each had them take an inventory of their property. Mark's attorney suggested he keep his communications with Beth to a minimum. Mark had mentioned his tendency to bicker with Beth when they tried to settle differences on their own. His attorney was particularly concerned about property issues. She did not want to be surprised with any out-of-court agreements that would prejudice Mark's position. She also advised him to close all joint savings and credit accounts as soon as possible to prevent unreasonable last-minute expenditures by Beth.

Beth was stunned by Mark's cautious, almost distrustful attitude toward her after he saw his attorney. When Beth went to draw some money out of the joint savings account and found it had been closed by Mark, she was irate. Beth told her attorney to file for the divorce. Beth's lawyer had papers served on Mark.

As the divorce progressed, both Mark and Beth became increasingly concerned about how they would divide their marital property and finances. Beth had started a part-time job when Sheldon began kindergarten, but she was not yet feeling financially self-sufficient. When Beth's attorney suggested that she ask for $500 per month in child support, Beth was a bit surprised, because she felt that $350 would have been fair. Her attorney explained his strategy: "We need to start negotiations with a high, but not unreasonable, figure, so that we have room to bargain. If we go to court, the judge will probably settle on a figure between what we and your ex-husband propose." When Mark heard about Beth's request for $500, his reaction was typical. He and his attorney agreed to offer $200, a figure which he knew to be low. Beth was appalled.

There are a number of problems with Mark and Beth's situation:

1. They may pay a needlessly high amount in professional fees in agreeing to a figure which was never really in dispute.
2. Mark and Beth may be creating anxiety and hostility damaging to both themselves and Sheldon.
3. Playing this game might not ultimately lead to an appropriate and mutually satisfactory out-of-court settlement.
4. If the issue is decided by a judge, there is no saying what will happen. The judge might have a bias for high child support, or conversely, against the supporting spouse being tied by weighty financial burdens.

THE DANGER OF NEGOTIATION THROUGH A THIRD PARTY

Mark and Beth are an example of good intentions getting lost in the scramble for a good legal position. Attorneys frequently explain that unfeeling actions taken on behalf of their clients are an unpleasant, but necessary, duty. Clients contend that their attorney is soley responsible for unsavory legal maneuvers. In this manner everyone avoids taking responsibility for his or her actions. Attorneys often inadvertently initiate proceedings, ask questions, or ignore situations that would be more sensitively handled by the separating spouses themselves. The following is an example of this kind of mismanagement.

When Mark and Beth got married, Mark owned a valuable rocking chair. Over time Beth became very attached to the chair. When discussing the property division with his attorney, Mark stated that Beth could have the chair. The attorney explained that legally the chair was Mark's separate property, because he owned it prior to the marriage; the attorney then suggested that Mark list the chair as separate property and use it to bargain for an item he wanted in return. Mark failed to convey the symbolic significance of the chair to his lawyer. Mark knows that despite his legal right to the chair, including it on a list of separate property is apt to surprise and offend Beth, who feels that they have an understanding about marital property that has special significance to either of them. However, because Mark is paying $80 an hour for his attorney's advice, he reasons that it is appropriate for him to follow it. Mark has turned his case over to his attorney and chooses to wait passively for the results his attorney delivers.

If Beth feels betrayed or attacked by the posturing of Mark's attorney, she may retaliate in any number of ways: hiding other property, claiming ownership of one of Mark's prized possessions, or using forgotten joint credit account with abandon. Many a quiet divorce has escalated into a bitter battle in this manner. Lack of attention to emotional issues, and the resulting distrust, can transform a divorce into a painful battle.

Numerous divorced persons recount bitter tales of their divorce, of good intentions and tragic results. Mary was divorced five years ago. She has two children and works in a hospital. When asked about divorce lawyers, her response was unhesitating: "They don't care. They don't like divorces. They bring all their past bad experiences with them. My husband and I had almost everything worked out and we went to an attorney to draw up an agreement. I chose a woman because I thought a woman would be more sensitive. She said she couldn't represent both of us. My husband got another lawyer . . . it was just awful."

"My husband was smart. He got his lawyer to commit to a flat fee. Mine kept sending letters, trying to negotiate, his would send back a brief question every now and then. Lawyers don't think about the money, even when we're just barely scraping by. They just keep sending out the letters. . . . We had gotten houses near each other so the kids could go back and forth freely. We almost had to sell them both it cost so much. . . . Now I wish he lived in another state."

ATTORNEYS, ORCHESTRATORS OF THE TRADITIONAL DIVORCE

In 1978 four psychologists attempting to define the lawyer's role in assisting divorcing couples conducted a series of interviews with seventeen lawyers.[3] Much to the researchers' surprise, they discovered that attorneys have very different concepts of their role in divorce. These are apparent in their attitude toward

1. The client
2. The objectives of legal intervention
3. The nature and value of collaboration with mental health professionals

Based on these differences, the researchers defined six stances adopted by lawyers who handle divorces.

1. The narrowest, most legalistic stance has been termed *the undertaker* approach. "The analogy rests on two points: (a) it is assumed that the job involved is essentially a thankless, messy business; and (b) it takes for granted that the clients are in a state of emotional "derangement."[4]

These lawyers have an obvious distaste for divorce. They might be businesslike and effective, but they are unlikely to lend a sympathetic ear. The pessimism characteristic of the *undertaker* is not conducive to realizing the constructive aspects possible in divorce.

2. The *mechanic* assumes a technical orientation. He or she is merely a tool with which to accomplish the client's wishes. The emotional issues of the divorce are not relevant to the *mechanic*.

> If a husband says he wants to give $25,000 a year to his wife, I don't think it's the duty of the lawyer to say to him "You're out of your mind." I think that if a lawyer is asked, "What risk do I run in the courts?" then he has a professional responsibility to give his opinion as to what the risk is.
>
> When all is said and done, one of the most important things you do is what you do as a lawyer—not as a comforter, not as a surrogate father—it's what you do professionally to get the best results.[5]

A *mechanic* is the attorney to use when a couple have a clear idea of their intentions and desires. Such an attorney will write up their agreement without questioning its validity, except on a strictly legal basis.

3. The *mediative* attorney displays many of the attitudes an actual mediator exhibits, focusing on rational problem solving, fairness, constructive outcomes for both parties, and concern about the spouses' welfare. Such attorneys downplay their adversarial role and negotiate the settlement out of court whenever possible.

4. Attorneys who have adopted the *social worker* stance focus on clients' overall welfare. The assistance of mental health professionals is welcome. Long-range plans for the children and for the unemployed spouse are within the realm of this attorney's concern.

5. The *therapist* attorney recognizes that the emotional issues of divorce are an inseparable aspect of the divorce process and helps clients cope with them as well as with the legal aspects of the process. One attorney related that he delayed bringing a lawsuit for over a year, due to concern that his client could not handle the pressure of her divorce. He did not go forward with the suit until her psychiatrist said she would be able to cope with the stresses it entailed. Attorneys with this stance tend to view the legal system as having a detrimental effect on divorcing couples.

6. The *moral agents* involve their personal sense of justice when handling a divorce. Very often, when children are involved in a divorce, an attorney will adopt this stance. The attorney may encourage parents to consult mental health professionals in order to strengthen their position regarding the welfare of the children. The *moral agent* wants a fair outcome.

The diversity evident in attorneys' perceptions of their function in a divorce is attributed to "role strain." (Komarosvsky, 1976, has defined role strain as a "felt or latent [not fully recognized by the person] difficulty in role performance and perceived paucity of rewards for role conformity.)[6]

> The lawyers described or alluded to crosscutting pressures that they experience in their work with the divorcing. Formal legal codes of conduct and training provide little relief from these pressures; indeed, they appear to contribute to them significantly. Each practitioner, therefore, is obliged to solve the professional dilemmas of matrimonial practice as best he can. . . .[7]

The researchers point to six major sources of role strain.

1. The adversary nature of the legal proceedings. The divorce settlement negotiations can be like the children's game of telephone. The husband tells his attorney something, his attorney calls the opposing attorney, and the opposing attorney calls the wife. By the time the final message is received, it can be substantially distorted. This natural process in the breakdown of communication is exacerbated by the traditional psychology pervading the legal profession—holding that every issue provides ammunition for either an out-and-out battle or "hardball" negotiation. This legal mind-set finds its origins in what has loosely been defined as the adversary process.

When a marriage is breaking up, communication frequently becomes strained. Minor differences may be exaggerated into major battles. The less a couple communicate directly, the greater the possibility that some misunderstanding will arise when they seek to finalize their separation. Facts and intentions are often distorted when a third party—for example, an attorney—takes to the forefront in the settlement of these issues.

In an effort to exercise exclusive control over the flow of information, attorneys often advise divorcing couples to keep their communications with each other to a minimum. This approach prevents the confusion caused by unrecorded understandings of which the attorneys are unaware. However, this system causes distortion and is an unnecessary waste of time and money for couples who can communicate directly.

2. The one-sidedness of the lawyers' view. Many respondents complained about the difficulty of gaining an accurate picture of the marital situation from their clients.

Most states prohibit attorneys from speaking to opposing parties without the consent of the latters' lawyers. This makes it virtually impossible for an attorney to gain a balanced picture of any divorce. California Rule of Professional Conduct 7-103 states: "A member of the state bar shall not communicate directly or indirectly with a party whom he knows to be represented by counsel upon a subject of controversy, without the express consent of counsel."

In other words, Beth's lawyer cannot talk to Mark without first obtaining permission from Mark's lawyer. Mark's lawyer will probably refuse to grant the request because:

a. Mark could say something that would hurt his case.
b. Mark's lawyer does not want any deals or understandings to be arranged without his knowledge.

c. If Mark does say something inadvisable during an interview which has been permitted by his attorney, the attorney may be held accountable. (Attorney malpractice cases are becoming common, and Mark's attorney does not want her already expensive malpractice insurance to become prohibitive as a result of Mark suing her for not adequately protecting him from Beth's lawyer.)

It is increasingly difficult to avoid the formalities and expense of the adversary system. Mark's lawyer will probably insist on attending any kind of "informal" interview Beth's lawyer suggests, and thus the atmosphere is apt to remain formal and distrustful. Beth's lawyer will soon decide that there is little or no chance for him to acquire a balanced perspective of any divorce and will thus cease to attempt to arrange such informal meetings.

This rule prohibiting attorneys from contacting the opposition directly has a sound foundation. Beth's lawyer could, theoretically, take advantage of Mark's legal ignorance. In the past attorneys have secured damaging statements from opposing parties who did not have the benefit of counsel's presence. So many attorneys resented this unscrupulous behavior that the bar associations constructed a rule to prevent this situation from occurring. This rule is appropriate for criminal, tort, business, and other adversarial cases. In nonadversary divorce this rule restricts the ability of counsel to acquire a realistic picture of the divorce or to gain rapport with the other spouse. While some bar associations are now considering the case of divorce mediation separately, attorneys will tread cautiously until some kind of definitive precedent is set.

3. The shortage of material resources. A family with two children which grosses only $16,000 per year is in serious economic difficulty when that income must be split between two households. One attorney noted that money would be far more useful than equity in this situation. The lawyer's fee merely exacerbates this problem; and because much of the lawyer's work is done when the client is not present, the bill often seems excessive.

4. The economics of the law office. The lawyers interviewed pointed out two potential conflicts of interest between the lawyer and the client: (a) Lawyers get paid to litigate; thus, the client's loss is the attorney's gain in this situation. (b) Often the husband pays the wife's legal costs; thus, the wife's attorney may feel some sense of responsibility to the husband.

5. The nonlegal nature of many of the issues and the training of lawyers. In law schools counseling and negotiation training is seldom required and is frequently ignored altogether. A law school's primary goal is to train the law student in the theory and practice of the law. Hidden behind the goal of "understanding the law" is the need to prepare the student to pass the bar exam. A second objective is to train students to prepare for an adversarial contest in court. Law schools apparently believe that attorneys should develop the skills of legal academic reasoning and technical precision. This is appropriate for certain areas of the law—but family law is not one of them. It is unrealistic to expect or desire a family lawyer to remain detached when faced with hysterical phone calls from a distressed client.

Despite the unique counseling skills needed by family lawyers, the practice of family law requires no specialized training. A few states certify family law specialists. Depending upon the particular requirements of that bar, those attorneys may undergo special testing; or they may be "grandfathered" in as specialists because of experience in the field; or they may participate in additional bar-approved family law courses. Continuing education courses on family law generally cover subjects such as taxes, pension rights, and litigation. While family therapy and child psychology courses might be useful to family lawyers, the need for this additional education has not yet been commonly recognized. This is not to say that many family law specialists do not have psychological expertise, only that it is not a prerequisite for the job or even an officially encouraged skill.

(Despite the existence of certification, potential clients should not feel precluded from inquiring about a noncertified attorney to represent them in a divorce. Family law practitioners whose practices prospered years before any kind of certification was available often consider certification an unnecessary burden. The overriding consideration is whether the attorney can view his or her client's problems not only as a legal dispute but also as a human dilemma, often requiring an emotional sensitivity and psychological insight not required in other areas of the law.)

6. The difficulties in the lawyer-lawyer relationship. If one accepts that attorneys doing divorces may adopt any of the six stances defined by the researchers, it is apparent that there is a high probability that most lawyers do not see eye to eye with opposing counsel when handling a divorce. A *mechanic* representing husband and a *therapist* representing wife will have a difficult time negotiating a divorce settlement.

The remarkable disparity between different attorneys' attitudes partially explains why people have such varied opinions of attorneys. Persons considering employing an attorney for their divorce should decide what kind of divorce they would like to have and what kind of attorney would best meet their needs. They should also evaluate the advantages and disadvantages of ending the marital relationship in an adversary setting.

Divorce attorneys are frequently maligned. Many divorcing clients have unrealistic expectations that no attorney can satisfy. Some attorneys are not prepared to handle the emotional demands of their clients. Common complaints of clients are caused by poor communication between attorney and client, clients' imagined or real experience of lacking control over a process that deeply affects their personal lives, and inappropriate competition for money and position. In all fairness, the blame for those problems does not land squarely on the attorneys. The law schools, the adversary system, and clients themselves all contribute to the shortcomings of adversary divorce. Sometimes it is the divorcing spouses who will not negotiate in good faith, insisting that their attorneys take their case to court in order to vent their own hostility and antagonize their former spouse. It takes only one irate spouse or overzealous attorney to spark a hostile divorce.

ATTORNEYS AS CHAMPIONS OF THEIR CLIENTS

The most prevalent public image of attorneys is as champions—well groomed, articulate, affluent, and quite possibly unscrupulous. Anyone who chooses a lawyer because of his or her reputation as a courtroom barracuda is likely to have a legal battle. Beth may go to a "good" lawyer with no clear idea of how she wants to proceed and find that "good" means a tough adversary who is fiercely partisan and unconcerned about the welfare of the rest of her family. Initially it is hard for her to recognize the attorney's "strong support" as detrimental to her ultimate best interests. She feels weak and confused and appreciates the "protection" her attorney provides. By the time she recognizes the disadvantages of a strong adversary stance, the tone of her divorce is set. Her attorney's competitive strategy will probably result in a like response from her husband and his representative.

The warrior attorney assumes the worst of the opposition. This often creates a self-fulfilling prophesy. An atmosphere of distrust prevails as each attorney attempts to secure the lion's share of the marriage's assets. Opportunities for the mutual satisfaction of needs are frequently overlooked in the heat of competition, or even out of spite. Negotiations break down under unreasonable demands as hostility spirals.

THE POWER OF ATTORNEYS

Clients initiating a divorce often have lowered self-esteem, rapidly fluctuating moods (anger, depression, exhilaration), and a minimal knowledge of the legal process they are about to begin. As a result, they are extremely open to suggestion. George Norton, a divorce attorney and mediator, has commented that all persons in the midst of a divorce are suffering to some extent from "diminished capacity" (a legal defense used to mitigate criminal penalties and escape contract liabilities–for example, a drunken woman is not as responsible for her actions as a sober woman). In other words, the actions of individuals experiencing divorce are colored by the intense emotional atmosphere surrounding separation. Divorcing couples under the pressures of separation and confrontation with the legal system tend to turn to attorneys as protectors. Thus, many clients delegate responsibility for their divorce either deliberately or unconsciously.

Attorneys' efforts to ascertain their clients' desires are not always successful. If the client does not know what he or she wants, is too burdened by guilt to express his or her wants, or is not skilled at communicating his or her needs, the attorney may be misdirected. Furthermore, the attorney inevitably interprets the client's words according to his or her own personal understanding of divorce. All too frequently the attorney is unable to intuit the client's needs, and the client becomes dissatisfied.

An important part of an attorney's or a mediator's job is helping clients understand and come to terms with financial and legal realities of divorce so that they can make intelligent choices and more gracefully accept the final settlement agreement. For example, as a rule, both spouses' standard of living will be temporarily lowered following a divorce. Knowing this, the client is better prepared to adjust. The attorney helps the client evaluate and decide upon priorities. How much alimony should Beth ask for? What might happen if she trades the right to alimony for ownership of the house? Can she afford to do that?

Traditionally, fathers were advised to request visitation every other weekend and for a few weeks in the summer, since this is what the courts tended to order. In some jurisdictions encouraging a father to litigate for a court order granting significantly more visitation might have been considered unethical. The expense involved, coupled with the poor prospect for success and the reduced chances of the father receiving generous visitation rights, deterred such encouragement. Custody battles are expensive as well as devastating for both parents and children. Frequently they result in a rigid visitation schedule designed to minimize the contact between hostile parents. Attorneys therefore had to explain to fathers that generous visitation was more likely when circumstances were congenial—that is, when fathers did not demand it. Fathers were caught between a rock and a hard place—they were understandably reluctant to oppose their attorneys' expert advice.

THE CLIENT'S BEST INTERESTS

Beth had a conscientious attorney. He suspected that her husband was hiding funds. Mark's bank records showed that he had done a great deal of shifting of assets between accounts during the past six months. Beth's attorney conducted extensive pretrial investigation. Depositions, interrogatories, requests for production of documents, and the like were employed to discover just how much money Mark might be hiding. Before the case reached the courtroom, Beth and Mark could no longer afford to litigate. Jointly they had already paid over $15,000 in attorney's fees and other related court costs. Beth had spent $11,000 of the $15,000, expecting the bill to be paid by the extra money she would receive from Mark. Their money and anger spent, Beth and Mark agreed to try to mediate. The mediated agreement cost them a little over $1,000.

Did Beth's lawyer attend to her best interests? If Mark was hiding $500,000, it might be worth $11,000 in attorneys' fees for Beth to realize her half of the money. (However, this does not allow for the emotional turmoil, prolonged anxiety, and additional hostilities the children may have to cope with.) If Mark was hiding $20,000, Beth might be somewhat better off financially, depending upon how the judge split the money. Is it worth it? Clearly, if it was anything less than $10,000, the moral victory might be the only victory realized—at a ruinous financial cost.

The attorney as advocate must consider the best interests of his or her client in both economic and emotional terms. The adversary-litigant nature of the law places major emphasis on economic considerations, since money is a tangible and accepted medium of exchange and can rationally be seen as an appropriate stake to be fought over in a divorce that does go to trial. The legal issues that confront lawyers in the vast majority of civil cases are, after all, economic issues. This being the case, most attorneys will proceed with caution in downplaying the economic stakes involved in a case. A majority of attorneys sued for malpractice have made financial blunders.

Assuming an attorney defines her client's best interests in economic terms, the attorney has to decide whether the expense of investigation and/or litigation is justified. The attorney is obligated to be thorough and at the same time to recognize the point at which work and effort expended will result in diminished returns. When the attorney is short of work, her interests are in conflict with those of her client.

The attorney often acts as the interpreter of the needs as well as the words of the client. The client may not be able to convey exactly what those needs are, due to lack of knowledge, emotional involvement, or ineffective communication. For example, many individuals have no concept of how much money is needed to live separately. Highly emotional, guilt-ridden spouses have been known to offer their spouses wildly disproportionate amounts of property and support, then to feel used and incredibly burdened two years later when the reality of their situation finally becomes clear. Other clients give their attorneys conflicting or incomplete information, due to their own confusion.

Attorneys risk legal liability and damage to their reputation when they are unable to decipher their clients' desires and needs or when they follow legally unsound wishes of a client. When clients are informed of their rights, they are urged by their attorneys to take advantage of them, particularly in light of the uncertainty of court outcome. Spouses who voluntarily offer to give up property they have a right to—not knowing how much more may be taken against their wishes—have a great deal of faith in their spouses and/or the legal system. A client must be exceptionally determined to give his or her spouse more property or support than the law requires in the face of contrary professional advice. For the protection of his or her own reputation, as well as the protection of the client, the attorney may feel professionally obligated to dissuade clients from making overgenerous, hasty, or emotionally charged decisions.

A husband may wish to leave the family house to his wife and children because of his greater earning power. His attorney advises him that he has a right to half of the house's value. The husband decides to honor his original intention despite his right to a share of the house, and the attorney follows those generous instructions, believing them to be the true and uncoerced wishes of her client. Two years later, when the husband wants to start a new family, he may regret his decision. He may then attempt to void the settlement, accusing his attorney of malpractice, claiming she should have prevented him from agreeing to an unfair settlement at a time when he was emotionally distraught. Despite the perfect propriety of the attorney's actions, her professional stature may be threatened. Little wonder attorneys are cautious.

Another example of commonly given and reasonable legal advice is the suggestion that clients cancel any joint credit cards and close joint bank accounts, since distraught or vengeful spouses have been known to go on buying sprees. Yet even this terribly sensible act can cause distrust, especially if the other spouse is not diplomatically informed of the action. At any point during the adversary divorce process, either the husband or the wife can take some of the legal posturing of the other party to heart. When either party concludes that the other is acting unreasonably or insensitively, the spiral of escalating hostility is likely to occur.

Occasionally, in especially bitter cases, attorneys lose their objectivity and become emotional as well as legal advocates. Such overzealousness complicates matters further. One such case is described by Richard Wolman of Harvard Medical School, who is occasionally employed as a guardian ad litem (a court-appointed professional representing a child's best interests in court). Several years ago he was assigned to a boy named Robert Smith. He had an appointment to meet the child's parents in the judge's chambers. When he entered the waiting room, a man and a woman were arguing quite loudly.

WOMAN:	You agreed to pay all the medical bills! We've got a $1000 orthodontist bill that has not been paid for three months.
MAN:	Orthodontia isn't covered under the company medical policy. There's no money for that bill.
WOMAN:	Well, we certainly can't pay it!
RICHARD:	Excuse me, Mr. and Mrs. Smith. . .
MAN AND WOMAN:	(in unison) Oh, no. We're the attorneys.

Attorneys take great care to avoid emotional involvement in their clients' causes. Strong identification with a client, or ego commitment to "winning" a case, can involve attorneys more than is appropriate. As representative of his or her client, the attorney is both participant and observer in the divorce process. When an attorney becomes too enmeshed in emotional issues, the proper execution of the case suffers. Unfortunately, the line between proper and unreasonable involvement often is evident only after things have gone too far.

Mediators also run the risk of becoming emotionally enmeshed in their clients' problems. However, many mediators try to minimize the amount and kind of advice they give. Also, because the parties themselves are doing their own negotiating, much of the gamesmanship is avoided. Negotiations can be quite straightforward, and the mediator's advice tends to be discussed and evaluated by both parties together. There is far less opportunity for the mediator to impose his or her values on either spouse.

THE NEGLIGENT ATTORNEY

Many people resent their attorneys because they don't appear to spend sufficient time on their case. Calls to their attorneys are not returned, papers are not filed, and questions go unanswered. An attorney who has three major cases pending may seem preoccupied, as if he or she has little interest in a relatively minor divorce. This may or may not add to the hostility between the parties being divorced. It most definitely adds to the anger and frustration of the spouse who is not satisfied with his or her lawyer.

The fact that the client perceives indifference or negligence on the part of the attorney may be attributable to the client's heightened sensitivity; in fact, the client may sustain no actual legal injury. On the other hand, when papers are not filed on time or information is not gathered effectively, clients suffer substantial losses. Few clients have sufficient knowledge of their lawyers' daily activities or know enough about the law to evaluate their attorneys' performance early on in a case. This means that most clients are well into a case before it becomes evident that they need a different attorney. Clients who switch attorneys in the middle of a case must balance the cost of educating a second attorney against the cost of keeping the one they have. Finding a new attorney is disruptive, and having already made one bad choice, there is no guarantee that the client will avoid a second error.

If a client discovers an attorney's negligence after the fact, after getting a clearly inadequate settlement, will that client try to recover his or her losses through a lawsuit reopening the divorce case, or will the client institute a malpractice case against the attorney? Neither action is likely, since they both take time and effort. Having recently been burned by an attorney and the legal system, the client is more likely to drop the matter and join the ranks of those people who disparage attorneys.

GOING TO AN ATTORNEY

The decision to go to an attorney or a mediator is a big, often traumatic, step. It is necessary to understand each alternative in order to make an informed choice about which is more suited to your needs. At the same time, familiarity with what you might expect in either situation tends to reduce nervousness about the initial interview at the office of an attorney or a mediator.

Professionals discuss fees and fee arrangements with potential clients at the first meeting. If the first interview is free or half price, it should be clearly stated. At this same meeting, the professional will describe the service offered, and he or she can begin to find out what kind of assistance the client wants and/or needs. (Particularly in the case of divorce, a client's desires and needs may not be the same.) Some mediators and attorneys provide written descriptions of their services and of how best to utilize them. Both mediators and attorneys request detailed financial and personal information from divorcing clients in order to develop a marital settlement agreement.

Barbara DiFranza is one of a growing breed of family law practitioners who are familiar with and respect the uses of mediation in divorce. An important aspect of her initial interview with a divorcing client is a discussion of her client's options—one of which is mediation. At that juncture clients are better able to make an informed decision regarding the manner in which they want to dissolve their marriage. Clients who choose to have Ms. DiFranza represent them receive a set of four brochures and questionnaires designed for divorcing clients to read and fill out at home. These help prepare clients for what lies ahead. Also, they encourage clients to participate more actively in their own case, which often results in more efficient use of professional time.

1. The Confidential Questionnaire is self-explanatory. It provides the professional with ready information as to the couple's history, and begins the process of assessing the issues to be dealt with. Used as a checklist, it ensures that all factors that are likely to affect property and support issues are covered in the interview and in the handling of the case.

2. Suggestions for Reducing Fees conveys a sympathetic, yet realistic, appraisal of the pitfalls inherent in adversary divorce. The uncontrolled emotionalism of either spouse can force both parties into a destructive and expensive courtroom fiasco. Ms. DiFranza discourages this kind of behavior while encouraging rational,

productive activity. Clients are urged to participate in preparing their own case by conscientiously providing relevant information, answering "interrogatories" (questions sent by the opposing side which must be answered), and maintaining an organized file on their case. The final paragraph in the brochure explains why it is in everyone's best interest to settle the case out of court. Thus, it prepares the client to negotiate a settlement.

WESTPHAL, ELLNER, DIFRANZA & PORTMAN
ATTORNEYS AT LAW
1666 THE ALAMEDA
SAN JOSE, CALIFORNIA 95126

BARBARA A. DIFRANZA
KENNETH B. ELLNER
MARK PORTMAN
RONALD B. WESTPHAL

(408) 297-1600

SUGGESTIONS FOR REDUCING FEES

Divorce often comes at a time when a family is going through a financial as well as emotional crisis. Sometimes the emotional crisis can precipitate the financial one further by upping the attorneys' fees and costs expended. For example, if a spouse is vindictive, or just plain upset, that spouse can refuse to negotiate in good faith, or act in such a way as to provoke numerous court appearances or otherwise delay the proceedings. Obviously, this would be beyond your control; and we would have to cope the best we could through the mechanisms provided by the court. Frankly, it can be expensive and wearying.

However, my client is capable of reducing fees through following these simple rules:

(a) Remember the high costs of telephone calls. Always call the person whose billing rate is most appropriate for the matter. As a general rule, call my secretary first. If legal advice or intervention is needed immediately, she is trained to recognize it and she will probably get my attention alot faster than a message to call back which I might not find until the next morning when I spend a full day at court. Better yet, she can often handle the problem right then and there. If you wish information on status of service or filing of papers, or on billing, my secretary has primary responsibility for these matters. Also, if the matter requires my intervention, she will see to it. Finally, if you merely wish to leave some information such as an address or telephone number that I have requested, it is best that you leave the message with anyone answering your call.

(b) Remember that our services are primarily legal. Certainly, unless I understand the underlying nature of your interaction with your spouse, I cannot represent you as well as I might. Also, recognizing that Family Law matters, especially those involved in dissolution, represent one of the most stressful times of a person's life, it is to your best legal interest that you are coping with these stresses. Unless you are thinking clearly, you may be inclined to make some decisions on settling or not settling the case which will ultimately be extremely costly to you. For that reason, I will spend some time with you exploring this interaction, especially toward the beginning of the case. From what you tell me, I may be able to point out some of the "games" that are being played and how to avoid being one of the players.[1] However, at some particular point, my listening to your experiences will fail to generate a return worth the added costs that will appear on your monthly statement.

(c) Participate as effectively as you can in your own case. Your time

---

[1]Highly recommended is Games People Play a paperback book which has been around a long time. Author: Eric Berne.
Also, The Custody Handbook. Author: Persia Woolley

is likely to be less expensive to you than ours. Therefore, we will request that you obtain as much of the information and documents for your case as possible, consistent with its proper and expeditious handling. For example, we may send you a long set of questions called "Interrogatories". The other party is legally entitled to request the information asked, although it may mean hous of painstaking research through your records. It is our responsibility to see that the information asked for is supplied, especially since many of the questions are legal in nature, and you will need our guidance in answering some of the questions. However, if we have to do "the whole thing" on answering such a set of interrogatories, your case will become extremely costly. Also, if there is a delay in answering such documents, the other side could apply to the court for sanctions in the form of a money judgment against you, or use the delay in answering as an excuse to gain a continuance.

(d) Organize and file the papers involved in your case, and bring them to all conferences and hearings unless otherwise directed. This way client and attorney will be on the same wavelength when settlement negotiations are attempted. Both will have a full set of the papers to refer to.

(e) Organize your questions and concerns so that they may all be discussed at one time rather than on separate occasions.

(f) Think positively toward the settlement of the case. I can hardly remember a case where husband and wife had the same memory as to the understandings with respect to their acquisition of assets and numerous other matters. As a result of these many disputes in fact, and as a result of still other disputes as to what the law is in these areas, I cannot give you percentages of probability of outcomes, nor can I guarantee any single result in the case. For that reason, and because a judge can often dispose of a case in such a way as to enrich the Internal Revenue Service rather than the parties it is almost always best to settle the case if one can obtain a reasonably fair settlement. Therefore, as soon as we have enough information to understand what is at issue, I will seek your authority to negotiate a settlement.

---

3. Approaches to the Division of Tangible Personal Property provides excellent suggestions as to how to divide property. When clients come to their lawyer or mediator with a completed property agreement, they can save from hundreds to thousands of dollars in professional fees. A partial agreement can be incorporated into a mediated or legally negotiated settlement benefiting both parties.

4. The Compleat Dissolution Threat List might at first glance seem frightening in its implications. Yet enumerating typical threats of irate spouses and describ-

---

WESTPHAL, ELLNER, DIFRANZA & PORTMAN
ATTORNEYS AT LAW
1666 THE ALAMEDA
SAN JOSE, CALIFORNIA 95126

BARBARA A. DIFRANZA
KENNETH B. ELLNER
MARK PORTMAN
RONALD B. WESTPHAL

(408) 297-1600

THE COMPLEAT DISSOLUTION THREAT LIST

(The divorcing person's guide to the psychological warfare of words that may be expected over the next several months)

"I will tell them x, therefore, you will never get the children." [x can be an affair, the fact that you are seeing an analyst, an addiction to two or three glasses of wine per day, or many another situation. Chances are, x has little or nothing to do with the best interests of the children and therefore will be disregarded in any planning for the children's lives.]

"Your attorney is a dud, or out to get our money, or why don't we use one attorney and save money, or your attorney is really partial to me, etc., etc."

[These are divide and conquer tactics. If there is a way to save attorney fees and costs, we are looking for it as well and will be glad to discuss it with you.]

"Unless you play this my way, you'll never get a dime."

[The threatener has been used to being in charge of things. That is no longer the case. The property will be divided evenly. Support will be awarded, probably in accordance with the schedule.]

"Why are you trying to take my money? (my pension, my children, etc.)"

[The answer is simply because you are entitled to it and you are willing to share.]

"I'll go to jail before I'll pay you a dime."

[So be it. There are various ways to enforce support obligations through wage assignments; ultimately, contempt of court can mean a jail term. However, this is very rarely the case and most of these people end up paying voluntarily.]

"I'll quit my job before I'll pay you that kind of money."

[Attempt to get a witness to this kind of a statement. If intent can be proven to avoid support obligations by quiting one's job, these support obligations would continue at the same level.]

"When the judge sees my expenses, he will award less (more) than the support from the 'schedule'."

[This is not true unless there are extraordinary expenses. It should be remembered that the supported spouse will get less money than needed and the supporting spouse will pay more money than can be afforded.]

"You'll never see the kids again."

[There are uniform acts to prohibit childnapping. A parent who attempts to move to avoid visitation will find that the visitation becomes for much longer periods of time and involves additional expense of airplanes. Failure to allow visitation is one of the reasons why the courts change custody from one parent to the other.]

"I will consider reconciling with you only if you sign this agreement."

[If you are going to reconcile, why do you need the agreement? or why must the agreement be in favor of the party making such a demand? Be extremely suspicious of any such statements.]

"If you don't see this thing my way, the judge will order that we sell everything".

[The Court will not order the sale of an asset unless there is a good economic reason for it in the best interest of both parties. Instead, the court will generally do all or a combination of the following:

(1) Award individual assets or obligations to one or the other party;

(2) Award an asset to both parties 1/2 and 1/2 because the asset, such as a limited partnership, cannot be valued, or,

(3) Provide that one party receive an asset such as a residence conditional on an equalizing payment or note to the other. Where there are minor children and tight economic circumstanes the court may also temporarily award the family residence to the custodial parent with sale and equal division to occur later.]

It is suggested that anyone suffering unduly from these kinds of comments and threats, keep a running diary with dates, places, occasions and summaries of conversations occurring. (Do not tape record a conversation without consent; its a felony with a heavy fine!)

It is not recommended that you phone your attorney as each of these threats come in. The purpose of listing them here is to show how common they are and that the best thing to do is ignore them and go forward with attempting to reach a reasonable resolution of the case at hand.

ing how these threats are actually handled by the courts relieves a lot of the anxiety the threats would otherwise cause. Forewarning the client reduces the impact of these threats when they actually occur, and provides constructive ways of responding to some of them; for example, clients are told to make a written memorandum of the date, substance, and circumstances that occasioned the threat.

JUDICIALLY IMPOSED SETTLEMENT

A surprising number of cases are settled immediately before trial, when the harsh realization of what may happen in the courtroom becomes vivid and imminent. The possible gains of "winning" may no longer seem sufficiently attractive to justify the risks of having a judge determine who will raise the children, get the house, pay support, and so on.

Legal trials are not terribly glamorous in reality. Court calendars are crowded. Because many disputes are settled immediately before trial, many court clerks overschedule court time as a matter of policy. Couples sometimes wait for hours with their attorneys at the courthouse.

In some jurisdictions judges must piece together all the information they can glean in as little as ten to fifteen minutes. Though $200,000 or more may be at stake, less time is allocated for the typical divorce than for a business dispute involving the same number of dollars. The final rulings are a product of experience and intuition, as judges attempt to compensate for a paucity of information.

Despite the demise of the fault divorce statutes, the physical structure and intended purpose of the courtroom makes it clear that the husband and wife are opponents. They are placed on opposite sides of the courtroom. Though they are in the same room, they do not speak to or face each other, but use intermediaries (attorneys) to speak for them. Even the intermediaries do not speak to each other; they address the judge. In this atmosphere cooperation and conciliatory interaction are unlikely.

THE JUDGE AS DECISION MAKER

Some couples take their case before a judge because they view this functionary as a figure of respect and authority and as one who will pass judgement objectively and fairly. These couples feel unable to make their own decisions. For some, the courtroom appearance together has the symbolism and significance of the wedding ceremony. Other spouses want an opportunity to publicly attack and humiliate their spouses. (Unless it is a custody proceeding, these spouses will probably be disappointed.)

Judges may or may not have a chance to review trial briefs supplied by each spouse's attorney before trial. Arguments in court seldom allow time for either spouse to be heard in any detail. This is anger provoking and frustrating to the litigating spouses. Based on this meager information, judges make the most equitable decision they can. Because so many family court judges are unable to satisfy divorcing couples, and because they are overworked, frustrated by their inability to make thoroughly informed decisions, and tired of the emotional turmoil they deal with day after day, family court is considered the least desirable assignment available in many jurisdictions.

Being human, judges are influenced by many things. It is the attorney's job to know if the judge has any personal biases that are apt to have a negative effect on the case. Judges can gain reputations for being sympathetic to women, marines, or any class of litigant. They may be known for awarding joint custody or custody to mothers. There are attorneys who believe that the quality of the judge's breakfast is crucial to the quality of a ruling on any given morning.

If one party appears to be untrustworthy, the judge is often influenced despite a lack of conclusive evidence. For instance, a husband who has been shifting funds a great deal prior to the divorce appears suspicious. Has he been trying to hide away funds that should be taken into account when dividing the marital property? Though the wife's attorney is unable to uncover concrete evidence of misappropriation of funds, the judge may be a bit more generous with the wife after hearing about the husband's recent activities.

Helen is still angry about the judge who presided over her divorce. "When we went to court, I was sorry we had failed to negotiate our own settlement . . . but I thought that the worst that could happen was I'd be awarded half of the property and reasonable child support. I was wrong. My attorney was from San Francisco and didn't know anything about the judge. I found out six months later from an attorney that practices in Alameda that my judge hates women. He would have gotten my case rescheduled with a different judge."

Judicial findings and resulting orders are more subject to arbitrary circumstances and the limitations of the court proceedings than is commonly believed. The judicial system itself recognizes the impossibility of providing unbiased judges. In most jurisdictions an attorney has the option of changing judges once without any justification, and with cause subsequently. Perhaps if couples understood the risks of the courtroom, they would be more reluctant to resort to it without first attempting meaningful settlement negotiations.

CHILDREN AND DIVORCE

No description of divorce in the shadow of the law would be complete without a discussion of its impact on children. Often couples enter their attorneys' or their mediators' offices with a fairly clear idea of how they would like to arrange their parenting responsibilities. Couples who have not yet decided this may wish to know how the law can affect their decisions. Certain changes in the law and in society have heightened the opportunity for parents to fight over children.

Mothers who work as many hours of the day as fathers and who have no more time to spend with their children than do the fathers have no reason to believe that they will gain custody of the children. True, mothers are awarded custody of the children in 90 percent of the cases where one parent has custody. This is largely because most fathers do not ask for custody of their children. When fathers do ask for custody, in most states they stand a 50 percent chance of gaining it. Equal rights advocates have forced the courts to abolish any presumption that mothers are more appropriate custodians of children. Judges must now rely on more objective criteria when making custody decisions: Who has provided the most child care in the past? Who has more time for the child? What arrangement will least upset the child? And perhaps, Who does the child want to be with?

Fathers are becoming "liberated," learning that they are important to their children and recognizing their own need for intimacy with their children. Recent research indicates that the traditional "every other weekend and a few weeks in the summer" visitation schedule is not adequate for a sustained relationship with a father. Children complain that they don't see their fathers enough; many feel hurt and rejected. Studies are only now beginning to explore the importance of the father's role in raising the children. A strong correlation between frequent contact with the father and success in school has been established (especially for boys). Some fathers back away from their children after a divorce because the limitations on their contact with their kids is too painful for them to tolerate. Rather than reopening their wounds on a regular basis, they see their children less and less. The situation is agonizing for both father and children. It is not surprising that more and more fathers are asking for joint or sole custody of their children.

This increased equality for fathers, and the encouragement of cooperative parenting arrangements, are good for families when divorcing parents do cooperate. Joint custody is a boon for everyone. It eases the tremendous burden on the typical single working parent, provides children with meaningful contact with both parents, and alleviates the noncustodial parent's sense of loss and isolation. When mothers recognize the value of the father's contribution to the children's upbringing, even after he has left the marital relationship, most will begin to encourage the father's interest in the child.

However, when couples cannot agree upon a custody arrangement, these changes in the law can heighten the conflict. Unfortunately, some mothers feel negligent or inadequate if they willingly give up time with their children. Pressure from relatives and friends frequently reinforces these feelings. Regrettably, some fathers are relieved to be released from the duties of child rearing.

The difficulties that arise when parents cannot cooperate are staggering. Custody battles are easily the most disturbing aspect of divorce. Everyone has heard the tale of King Solomon, who ordered a baby cut in two when confronted by two women, each claiming to be the child's mother. Solomon awarded the baby to the woman who relinquished her claim to the baby so that it might live. Unfortunately, psychologically cleaving a child in two is less apparent to divorcing parents, who too often fail to see the stresses they are creating in their children until they have already done irreparable damage to the child's psyche.

No-fault divorce statutes have been of little benefit to children whose parents choose to fight over them. Once custody of a child is in question, the character assassinations and blaming behavior of contested divorce rears its head. Typically, each parent attempts to denigrate the other in order to prove him- or herself the more appropriate custodian of the child or children. During a divorce most individuals have difficulty coping with a sense of marital failure. Vicious attacks on parental abilities do little to enhance already damaged self-esteem. Custody disputes are a destructive experience at a time when positive steps toward creating a new life should be underway. The children have hostile, demoralized parents at a time when they need all the love and stability they can get.

Many judges have custody evaluators make recommendations, because they realize that they have very minimal access to information with which to make a well-reasoned custody decision. When custody fights are bitter, three separate custody evaluations may be presented to the court: one on the mother's behalf, one on the father's behalf, and one on behalf of the court, which is acting as protector of the child. This is a wasteful and often destructive process. The child is pestered by a barrage of professionals, and the judge may have three conflicting professional opinions to evaluate.

John and Mary have been divorced for three years. At the time of the divorce, Mary took custody of the children. John worked all day and the children were young, so he accepted his role as noncustodial parent. John remarried recently, and he has been told that men now gain custody of their children more frequently. He resents the fact that he only sees his children on weekends, and fears that he is missing out on the most important part of being a father. Mary is a loving mother, but she has had a series of unsuccessful relationships after the divorce and is frequently depressed. Mary has had sole custody of the children for three years. John believes he can provide a better home for the children than Mary can. Mary does not agree.

John went to court to get a change in custody. John and Mary emerged from a particularly bitter custody battle $10,000 poorer, with two extremely unhappy children. John lost. The court did not consider John's reasons for changing custody sufficiently compelling. John received a strictly outlined visitation schedule to minimize the amount of contact he would have with Mary. Mary has the children but feels shaken, battered, and bitter.

A noncustodial "loser" often feels judgment has been passed and that she or he has failed as a parent and as a human being. The "winner" may have only a shaky sense of security, fearing future custody battles should she or he take a false step.

The most damaging aspects of custody battles are often not realized until after the divorce. Child snatching has become all too common. The separate states have joined together to create the Uniform Child Custody Act, which provides as much legal protection as possible to parents who have their child taken by an ex-spouse. For example, a mother who takes a child from its father and who tries to get custody of the child in another state's courts will fail, unless she can convince the judge that sending the child back to the father is dangerous to the child. (This is small consolation to parents who have children taken and who have no idea of how to find them.) Small children are snatched and countersnatched by loving parents who cannot live with court orders and who somehow rationalize their actions. Both parents and children are left with deep psychological scars and are haunted by insecurity and potential loss.

On a less dramatic level, continued tension between parents is stressful for children. Immature parents sometimes spy on one another or sabotage each other's plans and authority through the children. For example, when a mother deliberately feeds her child before he goes out with his father for a surprise picnic, the child suffers right along with the father. Many children live for years with loyalty conflicts that they cope with in a variety of ways. Some children find it necessary to choose one parent over the other, shutting the other out—a terrible loss to both child and parent, whether or not they will admit it at the time. A child who regards his or her mommy or daddy as bad lives with that reflection on his or her self-image. Other children carefully neglect to talk about activities done with the other parent, or become obsessed with being fair to each parent. Even very young children learn to avoid certain subjects, disguise their feelings, or carry tales, depending upon the demands of their circumstances.

Custody battles force judges to impose strict visitation schedules on parents. Ultimately, this is difficult for both the parents and the children. Inevitably, parents' situations and attitudes change in the first few years following a divorce; wounds heal, new lifestyles develop, and many divorced persons remarry. At the same time, the children grow. The ten-year-old is now thirteen and busy with sports on weekends. Children resent inappropriate visitation schedules as they get older. Custody and visitation may be frozen in time, indifferent to changing needs and personalities. Many boys go to live with their fathers in late adolescence. Some children thrive in a situation where they may move freely between their parents' households. Other children, particularly young children, need the stability of a primary home and frequent contact with the other parent. Parents need a good working relationship with each other in order to meet the changing needs of their family.

Mediated and negotiated agreements permit parents great flexibility. Mediation in particular encourages cooperative behavior for future parenting. Parents discuss the needs of their children in a supportive atmosphere, often creating schedules that would never be ordered or enforced in a court setting. For example: Cathy has children by two husbands. She negotiated parenting agreements in which she shares time equally with both of her children's fathers. She wants her children to have a sense of family. She also wants some time alone with the eldest, because her younger child is at a stage where she demands a great deal of attention. Right now the children spend 50 percent of their time with her together, and 50 percent of their time with her alone. The children get both individual attention and shared time. Cathy even gets 25 percent of her time for herself. "Sometimes it's too good to be true . . . then I have scheduling problems with one of the dads. It's worth it though! I can't imagine not having their dads involved."

There are a wealth of options open to parents designing a parenting agreement. Numerous books and counselors are available to assist parents looking for workable means of co-parenting their children.

In addition to the emotional strain of divorce, a huge number of children also suffer financially. It is not merely that their standard of living declines along with that of their parents. A tremendous number of noncustodial parents stop providing child support on a regular basis within one or two years after the divorce. Many parents have experienced the hollow victory of being awarded child support, only to find that the support checks do not arrive and that legal procedures to enforce their order are to expensive or are not possible because the supporting spouse has left town. Two-thirds of divorced mothers with children receive minimal or no child support. Approximately 40 percent of these women have incomes below the poverty level. Many end up on welfare.

A mediated divorce settlement does not ensure that support payments are going to be sent on time and in full; however, it makes this more likely. If Mark has fought with Beth tooth and nail, he is apt to resent sending her money, even if it is for Sheldon. If they have worked out a budget together, he knows just how necessary his support is; and if he has agreed to the settlement voluntarily, that payment is apt to be quite reliable.

FOOTNOTES

[1] Robert Mnookin published the first article on this subject: "Bargaining in the Shadow of the Law: The Case of Divorce," *Yale Law Journal*, Vol. 88, April 1979.

[2] Charles E. Sherman, *How to Do Your Own Divorce in California* (Occidental, Calif.: Nolo Press, 1982).

[3] K. Kressel, M. Lopez-Morillas, J. Weinglass, and M. Deutsch, "Professional Intervention in Divorce: A Summary of the Views of Lawyers, Psychotherapists, and Clergy," *Journal of Divorce*, Vol. 2, No. 2, Winter 1978.

[4] Ibid., p. 123.

[5] Ibid., p. 124.

[6] Ibid., p. 127.

[7] Ibid.

THREE

MEDIATION

MEDIATION: AN OLD ART REVITALIZED

> I had learnt the true practice of law. I had learnt to find out the better side of human nature and to enter men's hearts. I realized that the true function of a lawyer was to unite parties riven asunder. The lesson was so indelibly burnt into me that a large part of my time during the twenty years of my practice as a lawyer was occupied in bringing about private compromises of hundreds of cases. I lost nothing thereby—not even money; certainly not my soul.[1]

Written in the first half of this century by the Indian attorney and leader Mohandas K. Gandhi, this quotation reflects the universal appeal of mediation. The practice of having respected third-party neutrals intervene in community and family disputes is as old as society itself: it was recorded in the Bible and the Koran, and was practiced in ancient tribal cultures as well as in modern ones.

Mediation is a human response to both intra- and intercultural disputes requiring peaceful, mutually acceptable solutions. Both labor mediation and international mediation are essential forms of dispute settlement in our society. Managers mediate conflicts between employees; mothers mediate disagreements between siblings. Historically ministers, family members, friends, counselors, and attorneys have mediated family disputes. Mediation in the 1980s has been compared to sex in the 1960s—it has always been done, yet only recently has it attracted public awareness. Divorce mediation is gaining acceptance in the legal, therapeutic, and lay communities. Today mediation is becoming the theme of books, professional training, and services.

THE ORIGINS OF DIVORCE MEDIATION

Divorce mediation is an interdisciplinary profession. Lawyers and mental health professionals collaborate to meet the needs of their divorcing clients. Lawyers value mental health professionals' ability to help couples with emotional issues that arise during divorce; mental health professionals respect lawyers' ability to advise clients about the legal aspects of divorce.

The idea of divorce mediation was conceived by lawyers and counselors who were frustrated by their inability to meet the needs of those divorcing clients who did not want a traditional adversarial divorce. Most mediators are either practicing lawyers or mental health professionals who risked stepping out of their conventional role to help their clients get what they wanted. Family law practitioners were angered when divorces needlessly escalated into petty wars due to contentious attorneys. Attorneys such as O. J. Coogler, the president and founder of the Family Mediation Association, became committed to developing a mediation process after a harsh personal experience with adversarial divorce.

Mental health professionals often work with couples and families prior to the spouses' decision to divorce. They spend months, and even years, with couples concerned about marital difficulties. Traditionally, when it became apparent that the couple should separate, the mental health professional felt compelled to recommend that two attorneys be consulted. Soon the couple would be unwilling to speak with each other, though they had worked together on their problems with the counselor in the past. While the mental health professional could continue to counsel the couple, helping them adjust to the divorce, he or she could not help the couple resolve their legal differences without risking attack by the local bar association.

No-fault divorce was first introduced in California and was rapidly adopted by most states. This procedure made it possible for couples to do their own divorces and eliminated the necessity for an adversarial orientation toward divorce. However, most couples still sought attorneys when they could not do their own divorce; and the approach of these attorneys was of adversarial jockeying for advantages. Thus, in a large percentage of divorce cases, no-fault divorce failed to reduce significantly the animosity and self-serving manipulation of facts so common in divorce. No-fault divorce was not enough in and of itself. It was necessary to set up a new process, with different expectations. Divorce mediation was the most obvious solution to this problem. Especially in California—where divorce was a highly visible social problem and no-fault divorce was first available—and elsewhere around the country, lawyers and mental health professionals began helping their clients avoid the adversary process through self-determination/mediation.

Mediators were (and are) drawn into the field for a variety of reasons:

1. A couple would seek a lawyer (often a friend) for help in drawing up their final settlement agreement. They were reluctant to go to separate attorneys because

a. They knew what they wanted and saw no need for separate counsel
b. They had begun doing their own divorce and had run into some snags; they wanted legal information—not representation
c. They had seen divorcing friends become hostile and inflexible following visits to attorneys
d. They needed to save money

The attorney was in a bind. Technically, the attorney could represent only one of them; yet the couple's desire to work on their divorce settlement cooperatively was reasonable, even admirable.

2. Couples who had been in counseling together and were having difficulties negotiating their divorce settlement would return to their counselor, wanting help in working out the details of their divorce.

3. The professionals themselves were disturbed by the counterproductive activities promoted by the adversary system. They decided to provide couples seeking a nonadversarial divorce with the needed professional assistance.

Most mediators started out cautiously, not advertising, and working only with their clients or with couples who sought them out. They developed their methods by trial and error and by intuition. When their efforts were successful, they began to share their knowledge and expand their horizons. Mediators now have outside resources available in the growing volume of divorce and mediation literature and training. Mediation courses are beginning to appear in law schools, social work programs, and psychiatric curricula. Some lawyers have earned counseling degrees, and some mental health professionals have gone on to get their J.D. A few schools have proposed offering a joint degree. Soon there will be lawyers and mental health professionals with degrees in mediation.

WHY MEDIATE?

Tremendous efforts are being made to inform fellow professionals and the lay public about this underemployed option for divorcing couples. Why this urgency? The massive divorce rate has created a demand for more humane ends to the marital relationship. Today increasing numbers of divorcing couples wish to minimize the needlessly destructive and painful aspects of their separation.

Hurtful as divorce is, potential benefits may result from this process:

1. Parents often develop richer and more rewarding relationships with their children after divorce. This is particularly true of men who have played the traditional fatherly role of providing financial support, leaving child rearing to their wives. These fathers may actually spend more time with their children after divorce than when they were married.

2. Individual spouses recover old skills and strengths that were lying dormant and discover new ones. Spouses who were performing traditional male and female roles in the nuclear family may learn that they enjoy working on cars, cooking, car-

pentry, gardening, shopping, bookkeeping, or whatever they might have previously considered the exclusive realm of the other spouse.

3. Divorce is frequently a catalyst for reevaluating values and lifestyles. People often change jobs, go back to school, move, or develop a new internal perspective on life after a divorce.

4. Destructive and nonfunctional communication patterns that existed between the spouses are terminated and, if recognized, may be avoided in future relationships.

People who divorce through mediation tend to realize more of these benefits and experience less trauma. Mediating a divorce may salvage a relationship that was unsatisfactory as a marriage but is rewarding as a friendship.

Even when the mediation is terminated prior to reaching a final agreement, the effects of the attempt to mediate may be profound. Mediator Henry Elson tells of a couple who had started adversary proceedings but were dissatisfied and came to him. Ultimately, however, they were unable to mediate, because they found working together too painful. The woman called him later to thank him for the change of attitude he inspired. She claimed her present attorney was very much like him. Their lawyers were doing their negotiating for them, but they now understood that they wanted cooperative, fair negotiation. It is misleading to define only completed final agreements as successful mediations. A change in attitude, or a partial agreement, can be very valuable.

One study, "An Evaluation of Court Mediation: A Comparison in Divorce Cases with Children,"[2] reported very encouraging results. According to the study,

1. The children of mediated divorces adjust more readily after the divorce is over. This is probably because their parents hold less hostility toward one another, have a greater understanding and acceptance of their divorce, and are more careful about protecting the children from whatever animosity they still feel.

2. Settlement agreements resulting from mediation are more frequently honored, and the likelihood of future cooperation is greater. This means fewer post-divorce court appearances.

3. Spouses have a greater degree of self-determination and resultant self-respect after mediation.

4. Less money is spent by the couple and the state on the divorce where mediation is employed.

5. On the whole, mediating couples tend to be more satisfied with the outcome of the divorce. Furthermore, they are both economically and emotionally better able to begin building their new lives.

THE BEST POSSIBLE DIVORCE

The ideal divorce costs nothing and hurts no one. The spouses remain friends, no children are involved, and the couple part wiser for their experiences together.

The do-it-yourself divorce occasionally comes close to this ideal. For couples who already have an understanding about who owns what and who merely need to sever the legal bond, a divorce kit may be all they need. When done thoughtfully, doing your own divorce is the least expensive means of obtaining a divorce. The only costs are filing fees and the cost of the divorce manual or kit for the state in which you live. More and more couples decide to process their own divorces each year. Couples who handle their own divorce competently and without rancor show exceptional ability to cope with one of life's most traumatic experiences.

Many people are unable to do their own divorce. After years of marriage, emotions, property, and finances are generally too entangled for a couple to sit down and come to an agreement without any professional help. Couples seek assistance negotiating the details of the divorce for one or more of the following reasons:

1. The parties lack the legal information needed to make informed decisions. For example: Kate and John don't know how much Kate's pension is worth or how they can fairly account for its value in their divorce settlement. A mediator can help them value the pension or can send them to an actuary and make sure they are aware of all their options when they divide the pension.

2. One or both spouses need protection because emotions are still volatile and certain issues touch off emotional fireworks, old arguments, new arguments, or recrimination and guilt. For example: Greta was divorced four years ago in a jurisdiction that did not yet offer no-fault divorce. After consulting attorneys, she and her husband decided that they wanted to avoid any kind of adversarial proceedings. They parted on friendly terms, but the price was considerable.

Today she regrets her lack of protection. "I was leaving him. I gave him my car . . . I called it our car then. I left the marriage with a single bed and nightstand. A mediator could have protected me. I needed protection from myself." A neutral third party can prevent this type of situation by helping spouses overcome their feelings of guilt and by encouraging them to discover their actual needs and to decide what is fair.

3. One or both spouses avoid addressing sensitive issues that must be resolved to finalize the divorce. A mediator can take the couples through all the issues necessary for a couple to create a divorce settlement. If the couple resist discussing child custody, the mediator helps them face their fears and makes the problem seem more manageable.

4. Property, custody, or financial issues are in dispute. Dividing one house and one piece of investment property is hard work even when you understand all your options. When each spouse has a different understanding of the options available and/or wants a different outcome, the problem may become insoluble without help. The presence of an attorney/mediator introduces a knowledgeable third party who can answer questions and structure negotiations to increase the likelihood of reaching an agreement.

5. The financial issues are too complex to handle without professional assistance. Couples with a great deal of money and property need to create an agreement that is fair and that considers the tax consequences of the division of property. If both husband and wife take stocks currently worth \$100,000, but the basis (amount spent for an investment minus depreciation claimed or plus improvements reported) for the wife's stock is \$50,000 and the basis for the husband's stock is \$150,000, the wife will be taxed on \$50,000 when she sells her stock and the husband will report a \$50,000 loss. Couples who want to maintain co-ownership of certain properties may need legal assistance in deciding how to best structure a co-ownership agreement. A family business may need to be rearranged.

The cost of professional help is well worth it when the help is appropriate. When problems occur, couples doing their own divorce have typically sought separate attorneys, convinced that they are unable to work without professional assistance. Many of these couples would have mediated their remaining differences had they known that mediators were available to assist them.

In some respects, having a judge or an attorney decide how to divide property and parenting rights is simpler than working the issues through. Reaching consensus takes time and effort. A neutral third party can make a decision without ever causing the spouses to consider what is fair in their eyes. Unfortunately, when spouses never figure out the actual monthly cost of raising their children, it is more likely that both spouses will feel overly burdened—one thinking he or she is getting too little, the other feeling that he or she is paying too much. Similarly, attorneys negotiating for their clients spare the clients the effort of confronting their feelings.

Sometimes parties themselves make hasty agreements in order to avoid dealing with conflict. This may be faster as well as less troublesome at the time, but the result will probably be harder to live with. If Kate wants to have her son Dave with her on Thanksgiving, and the court or her attorney arranges for her to have Dave on alternate years because John (Dave's father) wants Dave on Thanksgiving too, neither Kate nor John will be happy. When John and Kate work with a mediator, they have an opportunity to hear each other's needs; they might find them more compatible than they expected. For instance, if John primarily wants to have Dave in the morning so that they can go to church together, Dave can also attend Kate's big family dinner at 4:00 P.M. Even if their desires are clearly conflicting, for example, they both have family dinners at 4:00 P.M., Kate and John might prefer to modify the situation so that they are both somewhat satisfied.

Mediators urge couples to think about how they will structure their lives after the divorce, because this affects the decisions they make in their final settlement. How can they best regain their standard of living? How can they make more money? Many people change professions as well as lifestyles after divorce. Parenting and monetary agreements need to be composed with these possibilities in mind.

FIVE STAGES OF MEDIATION

The process of mediation can be broken down into five stages. The first and the last stage are quite distinct because specific goals must be realized to begin and end a mediation. The middle stages are less clearly defined, tending to overlap with one another.[3]

Introduction/Commitment Stage

During the initial one- or two-hour mediation session, the mediator discusses fees, describes mediation, sets ground rules, answers questions, and begins to gain a commitment to the process from the couple. The mediator may begin to develop an understanding of the more pressing issues that need to be resolved, gain a sense of the couple's personal dynamics, and try to ascertain whether the couple are ready and able to mediate.

One or both parties' resistance to mediation can be used as a means of gaining commitment to the process. Dan, who had been married for fifteen years, wasn't sure he wanted to be in a mediator's office; he didn't really want a divorce but saw no way to stop it. He was angry, repeatedly accusing his wife of callous behavior. (He had only learned of her intention to leave him one month earlier.) Dan needed to express his anger and wanted his wife to "pay." The mediator heard that Dan wasn't yet ready to mediate. He decided to share his insight with Dan so that Dan could choose to move on and mediate or else recognize that he wanted to fight.

MEDIATOR: This may not be a satisfactory process for you because if it works, she'll get what she wants. You'll also get what you want; but if what you want is to fight . . .

DAN: I want to mediate.

MEDIATOR: How did you get to there from three minutes ago, when you stated that you had an inclination to hire the best lawyer money could buy?

The mediator knows that Dan needs to make a conscious choice for the mediation to work. If he does not press him now, the mediation quite probably will break down in a later session.

The mediator both describes the amount of work required and tries to convince the couple that the benefits of mediation are worth the effort involved: "I know you are going to have to expose some very tender nerves and make difficult decisions. Mediating is a lot of work. I think it's worth it, and it seems that you do too, or you wouldn't be here. I congratulate you on your decision to take responsibility for your separation agreement. . . ."

Definition Stage

The mediator and the couple will define the areas on which they already agree and the areas where there are issues yet to be worked out. It may require a considerable amount of research to ensure that when they get to the negotiation and agreement-making stages, the couple have all the information they need to make intelligent decisions. For example, couples often itemize their income and compose budgets when support is an issue. The mediator may write crucial figures on a flip chart the couple can both see, thereby focusing their attention on the issue they need to resolve, and gaining agreements that the figures are realistic.

Negotiation Stage

The couple are ready to begin negotiating once they agree on basic facts and principles. The mediator keeps them focused on one issue at a time, helps them think of options, and encourages cooperative behavior. When issues are clearly stated and needs and feelings are aired, agreements are more easily reached. The mediator recedes into the background when discussions are flowing, and steps in when one spouse seems overwhelmed or spouses are overlooking cooperative alternatives by strictly adhering to a fixed position.

Agreement Stage

Once the couple have evaluated the facts and constructed options, they are ready to begin making agreements. Once again, the mediator's job is to maintain a cooperative atmosphere and to keep the couple focused on a manageable number of issues at any given time. The mediator closes areas of agreement, provides legal or other information necessary to a discussion, points out unrealistic attitudes or proposals, praises the couple, and gets them to praise themselves for progress made.

Contracting Stage

In the final stage of mediation, the couple review the agreements and clarify any ambiguities. Just who writes it and how it is written depends on the style of mediation being used. Mediators are careful to make specific agreements that are likely to prevent future controversy. "Try," "some," and other vague language is discouraged. Where possible, firm commitments are sought, rather than a loosely structured group of contingencies. The agreement is checked to make sure all reasonable contingencies have been considered. For example: John has agreed to pay $400 per month in child support. If John is unable to pay child support or is late in making a payment, what will happen? John and Kate can avoid many potential conflicts if they specify what will happen if payment is late. Millions of dollars in attorney's fees have been squandered by parents trying to enforce court-ordered child support and visitation rights. Legally, late payment or lack of payment has no effect on a parent's right to have contact with his or her child. Nonetheless, custodial parents often deny visitation when alimony payments are late. One solution for John and Kate would be to have John agree to notify Kate as soon as he knows he will be late or unable to pay support. He can then catch up on the payment within three months, or work out some kind of exchange.

The stages of mediation are basic guidelines for the manner in which a mediation will progress. During the middle stages of mediation, the free flow of negotiations moves forward one or two issues at a time. In some respects, each is a mini-mediation: defining the issue, coping with emotional blockages, establishing decision-making principles, and coming to agreements. The ultimate goal is an agreement in which no one is a loser and which all parties willingly abide by.

PHILOSOPHIC UNDERPINNINGS OF MEDIATION

Because of the diversity in professional training, the absence of contact between mediators up until the late 1970s, the lack of formal guidelines and professional standards, the newness of the profession, a shortage of data concerning individual conflict-resolution skills, legal and ethical barriers set up by the various bar associations, and the differing needs of the clientele, a wide range of mediation styles, theories, and practices have developed. Nonetheless, there are fundamental unifying characteristics and underlying beliefs that are common to most styles of mediation.

1. Mediation respects and supports people's ability to make decisions that affect their lives. Mediators believe that given the right atmosphere, the couples they work with are better informed, able, and equipped to make fair, intelligent decisions about their separation than is any third party.

2. Mediation encourages couples to rely on their own sense of fair play and justice rather than on generalized societal norms. In mediation, if a mother wants her child to go to a private school, she is likely to pay child support exceeding that which a court would order. She has acted on her own internal feeling of what is appropriate. This contrasts sharply with parents who waste so much money and energy fighting that they lose sight of their own and their children's needs.

3. Mediation provides a forum in which to develop cooperative win/win solutions that benefit everyone. Studies show that mediated settlements tend to facilitate the family's adjustment to new circumstances and to reduce the costs of divorce. Parents, children, and the extended family all benefit.

4. Mediators carefully maintain their neutrality, ever aware of their potential influence on mediating couples. If the mediator has had prior contact with either spouse, that fact should be disclosed, thereby exposing any potential bias and giving the couple an opportunity to find another mediator if they feel it is necessary. Because mediators are human, some clients will elicit strong negative or positive responses from the mediator due to purely personal experiences or beliefs. The mediator may be able to successfully put aside these prejudices. When a mediator cannot identify or overcome a negative or positive reaction to a client and fears that it will have an effect on his or her performance as a mediator, a referral is called for.

5. In mediation, the appearance of neutrality is as important as neutrality itself. Once a mediator is perceived as biased, he or she can no longer effectively work with a couple. Parties will fight the mediator or disregard the agreements made with his or her facilitation. Should this happen, the mediator must refer the couple to another mediator. (An attorney or mental health professional who has represented or counseled only one of two parties wanting to mediate will typically refer the couple to another mediator, because the other spouse may fear that the mediator will side with the spouse that he or she already knows.)

6. Personal growth is a secondary goal of mediation. Couples learn from the process. Not only do they learn to avoid past mistakes, but they learn how to cooperate for their mutual interest.

MEDIATION RULES AND TECHNIQUES

Typically, mediating couples talk, cry, yell, laugh, and hopefully end up thanking each other and the mediator in the course of ten hours of mediation. Helping a divorcing couple through this emotional mine field requires skill and courage. To successfully facilitate this process, a mediator must master a wide variety of communication techniques and sophisticated procedures with which to assist the couples.

Before getting into the later stages of mediation, the mediator needs to establish the procedures and rules the couple agree to work with.

1. The mediator controls the process, though not the substance, of the mediation. The mediator may ask spouses to speak directly to him or her when emotions are high and hostile. For example, John doesn't have the opportunity to yell at Kate "You slob!" Instead, he tells the mediator why Kate's messiness disturbs him. "Kate is a slob."

MEDIATOR: "Excuse me, John, but we've agreed to stick to the issues and refrain from name calling. What is it you're concerned about?"

JOHN: "It's bad for children to live in a dirty environment. Hygiene and. . . ."

Because John is no longer attacking Kate directly, she may hear John's concern for the children if it is a real concern of his. If it is just a ploy to strengthen his negotiating position, the mediator may recognize this and bring this out to get to the real issue, which may be Kate's boyfriend or John's guilt about leaving his family.

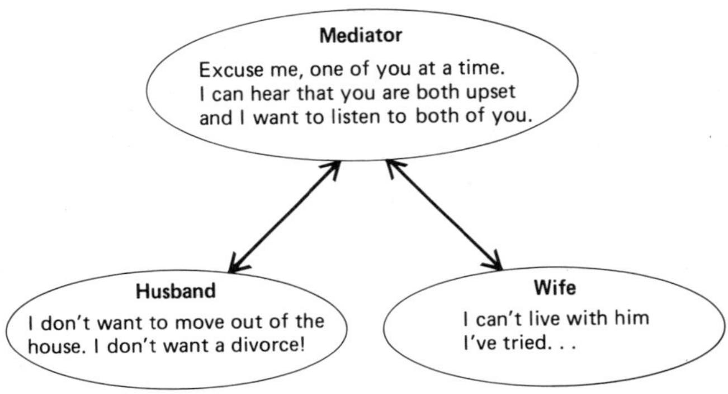

When a couple are communicating well, the mediator encourages them to talk to each other, intervening only when the discussion loses direction, the couple start blaming each other, or they become too hostile. Mediators specifically secure permission to interrupt when explaining their role in the process, paving the way for later interventions. The mediator will interrupt to help them clarify agreements, to redirect the conversation when they lose sight of their task, and to cut short arguments when they are not productive.

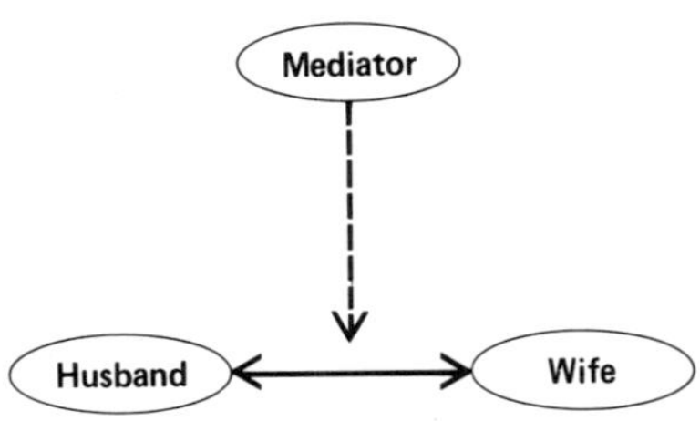

2. Openness and honesty are essential to successful mediation. This is discussed with parties as constituting one of the rules of mediation and is part of the initial contract the couple agree to in order to mediate. An agreement reached under conditions in which information was withheld is invalid and of no use to anyone.

3. Confidentiality is important in mediation. Many mediators have parties sign agreements to ensure that they will not be asked to testify in court or in any way divulge information revealed in mediation. Parties themselves often agree that their negotiations cannot be brought up in court should they only reach a partial agreement. Ground rules should specify the intentions both of the mediator and of the couple themselves.

4. The parties must agree to abide by their final decisions. Some couples agree to use binding arbitration should they reach an impasse on some issue in mediation.

5. There is often a rule prohibiting the use of outside parties to sway the other party. The most common rule of this nature forbids the parents from using the children as instruments to influence the negotiations for their custody.

In high-conflict situations the mediator may choose to have the couple address him or her to reduce the likelihood of fighting, or she may direct their attention to the chalkboard so that they will focus on the issues and gain mutual ownership of the suggestions as they are written on the board.

6. Mediators ask couples to look for a fair resolution of their differences. There should be no loser in mediation. Though most mediators attempt to leave all the decision making to the couples, when a mediator's sense of fairness is significantly offended by a couple's agreement, he or she will state that concern in some manner. Generally, a couple renegotiate; but should the agreement still be fundamentally unfair in the mediator's opinion, he or she may file a statement of nonconcurrence (which has no legal effect but which may serve to alert a judge to potential inequities). For example, fathers and mothers have been known to consent to give up all parental rights. The mediator may believe that the child has a right to have two parents.

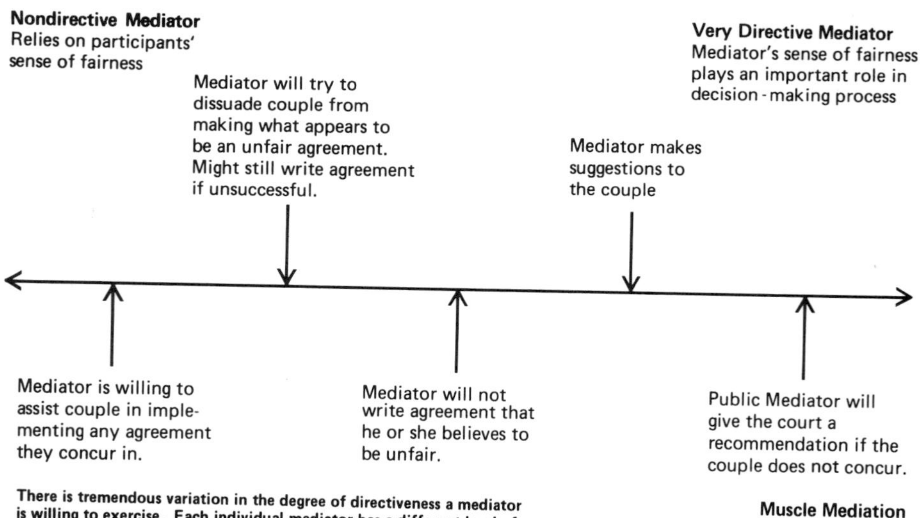

There is tremendous variation in the degree of directiveness a mediator is willing to exercise. Each individual mediator has a different level of tolerance for accepting a couple's concept of fairness. Children disparity in the division of assets, illness, and old age touch off chords of sensitivity in certain mediators.

7. Mediators frequently encourage couples to contribute rules they think would be helpful to the mediation process during the contracting stage. If trust is a problem, they may agree to bring in additional verification of finances. If one spouse is offended by certain old accusations, there can be an agreement that those will not be brought up in the mediation, and either that spouse or the mediator will be authorized to point out any breach of the agreement and stop it.

John Haynes states that a successful divorce mediation can be said to have taken place if

1. There has been full disclosure of all the economic assets of the marriage,
2. The economic division of the assets and the necessary support payments are

essentially equitable and designed to meet the joint needs of the family and the individual needs of each member,

3. There are no victims as a result of the agreement,
4. The channels of communication between the ex-spouses are open and direct; the mediator will have helped the couple organize a direct way to make decisions about the children,
5. The couple relate to their children as parents, not as spouses, through the acceptance of the permanence of their parental roles in the context of the ending of their spouse roles,
6. The children are able to develop and maintain an ongoing relationship with both parents; thus the agreement must provide for direct communication with both parents along with an appropriate range of access options regarding both parents,
7. The couple are empowered to make decisions and given the skills during mediation to continue the decision-making process in their respective futures.
8. The extended families, particularly blood relatives, are protected in their relationships with the children, and the children enjoy the same open access to them as to their parents.[4]

Once a basis from which to proceed has been established, the mediator's skills are used to keep the mediation progressing toward resolution.

1. Diplomacy, creativity, and the ability to inspire others to think creatively are mediative skills. Mediators have a great deal of influence; though they only have the authority the couple have given them. Most mediators refrain from making direct substantive suggestions because couples are more accepting of their own ideas than those of another person. One subtle means of conveying new ideas and messages with a minimum of pressure is storytelling. Stories that parallel a client's situation and show how other people have dealt creatively with similar concerns reveal a broader perspective. The couple unable to decide who gets the children may begin to open their minds to less traditional custody arrangements after hearing stories of other couples' unusual arrangements. (For example, a number of couples have given the children the house and have rented an apartment which the parent without the children occupies.)

Mediators who wish to make a point often convey their ideas or opinion by using carefully phrased questions. A mediator trying to convince a mother that her son would benefit from contact with his father on a regular basis would first confirm the mother's dedication to her son's welfare.

MEDIATOR: "What do you want for Dave?"
MOTHER: "I want to do what's best for him."
MEDIATOR: "How do you think Dave feels about his father?" and so on.

The mother is allowed to determine for herself that Dave will be happier and better adjusted if she makes it easy for his father to have frequent contact with him.

2. Mediation requires pressures and motivations. The need to continue raising the children together; a desire to avoid attorneys; the cost, time expenditure, and emotional turmoil involved in an adversary divorce; the belief that a cooperative settlement is more advantageous to both parties; and the desire for privacy, informality, and an understandable settlement convinces many couples to mediate. Mediators use these pressures and motivations to keep the mediation moving: "If you want to spend your time here arguing, I'm willing to listen. I'm earning $50 an

hour. However, I think we agreed to conduct the mediation in a businesslike fashion for your sake and for the children. I suggest we get back to. . . ."

3. Mediators teach couples to cooperate and emphasize the benefits spouses realize as a result of the cooperation. For example: Filling out budget forms separately is difficult for spouses who had split duties in the marriage. If the couple cooperate in the mediation session, the mediator may suggest that they assist each other with the budget between sessions. If they run into difficulties working with each other, they can simply stop, and continue at the next session. This is an opportunity for the husband to share his knowledge about the weekly shopping expenses and for the wife to share her experience in handling the monthly bills. This may be the spouses' first cooperative effort in months. When they recognize that they are working together toward a common goal, mediation seems all the more possible.

4. Mediators break down the issues to be decided until couples are capable of handling each issue separately or in discrete groupings. The mediator is constantly evaluating the couple's responses and trying to structure the mediation to meet their needs. The first issue the mediator chooses for the couple to mediate is generally selected because there is a high likelihood of reaching a satisfying cooperative agreement. Thus, the couple is quickly rewarded. Structured mediation (a style of mediation described in Section II of this book) suggests the mediation of a temporary agreement as the first order of business after agreeing to the rules. A temporary agreement is much less threatening because it lasts for only a limited period of time.

A custody agreement covering the next ten years is an overwhelming commitment for parents to make (not to mention an inappropriate commitment for the child, whose needs will change as he or she grows; and parents' needs will also change as they create new lives for themselves). A temporary agreement that covers a manageable period of time in a very concrete way—with guidelines provided for reaching another agreement when the first ends—is far easier to achieve. Six months, or until the end of the school year, is often long enough for a first custody agreement. When parents make the second custody agreement, they have a more realistic view of the commitments necessary.

As more and more small decisions are made, the couple become increasingly commited to mediation. They prove to themselves and to the mediator that they can work together for their mutual benefit. As the agreements mount up, they risk losing more and more emotional and monetary investments by abandoning the mediation.

5. Mediators provide an opportunity for spouses to vent some of their anger, pain, insecurity, and confusion about the divorce in a safe environment. After sharing their feelings, spouses feel understood, and they no longer need to repeat their positions. They can then move on to resolve conflicts. When a husband hears of his wife's pain and frustration, yesterday's cold, calculating actions may look less cold and calculating and more confused and angry. Sympathies for each other's fears and dreams sometimes develop.

6. Mediators pay close attention to a couple's balance of power. If the man is a practiced negotiator, for example, a car salesman or union representative, and the woman is a quiet scientific researcher, or if the man is feeling emotionally battered because his wife recently left him to move in with her boyfriend, the mediator may need to help balance the couple's negotiating abilities. The mediator can often achieve a better balance by openly recognizing an imbalance. For example: "John, you are an excellent negotiator. I'm impressed. Kate seems to be having a hard time expressing her needs. Would you be willing to help her out a bit?" Balance can also be restored by giving emotional support and ensuring that both parties let their needs be known: "John, you haven't said very much. What do you want to achieve today?" At the same time, the mediator must be careful to retain the appearance of neutrality. If one party has to be helped every step of the way, the couple are not good candidates for mediation.

7. Mediators help couples recognize and overcome poor communication patterns. For example: Many couples do mindreading. That means that rather than hear what their spouse is saying, they "read between the lines" and make assumptions about what the spouse "really" means; they then react to that. When John told Kate that he couldn't pick Dave up from baseball on Tuesday, Kate got mad. She assumed that John was unwilling to pick Dave up because it would interfere with his going out with his office mate after work. She further deduced that John didn't really care much about Dave. The mediator short-circuited this miscommunication.

MEDIATOR: Kate, what are you so angry about?
KATE: He always does this.
MEDIATOR: Does what?
KATE: Runs off to have fun, never thinking about Dave or me!
JOHN: Wait a minute. I want to pick Dave up. He's my son too, you know. It happens that I have a doctor's appointment that afternoon.

John and Kate cooled off and resumed talking. Ultimately, Kate started to feel pretty positive about parenting Dave with John.

8. Mediators use subtle body language and verbal cues to keep the negotiations flowing:

a. A raised hand can quiet a person (traffic cop imagery).
b. Prolonged eye contact encourages the speaker.
c. Refusal to make eye contact with an interrupting party discourages such interruptions.
d. A low, modulated voice has a calming influence. The mediator may merely lower his or her voice and speak slowly to gain attention or to cause the negotiations to become less volatile.
e. Polite, diplomatic interventions keep negotiations civil. "Excuse me, Kate, John is talking and we agreed that only one person would talk at any one time. Please write down your objections to the plan so that you don't forget them, and we'll talk about them in a moment. Thank you."
f. Mediators soften language, thereby altering spouses' attitudes. Consider the expression "my ex-wife," as opposed to "the mother of my child." The feelings elicited are quite different.

9. Mediators help couples expand their perception of their options. When a couple enter into mediation intending to decide who gets the children, you or me, there doesn't seem to be much room for negotiation. The mediator will explore possibilities with them. What real limitations do exist? Distance? Time? Money? The children's desires? The mediator will ask questions designed to encourage the mother and father to come up with new options.

Brainstorming is a technique used when couples are having difficulty creating a broad variety of options. Both parties are encouraged to make as many suggestions as they can, silly or practical. Neither party is allowed to criticize suggestions during the brainstorming session. The couple then pick their favorite options and proceed from there. For example, John and Kate both want to keep the dog. Kate argues that she should have the dog because it protects the house and their son Dave is fond of it. John says he should have the dog because he trained it; and since he is going to have Dave 40 percent of the time, Dave will still see the dog. When it became apparent that, given the chance, John and Kate would bicker about the dog, the mediator directed their attention to a chalkboard, explained how to brainstorm, and suggested two minutes of brainstorming imaginative or even silly solutions. For example:

a. John gets the dog, but Kate takes the dog on weekends.
b. Kate gets the dog, but John takes the dog on weekends.
c. John buys Kate a new dog and helps her train it. Their present dog stays with Kate until she feels safe with the new dog.
d. Kate buys John a new dog.
e. They switch custody of the dog when they switch custody of Dave.
f. The dog spends one week with John and one week with Kate.

Listing their options gave John and Kate a good chuckle and a sense of the wealth of options available to them. After that, it wasn't hard for them to combine a few of the ideas to come up with an arrangement they both liked.

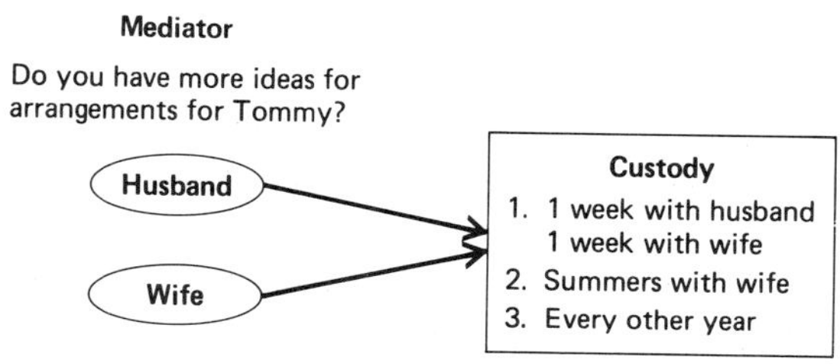

10. Preempting. Sometimes a mediator will know that a couple is likely to have trouble with a specific issue because their attorneys or counselors warned her. Some mediators attempt to subtley discover the more heated differences between a couple in the first session. With this foreknowledge the mediator has the opportunity to discuss this issue as an item of contention. For example, if the mediator knows that both the father and the mother are seeking sole custody and minimal visitation for the other parent, in the initial session, before open discussion has begun, the mediator can praise the couple for their concern for their child and discuss the needs of the child—studies that have revealed children's need for access to both parents, state law, and any other relevant information. Even if only one parent is seeking sole custody, this tends to be the least threatening way to convey the facts without having a parent decide that the mediator is biased. Ideally it is not apparent that the discussion is particularly meant for one parent's ears.*

11. When a spouse resists a particular agreement, the mediator may help the couple find a different way to structure the agreement so that it meets both their needs. If Kate needs $500 per month to live, and John is unwilling to pay Kate any spousal support because she is living with another man and he doesn't want this man to benefit from his support payments, the mediator can suggest options: What if John takes responsibility for buying Dave's clothes or for paying for day care or all medical and dental expenses? John may be far more willing to pay expenses specifically related to Dave.

12. When couples lack sufficient data or expertise to adequately resolve an issue, mediators send them to outside resources. The family business may need to be valued in order to be divided fairly, or couples may need more sophisticated tax advice than the mediator is able to give. One or both spouses often need outside counseling or the support of divorce classes offered in the community; or the couple may want some help bringing the children to terms with the divorce.

Mediators refer to other professionals, or to classes and books when they

*Donald T. Saposnek, *Mediating Child Custody Disputes* (San Francisco: Jossey-Bass Publishers, 1983), p. 200, 212, 219, and 225.

identify a couple's needs. For example, when parents want to tell their children about the divorce but don't know how, many mediators recommend children's books that explain divorce to children. These books provide an opening for parents to talk to the children about their own divorce.

13. During negotiations, and especially when a couple near agreement on an issue, the mediator does reality testing. Is the agreement practical? "How are you going to get Dave from the day-care center to John's before 4:00 P.M.? That's only fifteen minutes." Is the agreement specific enough? "Who is going to do the driving? What if Kate is late?"

14. Mediators are sometimes the spokespersons for one or both parties' deepest fears, bringing them to the surface so that they can finally be resolved. For example: John acts confident and self-assured in mediation; he talks as if he is well on the road to a new and better life. However, one thing doesn't seem to fit. Every time John and Kate talk about how to take care of their son Dave, they begin to bicker. As soon as the mediator recognizes this pattern, he or she will explore what is tripping John and Kate up. If the mediator discovers that John is deathly afraid that Kate's boyfriend is going to take his place as the father, the mediator can ask John about his concerns in an empathetic manner.

MEDIATOR: John, do I hear you saying that because Dave is so young, you feel he may adopt Kate's manfriend as a substitute father? I can see where that would be really scary.

When John faces this fear and talks about it with Kate he will then be able to ensure that he does retain his relationship with Dave.

15. Humor and timing are two of the most vital and least defineable elements of mediation. When the atmosphere is overly tense, the mediator can help the couple step back and view their situation as observers—sometimes the couple can even laugh at themselves. Knowing when to take a break or quit may save a mediation.

INDIVIDUAL CAUCUSING

Many people are familiar with labor mediation, in which the mediator works with the disputing factions in separate sessions. The parties privately develop proposals and counterproposals, some of which will be aired in group sessions. This is individual caucusing (also called shuttle diplomacy by some mediators). This process is sometimes used in divorce mediation, where it can be classified as either a distinctive technique or a separate style of mediation, depending on how a mediator uses the individual sessions. Some divorce mediators find individual sessions with the spouses helpful, especially when:

1. Parties have issues they are afraid of or embarrassed about or that they refuse to bring up in a joint session.
2. Parties can't occupy the same room without suffering severe emotional upset. The mediator may still be able to do successful shuttle diplomacy, conveying offers and counteroffers until the couple reach a consensus.
3. One party needs counseling that the mediator is best able to provide because of his or her knowledge of the dynamics of the divorce.
4. Parties need to decide upon priorities and develop proposals. For some spouses this is best accomplished in individual sessions.
5. Parties are extremely sensitive or are still quite hostile.

The individual sessions provide a forum for testing proposals without endangering the mediation or causing either party to lose face. For example, if John tells the mediator he wants the Volvo and is ready to give Kate the piano in exchange, the mediator can test Kate's reaction to the idea. If Kate thinks that is a terribly unfair idea but might consider trading for the dining room furniture, the mediator can set John onto a more productive track.

Individual caucusing gives the mediator an opportunity to develop a mediation plan based on knowledge of potential areas of agreement and disagreement. Early on, the mediator can have the couple negotiate items which he or she knows they are in substantial agreement about. Once the couple have developed a good rapport and have some agreements they want to preserve, the mediator will put tougher issues on the negotiating table. The mediator also has the chance to work on the parties' more rigid positions in individual sessions, suggesting that they may have to be more flexible or that they should think of other options that would be good for them. Some mediators like the advantages of individual caucusing so much that they use it in every mediation they do; others prefer to use it only in situations that specifically call for it.

Reasons for avoiding or doing a minimal amount of individual caucusing include the following:

1. Separate sessions cause some parties to fear that the mediator will become biased, create a closer affiliation with one spouse, or hear tainted stories.
2. The mediator takes on more responsibility for the outcome of the mediation when he or she talks to parties separately. The greater knowledge the mediator possesses gives him or her added control of what issues will come up, how they come up, and how they are resolved.
3. Spouses become concerned about secrets to which they are not privy.
4. A spouse is likely to divulge something in confidence that should be stated in a joint session. For example, if John reveals that he has saved $2000 that his wife does not know about for "a rainy day," in the privacy of an individual session, the mediator must convince him to disclose this in the joint session later.
5. When the mediator is confronted with a confidence he or she is not at liberty to divulge and the spouse refuses to disclose it in the joint session, the mediator may have to withdraw from the mediation.

Each system has advantages. A mediator who does not do individual caucusing may be essential for spouses who are very distrustful of each other. On the other hand, some couples are far more comfortable formulating plans for the future in individual sessions. The real issue is identifying which system is best suited to a particular couple.

CHILDREN IN THE MEDIATION SESSION

The mediator and parents jointly decide whether and when to bring children into the mediation session. The children's ages, maturity, ability to contribute to a better agreement, desire to participate, and need for reassurance—as well as the parents' ability to maintain a constructive atmosphere while the children are present—are all factors taken into account when deciding whether or not to include children. When parents are at an impass and ready to litigate, the mediator may decide that in the long run it is in the child's best interest to bring the child into mediation upsetting as that may be. Before children are brought into mediation, the mediator sets up guidelines for the session. The children's role is defined. The parents must be able to work together; often they may already have sorted out many of their ideas about custody arrangements. Quite possibly, they won't make any final agreements with the children present. Seeing parents work together, hearing the plans for custody, and experiencing their parents' deep concern is reassuring for many children.

There are a range of roles the children can assume in mediation. How much influence should a child have over custody arrangements? Some mediators and parents believe children should be actively included in the decision-making process. Others believe that while children's input is valuable for parents designing an agreement, it is the parents alone who ultimately make decisions regarding custody, particularly when children are young. More authoritarian parents feel it is their prerogative to make arrangements for their children regardless of the latter's ages. (Remember, a court would not presume to tell married parents where their children should live, except in cases of extreme neglect.) In this case the mediation session can be used as a controlled environment to inform children of their parents' arrangements and concern for their welfare. The age of the children, the orientation of the parents, and the professional opinion of the mediator are all factors in determining what role the children will play in a given mediation. A study conducted during the summer and fall of 1981, funded by the Divorce Mediation Research Project, revealed that 57.4 percent of the 256 private mediators who responded to their questionnaire do not ever meet the children in their average mediation.[5]

Children should not be placed in a position where they feel as if they are deciding which parent they shall live with. At the same time, a custody agreement that the children don't like will cause difficulties. A young child will become cranky, sick, or unmanageable; a teenager will simply sabotage any custody arrangement he or she doesn't like. A balance must be struck between working with the children and sheltering them from the turmoil of the divorce. Even the child who has expressly stated a preference for living with one parent may need protection from him- or herself. Given the choice, children often choose to live with the less emotionally stable parent, even alcoholic and abusive parents, because they feel that this parent needs them. Looking after the children's best interests is a difficult task with few clear answers.

When children participate in a mediation session, the mediator helps them air their fears and desires while trying to allay their anxieties. Very often parents are asked to express their love for their children, their desire that the children speak openly, and the reassurance that they will both continue to love and care for the children regardless of the change in their relationship with each other. The mediator can assure the children that they will not be asked to choose which parent they want to live with. If the parents do begin to pressure the children about their preferred living situation, the mediator will intervene on the children's behalf.

ATTORNEYS IN THE MEDIATION SESSION

As a general rule, the couple themselves are the only parties in the mediation, except for one or two sessions with the children. However, there are situations where including spouses' attorneys clarifies or speeds up the process. When couples are already involved in adversarial proceedings, some mediators will conduct one or more sessions with the attorneys present. Spouses get a clear picture of their adversarial alternative when each attorney explains his or her client's position and the legal rationale supporting it. The black and white "I own X" begins to take on various shades of grey as attorney A explains why X belongs to wife and attorney B explains why X belongs to husband. Mediating with attorneys is sometimes like a settlement conference—a meeting in which attorneys, clients, and a judge or family court master try to settle issues so that the case does not go to court. If it becomes obvious that one party's attorney is not amenable to mediation, that client can make a decision about whether he or she wants to mediate or to proceed with this attorney in the adversary system.

Some mediators (especially mental health professionals) encourage clients to bring their attorneys to one or two sessions in order to deal with specific legal questions, particularly when the attorneys support their client's efforts to mediate Attorney/mediator Gary Friedman comments that when attorneys attend, they usually come to only one mediation session because they end up sitting on the side-lines while the couple mediate.

Attorneys may be invited to join the mediation when one spouse wants to mediate but is slow to participate in the mediation because of nervousness, timidity, or an inability to remember legal information. After discussing the problem, the couple and the mediator may invite the attorney for the reluctant spouse to attend a mediation session so that the attorney can coach the spouse, leaving the mediator's neutral position unsullied. A second option is to invite both spouses' attorneys to one or more mediation sessions.

The expense of paying for three professionals may seem exorbitant, until one considers the alternative. Should the couple litigate, the costs of the divorce skyrocket. The hourly cost may be higher, but in terms of overall payments to professionals, the mediated agreement leaves the couple far ahead. If two attorneys and a mediator are necessary for the couple to negotiate an agreement that meets their needs and that they feel committed to and are satisfied with, the money is well spent.

HOW MEDIATION DIFFERS FROM COUNSELING AND THE PRACTICE OF LAW

Few people have trouble distinguishing between the role of an attorney and the role of an attorney doing mediation. The fact that a spouse may wish to have his or her attorney in a mediation session, even with an attorney/mediator, is ample evidence that clients understand the difference in the professionals' roles. Differences are manifest in the professional setting. Does the attorney have one client to represent or two clients trying to come to an agreement? Distinguishing a counselor or therapist from a counselor or therapist doing mediation is not so easy. Some mental health professionals do gloss over the differences between family therapy and family mediation; however, the more accepted trend in the field is to quite clearly distinguish between the two in both word and deed. "Mediation is a goal-focused, task-oriented, time-limited process. It emphasizes the present and the future, not the past. Crisis and short-term therapy share some of these parameters, but they differ from mediation in their goals, tasks, and issues and in the manner in which each commences."[6]

The most evident educational difference between a mediator and a therapist is their knowledge of the law. While both family therapy and crisis intervention techniques are used extensively by mediators, mediators possess greater legal sophistication. Many have studied their state's marital law so that they can offer limited legal information and know when clients need to seek legal advice. At the same time, mental health professionals who serve as mediators are careful to avoid engaging in the unauthorized practice of law.

Although the results of mediation are frequently therapeutic, divorce mediation is a goal-oriented process. When mediators work with individuals on emotional issues, this work is directed toward reaching an agreement. The mediator uses therapeutic interventions to help couples resolve hostile feelings that arise during the process. Counseling skills are used to direct couples back to the issues at hand, to evaluate a couple's ability to mediate, to determine their need for outside counseling, to establish when they need to vent their feelings and when they can move on, to facilitate the couple's future adjustment, and to help them reach a mutually satisfactory settlement. "The role of the therapist is to encourage exploration of the meanings and levels of dysfunctional psychological reactions. In contrast, the role of the mediator is to manage and contain emotional expression so that the process of reaching settlement can proceed. The narrow role of diagnosis in mediation, particularly with respect to power imbalances, and the conflict management techniques, bargaining skills, and negotiation strategies that are effective in mediation have been discussed."[7] As a rule, couples are not encouraged to explore past differences unless it helps them resolve current issues, or unless they have specifically contracted with the mediator to address these problems.

Individuals who enter mediation with the understanding that it is a practical, goal-oriented process for getting a divorce may feel tricked and angry if a mediator does extensive counseling in a mediation session. Many have had their fill of counseling, are working with a counselor elsewhere, or have an aversion to counseling. John is working with a counselor trying to understand why his marriage is ending, while Kate still denies the marriage is over. If mediation sessions were focused on helping Kate accept the divorce, John could become bored or annoyed, particularly if he has already spent hours discussing this very subject. The mediator's time is expensive, and if John has lost patience with Kate's doubts, he may be unwilling to share the expense of employing the mediator to work with Kate. Kate can express fears and talk freely in a private counseling session. Referral to a counselor or therapist satisfies everyone's needs in this case.

Mental health professionals who provide both therapy and mediation services to the same clients are generally careful not to confuse their functions. Because of the mediator's sensitive role, it is often preferable for the parties to do any extensive counseling in a separate setting. The professional may be able to effectively switch roles, but clients are often less able to distinguish between the two. They may expect counseling in mediation and mediation in counseling. Unless roles are clearly defined, those clients may not be satisfied with either process.

THE ROLE OF THE NONMEDIATING MENTAL HEALTH PROFESSIONAL

Mental health professionals provide services to couples undergoing a divorce that are often best kept distinct from mediation. For example, counseling is useful for couples not yet sure they want a divorce. When in the course of counseling a couple determine that their marriage should be ended, the counselor can refer the couple to a mediator. When these couples enter mediation, the sessions are more efficient, since many potential emotional blocks have already been worked out. With the couple's approval, some mediators will consult with the referring counselor or attorney prior to mediation, thereby expediting matters further.

Divorce creates a huge new area of uncertainty for a couple. Economic circumstances, emotional trauma, and procedural requirements are overwhelming. Divorce threatens parties' standards of living and demands that they find new, single identities. Financial and emotional security are simultaneously threatened. Many couples view the ending of their marriage as a failure. (Note the popular terminology surrounding divorce: broken home, failed marriage, split up, marital dissolution—all descriptions focusing on loss.) Individuals' responses are frequently parallel to those expressed at the loss of a close relation. Denial is usually the first stage. Spouses refuse to recognize or believe that their marriage will end. Once the end of the marriage is accepted as inevitable, there is very often a period of anger and then of grief. After this the parties become accepting and begin working with the future in mind. Individuals will vacillate from day to day and from hour to hour as denial turns to anger, anger to grief, and perhaps grief back to denial, until the couple are generally accepting of the divorce.

To complicate matters further, couples seldom experience these states simultaneously. A wife who initiates a divorce may already have experienced the denial and anger associated with the loss of the relationship; while the husband who was oblivious to her dissatisfaction with the relationship may not yet be able to believe or accept that she wants to leave. The spouse who feels rejected often takes longer to overcome the loss.

Counselors provide support and guidance through the emotional upheavals caused by divorce. They work at length with individuals concerned about themselves and their children at this critical time. Often one or both spouses need a separate support system while going through a divorce. A mediator can only supply a limited amount of support without compromising his or her neutrality. In a therapeutic environment the individual gets help in

1. Learning to accept the ending of the marriage
2. Understanding why the relationship did not work out, becoming aware of the causes of the various problems, and preparing to cope with these problems in a constructive manner upon entering a new relationship
3. Clarifying individual goals professionally and personally
4. Acquiring additional parenting skills and responsibilities suited to his or her new role
5. Overcoming feelings of guilt, failure, loss, blame, hostility, worthlessness, loneliness, rejection, anxiety, and denial, which often accompany a divorce

ATTORNEYS AS MEDIATORS

Traditionally attorneys are the head tactical consultants and choreographers of a client's divorce proceeding. As mediators, attorneys learn to abdicate control. They also pay greater attention to the feelings and emotional needs of their clients. They facilitate discussion by the spouses and learn to orient themselves toward the interests of the family rather than of any one individual. The attorney's training in achieving goals and in problem solving are invaluable in this context.

Divorce mediation has elicited a mixed reaction from the legal community. Bar associations are concerned because mediation poses ethical problems for the traditional attorney. Divorcing spouses' differing economic and personal interests present an insurmountable conflict of interest for attorneys who believe that sole representation of one party is the only proper role of an attorney.

American Bar Association Ethical Consideration 5-1 reads: "The professional judgment of a lawyer should be exercised, within the bounds of law, solely for the benefit of his client, and free of compromising influences and loyalties." This ethical consideration is satisfied only if the mediating attorney can view himself or herself as representing the family. The American Bar Association is still struggling with this issue. Some state bar associations do not accept this concept. Maryland takes a dim view of one attorney representing a couple in a divorce. An attorney may only mediate if the spouses also consult separate counsel or handle the legal proceedings themselves, without representation. Other bar associations have recognized the need for divorce mediation. They provide liberal interpretations of "conflict of interest," so long as the couple are fully informed of their right to independent representation and the mediator does not represent either party separately, should the mediation not result in a final agreement.

Bar associations are also concerned that mental health professionals practicing mediation do not engage in the unauthorized practice of law. Mediators have noted the paradox created by lawyers who claim that mediation is not lawyering and in the same breath denounce mental health professionals who mediate, accusing them of the unauthorized practice of law.

A lawyer-therapist team would appear to provide a solution to this problem. However, such a team is faced with two other possible objections by the bar. In addition to the lawyer's possible problem with conflict-of-interest issues, Ethical Consideration 3-8 states that lawyers should not practice law in association with laypersons, nor should they split fees with laypersons. Disciplinary Rule 3-103 provides that lawyers may not form a partnership with nonlawyers if any of the activities of the partnership constitute the practice of law.

Divorce mediation was far from the public eye when these rules were formulated. These considerations and rules were all created to maintain the legal profession's reputation and prevent any kind of unscrupulous partnerships. Today critics accuse attorneys of protecting a lucrative monopoly. However, the restrictions presently hampering attorney/mediators are gradually being relaxed and redefined, similar to the way in which the fault system of divorce evolved into the no-fault system which is now prevalent.

The American Bar Association's Young Lawyers Alternative Dispute Resolution Section is eager for attorneys to be aware of and to expand into this new field. While some attorneys do object to mediation on principle, or for fear that it will cut into their practice, many contend that mediation is the coming forum for divorce and that attorneys are the best-qualified professionals to mediate property, alimony, and support issues.

As for the fear that mediators are in competition with lawyers, the service provided is distinct and not to be confused with good lawyering. A couple who agree to mediate their divorce do not need adversarial representation. They may, however, want the advice of separate attorneys so that they can be fully informed as they mediate; or they may want separate attorneys to write up or review their final agreement. Mediators protect their own neutrality and ensure that couples have made fully informed decisions when they send them to separate attorneys. Attorney/mediators are particularly inclined to suggest separate counsel because it ensures that they are not regarded as either party's representative. The result is a solid legal agreement that will not be shaken by a subsequent revelation of information.

HOW ATTORNEYS WORK WITH MEDIATORS

Mediation has created new roles for attorneys. Clients mediating agreements jointly or individually employ attorneys as consultants, asking specific questions so that they may more knowledgeably negotiate. Or clients bring in mediated settlements for the attorney to evaluate. Some attorneys are uncomfortable in these less typical roles and are unwilling to work with mediating couples because of the ethical problems posed.

At the 1982 American Bar Association conference, attorney Dee Samuals complained that attorneys lack guidelines for reviewing mediated agreements. Her solution to this problem is to explain her approach to clients who request her services. The clients then understand precisely what services are being rendered and can request more or less professional assistance.

Attorneys can offer any combination of the following services:

1. Reviewing the agreement
2. Investigating the agreement
3. Drafting the agreement
4. Educating the client

Simply reviewing the agreement to ascertain whether it is legally binding is of questionable utility and may expose the attorney to liability if the agreement is challenged at some later date. Meaningful review of an agreement requires investigation as well. Clients can request different degrees of investigation. First, the attorney might want to look into how the agreement was reached. Was the agreement explained? Did anyone feel pressured? What does the agreement do for each party? By asking questions, the attorney is able to (1) evaluate whether the agreement truly reflects the intentions of the parties, (2) check to see if either party can later deny having freely and knowledgeably entered into the agreement, and (3) prevent hasty, unwise decisions. Of course, asking these questions may raise doubts in the minds of either or both spouses and may needlessly jeopardize the entire agreement. Clients may choose to renegotiate certain points, and the costs of the divorce may increase. On the other hand, the added precaution can result in a more trouble-free and satisfying agreement.

Mediating parties need to be thorough, but there is a point at which the cost of caution outweighs the benefits. Investigating financial aspects of the agreement by hiring actuaries and appraisers increases the costs of the divorce. Depending upon the parties involved and the amount of property, this may be necessary to create a solid, well-structured agreement. However, for those couples who have a minimal amount of property and money or have valued their property according to their own standard of fairness, trusting that they have each made full disclosure of all their assets, this caution is excessive. If clients state that they are satisfied with the property values they arrived at and trust their spouses' claims that there are no hidden assets, the attorney should generally accept the clients' assurances.

When an attorney agrees to draft a marital settlement agreement, he or she must work closely with the couple, and possibly with the mediator as well, in order to accurately transcribe the agreement. Choices in construction of the agreement (for example, the selection of particular wording) can be tricky. The attorney should explain the advantages of different constructions and allow the couple to choose the wording they prefer.

Reviewing, investigating, and drafting the agreement all require the attorney to educate clients to some degree. Some attorneys instruct their clients further, making sure that various options were explored in mediation and that the clients truly understand the consequences of their agreement. Once again, too much caution can be counterproductive. Telling clients about innumerable options after they have reached an agreement may be redundant or confusing. On the other hand, if the mediator overlooked a particularly advantageous means of dividing the property, the attorney provides an invaluable service by bringing it up. What if the attorney feels that the agreement is fundamentally unfair? This can be a difficult position for the attorney. How much pressure should or can consulting attorneys exert when they feel an agreement is disadvantageous to one client, or if they think they have a better solution? Essentially, attorneys evaluate the needs of clients to the best of their ability and provide them with as much professional assistance as clients desire.

The attorney's relationship with the mediator is also of concern to some professionals. If the mediator sends a letter requesting review and implementation of an agreement, might the lawyer's independent judgment be questioned? Understandably, a lawyer who continually upsets mediated agreements may not be called upon in the future. Also, some lawyers resent being presented with a final agreement which they had no part in creating. They feel pressured by what seems to be a fait accompli. They don't wish to rubber-stamp agreements, nor do they want to rehash unnecessarily a fundamentally sound agreement in order to change one or two small points. Once again, attorneys must determine how to best look after their clients' best interests.

Attorneys may advise clients about their legal position at any stage in the mediation process. By acting as legal consultants rather than as advocates assessing and planning strategies, lawyers ensure that agreements are well thought out and well written. The most conservative, arguably the most thorough, and the most expensive form of mediation employs attorneys from the start of the process. Spouses consult with separate attorneys so that they are aware of their legal rights and they know what an adversary approach would entail and how their attorney views the likely outcome in court. They are mediating "in the shadow of the law." The mediator explains that the attorneys are to be used as resources. The couple should not be controlled by the law, or by what they think they can get, but rather by their own sense of fairness. Using attorneys early on in the mediation allows the attorneys to contribute to the negotiations throughout and eliminates the likelihood of significant objections by the attorneys at the agreement drafting stage.

Settlements should be impervious to the reactions of family and friends. When Jane exclaims "You gave him the car!," Kate should be able to nod quietly, being quite clear in her own mind why John has the car, and being satisfied that the reason is good. Neither party will feel that they have made foolish choices due to a lack of legal information.

SIGNS OF READINESS TO MEDIATE

There are couples who can and couples who cannot mediate their divorce. Some couples just need time for the dust to settle before they are ready to mediate, while some will never be ready. For example, the spouse who hopes to take advantage of his or her mate in mediation is not an appropriate candidate for mediation. Nor are the quiet man and overbearing woman ideal candidates for mediation. The couple

1. Agreement to agree.	**2. Agreement responsive to the needs of the parties.**	**3. Agreement in accord with parties' sense of fairness.**
This type of mediation is more typical of labor mediation. The pressure to agree is so great that a meeting of minds is unlikely. One party may be overpowered. Each party's needs may or may not be met.	Parties' needs are met, and cooperative solutions have been found. However, parties may not feel a sense of closure and release if emotional issues relevant to the perceived fairness of the agreement have not been addressed.	This agreement entails the most work and is very solid once it is reached. Emotional as well as concrete needs are met.

Issues that must be Resolved ⟵ **Emotional Release** ⟶ **The Heart of the Matter**

Some parties want to get to the heart of what happened in the relationship; others only want to come to an agreement.

who come to mediate in order to save money probably do not have a strong enough incentive to mediate initially; but they may acquire adequate motivation. Mediators see couples at every conceivable stage of the divorce process and must determine whether the couples are able to mediate. The following questions must be considered:

1. Do they both want the divorce? Spouses are seldom ready to divorce at the same time. If neither spouse is sure about divorce, the mediator will recommend marital counseling. When one spouse clearly wants a divorce and the other is unsure, the mediator needs to do some extra groundwork with the unsure spouse. A spouse who doesn't accept the inevitability of divorce can sabotage the process by forgetting to do homework, missing appointments, refusing to negotiate in good faith, not participating actively in the mediation, refusing to abide by rules, or simply by finding objections to all proposed settlements. The reticent spouse may not even be aware of his or her motives.

2. Do they have sufficiently equal abilities to negotiate for themselves? If one spouse is overwhelmed by the other spouse, acquiescing to all suggestions and minimally participating in the discussions, the quiet spouse needs adversarial representation.

3. Is the couple able to put aside most of their anger and frustration so that they can mediate together? Couples who merely want to continue fighting in the presence of an audience are not ready to mediate.

4. What is the couple's motivation to mediate? The motivation must be strong enough to keep the couple working together even when the atmosphere is tense and they are not getting exactly what they want.

5. What is their style of communicating? When the spouses manipulate each other through guilt or silence, the mediator must help them develop more functional communication patterns.

6. Are the spouses flexible? If either party has rigid demands, there may not be room to mediate.

COUPLES WHO USE MEDIATION

Ted and Ellen's marriage was unsatisfactory for years. They owned a $120,000 house with a $40,000 mortgage. They shared two children, $8,000 in the bank, ten years of married life, one dog, a certain amount of bitterness, and the desire to separate in the most painless, least destructive manner possible. They wanted to protect the children from undue hurt, avoid the expense and emotional turmoil of a legal battle, and–if possible–avoid attorneys altogether. However, they were overwhelmed by the complexity of the issues they had to face when they sat down to write up a divorce settlement by themselves.

When they heard about mediation, the couple was curious and interested, but skeptical. What could a mediator do that they hadn't already tried to do themselves? The mediator they contacted explained that she would provide them with the legal information they lacked, help them with paper work, and prevent them from getting sidetracked when discussing issues; she might also be able to suggest solutions they had not considered. They decided it couldn't hurt to schedule one session. If they felt it was unnecessary to have the mediator help with the whole divorce, they could seek help with just one issue, such as custody.

Ted and Ellen mediated their whole settlement in less than eight hours. They learned to cooperate with each other for their mutual benefit, despite some powerful conflicts. Property issues were surprisingly easy to settle once the mediator had helped them get all the facts on the table. Support and custody required a good bit of thought and creativity, but ultimately both parties were satisfied by the arrangement.

Ted paid for Ellen's return to school for four years. After four years he would only be responsible for a fair share of the child-rearing expenses, a figure which they would determine annually according to their incomes and expenses. If during the annual assessment any obstacles arose, if they agreed that they were unable to negotiate alone, or if five hours of discussion passed without resolving their differences, they would again contact a mediator.

They decided to share custody of the two children and to reside in the same neighborhood so that the children would have easy access to both parents. Ted and Ellen want to talk freely and frequently about the children so that they never get lost in the shuffle between the two houses. They made a schedule to provide basic guidelines for who would get the children and when. They agreed to inform each other about any deviations from that schedule.

Ted and Ellen are proud of the control they took over their lives at a time when many couples relinquish control to attorneys and judges. They feel that they have grown and learned from an otherwise painful process. The children are sad that their parents separated, but unlike many children of divorce, they neither blame themselves for the divorce nor feel that either of their parents has rejected them. The children continue to love both parents without guilt; children subjected to an angry divorce often feel forced to side with one parent or to hide their love for the parent they are not with.

Divorce mediation provides a middle ground for couples who have good intentions but who are also faced with many complicated emotional and financial issues that make the divorce difficult to resolve without help. In many ways Ted and Ellen were ideally suited for mediation. They had not yet acquired competitive orientations toward one another. They were highly motivated by their children's welfare. Neither felt helpless or unable to represent himself or herself. The issues to be resolved were numerous and complicated, but the couple were honest with one another, freely sharing information and assisting each other.

Few mediations run smoothly. The fact that divorces are initiated means communication has broken down in some facet of the marital relationship. Mediation requires communication as well as honesty, trust, and cooperation. Many couples are relieved to finally clear the air and establish a firm groundwork for postdivorce parenting. Occasionally couples are so satisfied by their renewed ability to communicate that they no longer wish to divorce. As a general rule, any couple who might be able to mediate should attempt it. Couples who have children can mediate as regards parenting rights and responsibilities, even if they mediate over nothing else. Even when a couple are unable to mediate a final settlement, they will probably settle some issues and acquire a more cooperative attitude, which may ultimately save them a great deal of money and emotional upheaval.

Although any couple who want to mediate can do so, couples who choose to mediate display some typical characteristics. Couples who use private mediation tend to be better educated and in a higher income bracket than the average couple. Minimizing the financial drain and lessening turmoil for the children are common reasons why couples choose to mediate. Often they find out about mediation from a friend or through professional referral. Marriages typically last five to twenty years. In general, couples married under five years have not yet acquired the ties that would motivate them to mediate. Attorney/mediator Larry Gaughn of Washington, D.C., has identified eight common situations in which couples mediate:

1. The couple negotiate reasonably well with each other. All but one or two minor decisions have already been made. This couple just want the final touches done professionally. Mr. Gaughn calls this "Capstone" mediation.

2. Legal (or practical) issues are the couple's stated reason for seeing a mediator. Emotional issues are less important and may or may not be discussed.

3. The couple have come to the mediator because they cannot agree on how to arrange for future parenting of their child. Often there is only one child, who is under six years old.

4. The spouses are emotionally enmeshed. Often separation has not taken place at the time of mediation. This is the most difficult type of couple to work with. Approximately one couple out of five is in this category.

5. The spouses are at different stages in the divorce process. The noninitiating party has serious trouble coming to grips with the reality of the separation/divorce, or one party is very depressed and unwilling to look out for him- or herself.

6. The couple have serious value differences. These values may be political or religious, or may involve different ideas about childrearing, lifestyle, sex roles, and so on.

7. The couple are "autistic." They want the mediator to tell them what to do. Each wants to be fair, but not too fair. They do very little negotiation.

8. The couple are overresponsible/overdependent. One person is willing to let the other dictate the solution. The other person is usually quite willing to assume this role. Or one spouse may be excessively guilty and thus willing to give the other too much.

Sometimes it is not apparent that a couple are not ready to mediate until after the mediation process has begun. Couples come to an impasse on a relatively trivial item, such as a TV or an old piece of jewelry, because of an emotional issue. Emotionally entangled couples have been known to fight in court for years over petty items. This negative intimacy prolongs their attachment to one another, painful as it may be. Mediation can also be used as a means of prolonging contact with a spouse, if the mediator is not vigilant. If it becomes apparent that mediation is almost complete and one spouse begins to create difficulties, it may be that he or she is not ready to release his or her spouse. When mediators recognize the source of the reticence, they attempt to resolve the underlying difficulty. If the problem appears to require considerable counseling/therapy, the reluctant spouse is referred to a mental health professional. The mediation can be completed when both parties are ready.

In some instances the mediator needs to slow things up. For example, Sue and Jack decided to divorce after fifteen years of marriage. Both wanted the divorce to be as amicable as possible. When they first went to see the mediator, they were still living in their house together. The mediation went so smoothly that Sue and Jack had resolved most of the issues necessary to create a marital settlement agreement within three weeks of the first meeting. The mediator was reluctant to let the process end so quickly, because a couple who is still living together has not yet experienced much of the trauma of divorce. Though Sue and Jack were eager to sign a final settlement agreement, the mediator preferred to prolong the process so that they had a better sense of their needs and the impact of the divorce before the final signing.

As mediation gains wider recognition, different types of couples will mediate their divorces. What is apparent at this stage is that though mediation is not right for every couple, it is a tremendous improvement over traditional practices for those who can mediate—particularly when they visit a mediator before they become enmeshed in hostile proceedings.

MEDIATED AGREEMENTS ARE LEGALLY BINDING

When the marital settlement agreement is incorporated into the divorce decree, it is as binding as any court order. Some couples are concerned that an agreement they negotiate themselves will not have the same force or effect that a court-ordered decree has. In mediation, couples create a contract between private parties. The contract is as enforceable as any contract negotiated by lawyers, assuming it is properly written.

Other couples are concerned that the agreement they make will not be accepted by a judge. This can happen when

1. The judge believes that the property division is clearly unfair
2. One party needs state assistance because inadequate provision has been made for his or her welfare
3. There is reason to believe that one party was coerced or misinformed
4. The arrangements for the children do not appear to be in their best interests

In such cases a judge will inquire about how the agreement was reached and might suggest that the couple renegotiate. As a rule, however, judges are extremely pleased when couples settle their differences out of court.

Mediators and any consulting attorneys do all they can to assure that the mediated agreement is acceptable. Mediators try to alert couples to aspects of the agreement they are not sure a judge will accept. Often mediators know the policies of local judges, so the couple can be informed of any policy that threatens their agreement. If an attorney is asked to write up or double-check an agreement, he or she also advises the couple about any possible difficulties. The couple may choose to alter that aspect of the agreement, or—if it is truly what they want—they can be prepared to explain it to the judge so that the agreement will be accepted.

CHOOSING A MEDIATOR

Qualifications

Mediators, bar associations, and mental health professionals associations are presently embroiled in considerable controversy over the creation of ethical standards and licensing procedures for mediators. Everyone is concerned that unqualified persons calling themselves mediators will create a bad reputation for mediation. Standards and licensing are seen as one means of preventing this from occurring.

It is difficult to set standards and create restrictions on mediators at this time because divorce mediation is in a formative stage of development. Presently there is no group qualified or with authority to license mediators. Standards and rules would be arbitrary and possibly self-serving if bar associations or psychological associations were unilaterally to declare themselves licensing bodies.

The diversity that exists in the field of mediation is a sign of growth. If lawyers declare mediation to be a legal specialty, or if marriage and family therapists determine that it is a facet of marriage and family therapy that only marriage and family therapists can practice, mediation loses the benefit of other professionals' expertise. The religious counselor who is particularly suited to mediating for his parishioners would be unable to mediate. Skilled mediators who do not fit the licensing criteria may or may not be grandfathered in as mediators. The solution to this problem is not yet apparent.

Choosing a mediator should be done as carefully as choosing a doctor or a lawyer. Both couples wishing to employ a mediator and professionals who recommend mediators should assess their needs and list their priorities.

1. Do they want a therapeutic or a highly goal-oriented approach?
2. Do they want to do individual caucusing?
3. Do they want to mediate an entire divorce or just custody and visitation issues?

Couples who approach a mediator with a clear idea of the type of mediation they would like can ask the mediator to mediate in that particular manner. For instance, if Ellen and Ted know that they want to do individual caucusing, a mediator that ordinarily avoids individual caucusing might be willing to make an exception when confronted by a direct request. After all, mediation is founded on the belief that couples should take responsibility for resolving their own differences in a process that they have chosen themselves. If the mediator is unwilling to do individual caucusing, the couple can either find another mediator or keep this one—with no false expectations. In this way couples are more likely to be satisfied and to save both time and money.

Couples should consider composing a list of questions to ask mediators.

1. What are the mediation rules?
2. What role do attorneys play?
3. Are attorneys welcome in the mediation session?
4. Who writes up the mediated agreement?
5. Are the mediation sessions confidential?
6. How are children involved in the mediation sessions?

Does the mediator have any biases? Despite the emphasis mediators put on couples being given the opportunity to create their own marital settlement agreement, the mediator's personal convictions about child custody, spousal support, or property division are often apparent and extremely influential. Many mediators have a strong bias toward joint custody. If this is the case, the couple should be aware of it, particularly if they don't want joint custody. Many mediators believe both parties should be self-supporting if possible. Some women do not want to develop marketable skills, preferring instead to remarry. Couples should talk with the mediator, getting the latter to explain his or her own underlying beliefs about divorce and mediation. They should then determine if they feel able to work with this mediator after hearing this and after telling him or her their own desires. What are the mediator's qualifications?

1. How long has he or she been mediating?
2. How many cases has he or she mediated?
3. How long has he or she been practicing law or counseling?
4. What kind of training has he or she had?

Remember, divorce mediation is a new field. If you can find an experienced mediator that is great! However, it is likely that a mediator has only recently begun offering his or her services as a mediator. Nonetheless, this mediator may be an excellent choice by virtue of other professional expertise.

Couples should find a mediator they are comfortable with. They should be able to ask questions and be satisfied with the answer they receive. If the mediator is not meeting a couple's needs, spouses should voice their concerns. Ellen and Ted felt constrained by their mediator's methodical coverage of every issue of divorce. When they began going through the kitchen item by item, Ellen protested. The mediator thanked her for her honesty and checked to see that Ted also wanted to take care of the kitchen items outside of the mediation session. Ted did. The mediator helped them establish a few simple rules for dividing things on their own, making it clear that they could put aside any items they couldn't agree on and handle those in the next session. When Ellen and Ted began the detailed budget for the children, Ellen spoke up again. This time the mediator explained the usefulness of creating a support payment by working from a complete budget that both she and Ted agreed was accurate. Ted and Ellen were convinced that the time and effort of going over the budget in the mediation session were worthwhile. Remember, mediation is the clients' process and should respond to the clients' needs. Mediators try to work out a system that both parties can live with.

The cost of mediation varies depending on two things:

1. The number of hours spent mediating, the service couples are requesting, how many issues there are to address, and how ready couples are to negotiate with one another. "A Portrait of Divorce Mediation Services in the Public Sector" reports that "the average case in the private sector is estimated to take 8.7 hours. Fifty-two percent require 9 hours or more. In the public sector, the average case requires 6.3 hours and forty percent are handled in 4 hours or less."[8]

2. The hourly charge of the mediator(s). Public mediation tends to be free (funded by grants or filing fees) or cost in the neighborhood of $30 per hour. Private mediation fees range from $20 per hour to $180 per hour, the average price of a divorce being $440. "On the average lawyer/mediators charge $68 per hour while mediators with professional backgrounds as family therapists charge $52 per hour."[9]

Most mediators announce their fee when couples first contact them, and then talk about it again during the first mediation session. If clients find the cost of mediation a limiting factor, many mediators are flexible and will extend themselves either by adjusting fees or by recommending other mediation services. For example, some private mediators tell clients about free public custody mediation services that can be used in conjunction with private mediation of property agreements.

The following chapters describe five basic mediation models as well as variants likely within each of those models as practiced by individual mediators. Fortunately or unfortunately, depending upon how one looks at it, mediation models are not so clearly delineated in real life. I have isolated attorney mediation, mental health professional mediation, conciliation court mediation, co-mediation, and structured mediation because they are easily recognizable. There is, however, a great deal of cross-pollination, as indicated in the accompanying chart. Different stages of mediation are described in detail and are graphically illustrated by transcripts of mediation role-plays and actual mediations. Role playing is a common training technique in which participants are given a typical fact situation to act out in a practice mediation done before a class learning mediation techniques. The facts involved in the actual mediations have been altered so that individuals cannot be identified.

The next section begins by describing attorney mediation and then mental health professional mediation because most all mediators are from these two professions. In 1981 the Divorce Mediation Research Project mailed 200 questionnaires to members of the Association of Family and Conciliation Courts and 800 to mem-

TABLE 3-1

	MEDIATES CHILD CUSTODY ONLY	MEDIATES THE ENTIRE DIVORCE	PUBLIC MEDIATION	PRIVATE MEDIATION	CO-MEDIATION	STRUCTURED MEDIATION	INDIVIDUAL CAUCUSING
Attorney	2	1	2	1	1	1	1
Mental Health Prof.	1	2	1	1	1	1	1
Attorney/Mental Health Prof.	2	1	2	1	2	1	1

[1] Indicates that it is typical for this professional to practice this type of mediation.
[2] Indicates that this type of mediation is less common for this professional. (For example, attorneys generally don't specialize in custody mediation.)

This chart presents one way of defining types of mediation available.
Start by determining whether the mediator is a mental health professional, an attorney, or both.
Second, does the mediator mediate the entire divorce, or only child custody? (Many mental health professionals mediate only child custody.)
Third, is this private or public mediation?
Finally, does your mediator practice co-mediation and/or structured mediation, individual caucusing, or co-mediation and individual caucusing? (Mediators can practice co-mediation and structured mediation at the same time—they are not mutually exclusive styles; however, individual caucusing and structured mediation are mutually exclusive.)

bers of the Family Mediation Association. It received 256 responses from private services and 59 from public service. The responses suggested that social workers, psychologists, attorneys, and marriage family therapists—along with a smattering of others, in that order—are taking up divorce mediation.* (This may or may not be an accurate indicator of which professionals in what numbers are taking up divorce mediation. It may be that attorneys are less aware of these groups or less inclined to return questionnaires.)

FOOTNOTES

[1] Mohandas K. Gandhi, *An Autobiography*, 12th ed. (n.p., Beacon Press, 1971), p. 134.

[2] Stephen Bahr, "An Evaluation of Court Mediation: A Comparison in Divorce Cases with Children," *Journal of Family Issues*, Vol. 2, No. 1, March 1981, pp. 39–60.

[3] Sheila Kessler was the first mediator to publish a five-stage mediation model. Sheila Kessler, *Creative Conflict Resolution: Mediation* (National Institute for Professional Training, Calif., 1978).

[4] From John M. Haynes, *Divorce Mediation*. Copyright 1981 by John M. Haynes. Published by Springer Publishing Company, New York. Used by permission.

[5] J. Pearson, M. Ring, and A. Milne, "A Portrait of Divorce Mediation Services in the Public and Private Sector," *Conciliation Courts Review*, Vol. 21, No. 1, June 1983, p. 15.

[6] Joan B. Kelly, "Mediation and Psychotherapy: Distinguishing the Differences," *Mediation Quarterly*, No. 1, September 1983, p. 35.

[7] Ibid., p. 44.

[8] Pearson "A Portrait of Divorce Mediation Services in the Public and Private Sector," p. 12.

[9] Ibid., p. 4.

*J. Pearson, M. Ring, and A. Milne, "A Portrait of Divorce Mediation Services in the Public and Private Sector," *Conciliation Courts Review*, Vol. 21, No. 1, June 1983, p. 8.

FOUR

ATTORNEY MEDIATION

In many ways attorneys are ideally suited to mediating divorces. Attorneys are knowledgeable about property, support, and contracting. As mediators, attorneys explain the law and the relative advantages of in- or out-of-court settlement. When a couple disagree about how they wish to apply the law, attorney/mediators frequently role play, representing each spouse as an adversarial advocate in the mediation session. This role playing allows the parties to get a clear picture of what their attorney and their spouse's attorney might say in court, how the case could be argued, and the range of possible outcomes if the case should go to trial. What is the most support a wife of ten years might get? What is the least? Attorney/mediators are cautious about speculating, because there is no way to know what will happen in court. Many mediators cite examples of parallel cases and encourage couples to draw their own conclusions about the legal implications of a given situation. Some will predict the likely outcome, particularly when spouses are extremely unrealistic.

An attorney/mediator will alert couples to aspects of their agreement that are significantly different from the norm. This allows the couple to reaffirm their commitment to the agreement and gives them the chance to consider alternatives if their agreement seems too cumbersome. For example: Bill and Linda don't want to lose their house. Neither has money to buy the other out. They have tentatively agreed to hold the house in joint tenancy for the next two years. Bill will live in it the first year, and Linda will live in it the second year. At the end of the two years, they plan to reassess and to divide the house as best they can, hopefully allowing one party to buy the other out. The agreement has potential complications that need to be thought out. Their mediator carefully explains the ramifications of holding the house in joint tenancy, how that would affect inheritances and maintenance. He then has them begin to discuss how a buy-out would look in two years. Ultimately they decide that a simpler arrangement will be easier to handle. Careful examination of the agreement avoids potential dissatisfaction after the agreement becomes finalized in the legal process.

Individuals who are reluctant to consult mental health professionals because they feel they don't need a "shrink" are often less reluctant to use the services of an attorney, even an attorney/mediator. The mediator provides tangible services, such as legal information and possibly handling of the paper work. This type of client may inadvertently benefit from the therapeutic nature of the process.

Attorneys are often concerned that they are not adequately trained to deal with the emotional issues arising from divorce. Consequently, attorney mediators as a group have a greater tendency to be goal oriented and to make fewer purely therapeutic interventions. Some couples prefer this businesslike attitude.

THE CROSS-TRAINED ATTORNEY

A surprising number of attorney/mediators are therapeutically oriented. These mediators learn counseling skills as well as law. Many go so far as to get degrees in family counseling or clinical psychology. While still maintaining a legal format in their sessions, this group of attorney/mediators tends to be confident addressing the emotional underpinnings of divorce.

Gary Friedman and Henry Elson are respected Northern California attorneys who began practicing divorce mediation as early as 1976 and 1974, respectively, well before mediation had gained any kind of significant visibility. Today their practices attract a large number of couples, and they do twenty to thirty divorce mediations a year. (The average attorney incorporating mediation into his or her practice will do from zero to ten mediations in a year.)

Mr. Friedman and Mr. Elson became interested in alternative dispute resolution procedures because of their dissatisfaction with certain adversary procedures. Mr. Friedman looked into a wide variety of psychological movements when he was developing his mediation skills. Mr. Elson was trained as a marriage, family, and child counselor. Despite their considerable psychological expertise, they consider themselves to be attorneys first and foremost. Mr. Elson is quite adamant about his identity as an attorney: "I'm a lawyer and hold myself out as one in the mediative mode." Mr. Friedman is fostering a nontraditional, nonadversarial legal role for himself. It is instructive to note both their differences and their similarities.

The introduction of no-fault divorce in California caused Mr. Elson to question the necessity for the continued adversarial handling of divorce proceedings. Mr. Elson has been practicing law in the San Francisco Bay Area for the last thirty years. He became a licensed marriage, family, and child counselor in 1978. Ultimately he limited his divorce practice to nonadversarial divorces. Four days a week

Mr. Elson practices law in office space he shares with three other attorneys. One day a week he does counseling at the Pacific Child and Family Counseling Center.

Couples seeking Mr. Elson's services as a mediator come to a law office replete with secretaries, walls of legal tomes, and heavy oak business furniture out front. The inner office is furnished with three comfortable chairs, two of them separated by a small table (clearly for the clients), and a large desk. The introductory session begins with what Mr. Elson terms his Miranda warning. (In criminal law the police read the Miranda warning upon making an arrest to inform a person of his or her rights. Officer Joe Friday of "Dragnet" did it repeatedly: "You have the right to remain silent. . . .") This is outlined in the consent form he has all mediating couples sign. The couples are made to understand that he will not represent either party separately and that he will not testify in court. Further, the couple are assured that mediation does not interfere with the right of either party to seek independent counsel: "I really get an informed consent, to the point where they begin to rebel against listening to it."

Once this task is accomplished to his satisfaction, Elson is an extremely flexible mediator. He allows the couples to set the mediation agenda:

> I don't like to follow formulas . . . I try to combine the conventional atmosphere of the lawyer-client relationship with a kind of counseling/therapeutic atmosphere. So when people come up here for mediation they get treated the way all my clients do, except there happen to be two of them in the room at the same time. . . . I probably appeal to a certain kind of client, middle class, relatively articulate. . . . I want people to be thoughtful about what they do. I hope they might be able to learn something about themselves from this experience, not just get legal advice.

Mr. Elson often educates his clients about legal issues so that they can better weigh the decisions they must make. Some clients are greatly benefited by this intense participation.

Mr. Elson has no deadlines when he mediates. Some couples he has worked with have taken well over two years to finalize their divorce. They may come in to see him only once in six months. When neither spouse is anxious for the final decree, a slow separation may soften the process. Whatever the couple are comfortable with is fine for Mr. Elson; some mediators, however, like to establish momentum and have couples come in every one or two weeks until the settlement is mediated.

Mr. Elson does individual caucusing when it appears that a couple will benefit from it. He recalls one couple he met with together only two times. From then on they carried out negotiations on an individual basis, simply because it was more productive. The woman was much more open in a one-on-one situation, and both were happy to have Mr. Elson shuttle between them to reach an agreement. While this takes more time in general, sometimes it is the only way to mediate when one spouse is too upset to negotiate with the other spouse directly.

As a rule, Mr. Elson does not want agreements to be finalized at the time they are made in the mediation session. He feels that the pressures for agreement are too great in the mediation session. He encourages couples to go home and think about their decisions. When a final agreement is reached in mediation, Mr. Elson will write up the agreement in pro se form (indicating that the couple are representing themselves), encourage each spouse to have an attorney look over the agreement, and instruct the couple on how to present their case to the court.

Mr. Elson tends to be conservative about touting the benefits and uses of mediation. He contends that calling mediated divorces amicable is a misnomer. Couples do cooperate, but they are there to address conflicts. Many mediators feel a majority of divorcing couples could mediate their divorce. Mr. Elson is not so optimistic, but he does believe that couples that can mediate should.

Mr. Elson's demeanor and style are quick and friendly. Spouses often become tense and argumentative, yet Mr. Elson's humor and his good sense of timing as regards intervention keep discussions balanced and active. He moves from issue to issue in a businesslike manner, making sure that husband and wife thoroughly consider each issue.

HOUSE SETTLEMENT NEGOTIATIONS

Kate and David have been married for eight years. Both professionals in their early thirties, they have no children, and their heavily mortgaged house is their one major asset. Over the last four months, they have met with Mr. Elson three times. The following discussion took place during the last twenty minutes of their fourth session. They are close to settlement, but Kate and David have a significant difference of opinion as to how to divide the proceeds from the house. Kate contributed $10,000 of her separate property, money she earned before they were married, for the purchase of the house. She wants that contribution to be reflected in the division of the proceeds they realize from selling the house. David contends that the money she contributed was a gift to the community; he is pointing to the Lucas case (a defunct California divorce case which established that separate property used to pay for community property would be presumed to be a gift to the community absent an express agreement between the couple that the separate property was to remain separate) as his legal authority. Because of that, he wants a 50/50 split of the proceeds. Both have studied the relevant law. Kate has brought up her right to half the value of David's pension as a point with which she can bargain David is angry about this.

MR. ELSON: You have to make that conscious decision because David is saying, as a matter of principle, that he doesn't even want to discuss the pension. It makes him mad. There are tears in his eyes when he starts talking about it, and he gets angry at that.

DAVID: Well, I'm just not going to be part of a voluntary settlement in which . . .

MR. ELSON: Exactly. You're saying . . . "If we're going to talk about the pension, I'm not going to take part in the discussion voluntarily. It's going to change the nature of the thing."

DAVID: I'm not going to bleed. I'm not going to cut myself.

MR. ELSON: I don't think that kind of rhetoric is appropriate here, because we don't have that much at stake.

DAVID: I just want my position known, that I'm simply not going to be a part of voluntary settlement on that basis.

MR. ELSON: Kate said one of the reasons she's pushing to get a larger percentage, to get some reflection of her separate property contribution, is because she does not want to feel as though she sold herself down the river. Is that what I heard?

KATE: Right.

MR. ELSON: OK. And that is doubtless part of the dynamic between the two of you. I can see that as clearly as can be. There is a fight for autonomy, who's going to make the decisions in the marriage. That's a problem people have in marriage all the time. You two didn't handle that very well. I'm not saying you were the bad guy, David. I'm just saying she doesn't want to repeat what apparently she felt were some of the concessions she made to you during the marriage. (turning to Kate) I think that's what I hear you saying.

KATE: Yes. I'm sure David feels that because of the school issue he . . .

MR. ELSON: You don't have to state his position.

KATE: I think what you were getting to is that it wasn't going to be that difficult to make a decision.

MR. ELSON: Well, I was thinking, I don't see major economic hurdles, but I do think it's necessary for you to know how much the pension is, or to consciously say, irrespective of what it is, I don't care. Suppose the pension is worth $30,000? You're giving up $15,000 to get $5,000 or less. I want you to know that. I don't mind if you give it up, as long as you know you're giving it up, and you think about it outside this office, either with or . . .

DAVID: It's certainly not $30,000.

MR. ELSON: I know.

KATE: (to David) I thought you were investigating. I thought you found out.

DAVID: Well, I found out what my contributions were for my first job. I simply haven't got the figures for my current employer. $1,789 for when I worked for PG and E.

KATE: And that was how many years, two?

DAVID: Two and a half.

KATE: So maybe you have five or ten thousand? Anyway, I don't want to go 50/50. I want to go 75/25, and I don't care about your pension. I say forget your pension.

MR. ELSON: Irrespective of its value?

KATE: Irrespective of its value.

MR. ELSON: Even if it was $30,000?

KATE: Because here's what he'll do. I don't want to have this legal battle with him and I don't want to pay a lot of money out. I don't want to waste the money I was going to gain on a legal battle for the pension. If he doesn't want to pay me, I'll have to go back to court and say, "He's not paying me or I'm not getting this." I don't know exactly what he's going to do. Maybe it would be best for me to battle this out . . . for my own ego.

MR. ELSON: We don't each have to state our strong principles. I'll stipulate that each of you have strong principles (laughter). David, you made $1,600 in contributions for two years of work? And how many years have you worked during the marriage?

DAVID: I'll get the figures. I was on the verge of getting the figures when I got pretty angry. I said to hell with this. If she wants to find out what the pension is, she can go to court and find out. But I've cooled off. I apologize for not getting those figures. I'll make an attempt to get them as quickly as I can.

MR. ELSON: I don't want to rush you to a conclusion just to satisfy my need to get this worked out. (turning to Kate) You're saying that if the pension is something reasonable, you're not going to fuss about it, and that you would want 70 percent of the net return from the house and (to David) you're saying "I'll come up to 68 percent from 66.3 percent," so we're just two percentage points away. Are there any other issues? There's the Toyota. You're going to have to get the Toyota in there some place. That's the problem with quantifying something subjectively.

DAVID: Does it have to be quantified for the dissolution settlement? Just say that, you know, I will pay her fair market value as of April 1983.

MR. ELSON: You can do that. It doesn't have to be attached to the house or to the pension. You could just say, you get the Toyota, I owe you $1,000 or whatever it is, I'll pay you . . .

KATE: Don't we have to specify within a certain amount of time?

MR. ELSON: Oh yes, otherwise it wouldn't be realistic. What I'm saying is that it doesn't have to be glued to the pension or the house. You can deal with each asset separately. A lot of people don't do it that way, though. A lot of people just do a big balance sheet and then come out with a figure of, say, $5000 in favor of the wife. But you can do it item by item, that's OK. Any way that's comfortable and fair.

DAVID: I think both of us feel different about each item, stronger on some, less on others.

MR. ELSON: You certainly do.

DAVID: Unless you're at a real impasse, the balance sheet to me is very unimaginative. It doesn't take into consideration people's subjective feelings about things.

MR. ELSON: You are indeed a couple that forges your own way of dealing with things. That's fine with me. I'm happy about that.

DAVID: One other question. It's been very difficult for us to make the payments on the house. One very bad alternative which we have to realistically face is that we may simply default on the house. It's unthinkable, but it's a real possibility. So assuming that one defaults on the house, do you know if there's a tax loss we could take in the next year, or anything like that?

MR. ELSON: It's like selling it at a loss. You'd have a capital loss. I don't think there's too much you can do with capital losses. You set it off against capital gains. You might be able to use a small portion of the capital loss to set off against ordinary income, but I don't think it would be a bonanza. You could check with your accountant. I have a book here. I could look it up, but I don't think I'll do that now.

DAVID: I understand.

MR. ELSON: I'm just looking down the checklist of items, we have the house. We have it on the way to some solution. The furniture you said you've handled yourselves. Clothing, jewelry, and similar personal belongings the same thing. The Toyota you've talked about. The checking account I've got a feeling you're going to be using to pay me (laughter), and it's probably gone, anyway. The savings account is nominal. The pension we've talked about. The life insurance is not a big issue.

DAVID: We borrowed heavily against it. The policy was on me, with Kate as the beneficiary.

MR. ELSON: Does it have a value?

DAVID: I borrowed on the cash value of it.

MR. ELSON: Together or subsequent to the separation?

(In Unison): Together.

DAVID: Before we separated. I mean we needed some cash to get into the house and get established . . . about $900.

MR. ELSON: Well, the remaining value must be divided. You can cash the policy in if you want to, you could owe her half of its value, or you can waive it.

KATE: Well, I'll waive it. He's got his insurance and I've got mine.

MR. ELSON: OK, again you're getting to a situation where you're not examining the details. You feel it's about right, but I want to objectify it so that you know what you're waiving. I'm not trying to talk you out of waiving it. You should tell her what the value is and what it would be worth if you cashed it in. If you're saying, I'll keep my policy and you keep your policy, that's fine.

KATE: I don't think he has very much that is cash value on it. He's cashed it out.

MR. ELSON: OK. So it's not an issue. Moving on, have you consulted lawyers or talked to people who have read about the Sullivan decision? You have both come prepared to do some kind of bargaining? (turning to Kate) You talked about pension and spousal support, (turning to David) and you talked about Sullivan. Do you know what Sullivan is?

KATE: The school issue.

MR. ELSON: It's concerned with the monetary value of education and licensing. If one of you gets a piece of paper as a result of the community educating one member of the community, does the community have a right to get reimbursed if the community dissolves? The Sullivan case said yes in a big, long opinion. Then the Supreme Court plucked that case up and said "We're going to decide this case," and so the court of appeals decision is no longer valid. There is no law that covers it now.

DAVID: So it's pending.

MR. ELSON: It's pending. It's causing a lot of trouble with divorce cases, because people are waiting for the decision.

DAVID: I read the case and its very long opinion. It looks like it was set up for a state supreme court. (David and Mr. Elson discuss a bit about Rose Bird and how the case got to the Supreme Court of California.)

MR. ELSON: (laughingly) In this case it is reversed here. In this case Kate has the license.

DAVID: I think the Sullivan issue for me . . . hopefully its going to go away, we can work out something with the proceeds of the house and my pension. I might have a legal basis for Sullivan, but like my pension, I don't feel I have any moral or ethical right to ask her to pay me back for the school expenses. I don't want it. I didn't like putting her through school, but that's the way it was and that's water under the bridge now; and morally or ethically I don't think I'm entitled to reimbursement. . . . It's just tough shit as far as I'm concerned, but as she said, it's a bargaining chip. Quite frankly, it's a bargaining chip that I don't have the stomach to use. I really don't.

MR. ELSON: (chuckling) He says I've got a bargaining chip and I'm not going to use it against you.

DAVID: Well I would, but I abhor the thought of having to. So maybe it's not an issue. And again on the alimony issue. Not to worry about that. There is the disparity in our incomes. I think I could make an argument if I had to in court through an attorney that she shouldn't be entitled to alimony because she is more educated. Her earning potential will probably exceed mine one of these days. I don't think the current position she has is forty hours per week. Is it? It's thirty-five.

KATE: It's a full-time position.

MR. ELSON: It's thirty-five hours?

KATE: We work a seven-hour day.

DAVID: I could probably make a survey saying people with MSW degrees graduating this year currently make this kind of money, in this kind of position. Why should I give you alimony to keep you in a job you simply like to do? You like the hours; it simply doesn't pay you as much as you might otherwise earn. So I'm not too worried about the alimony. You could raise it, but quite frankly, I'm not going to take it that seriously.

KATE: OK. Again, I would like 70 percent of the return from the house when we sell it, and I would like that to be part of the written agreement. I think it's important to find out about the pension, but I doubt if I'll do anything with that.

MR. ELSON: So you're saying. I'm brushing things over a little bit. You're saying that you raised the questions of spousal support and pension as a way of bargaining to get 70 percent of the proceeds of the house in order to compensate you for the separate property contribution that you lost on the Lucas case (Lucas is the case that concerns the separate property gift to the community). (turning to David) You're saying that you raised Sullivan and you raised

Lucas on your side of the fence . . . but you're willing to consider a disproportionate division of the proceeds of the house, assuming there is any, if she waives spousal support and the pension. You'll take care of your personal property by yourselves.

DAVID: I think that is a fair statement. As far as the division of the proceeds of the house, I have to think about it for a day or so.

MR. ELSON: I don't like agreements to be reached here just because we both tend to want to be a good guy. Sometimes we don't want to be a good guy. Sometimes it's not in your interest. So let's all think about it. If you're willing to pay for my sending you a summary of this, I'll summarize it. I offer that to people because it takes me sometimes forty-five minutes to an hour to do that. I don't want to charge you for that unless you want it.

KATE: I think we know what we talked about. I would like to work on it. As I said in the very beginning in January, I'd like to set up something for early September.

MR. ELSON: To get to court.

KATE: Right.

MR. ELSON: Certainly. Taking a slow timetable, we should be able to get to court by September.

DAVID: If you're getting a court date, I've got some time I'm taking off toward . . .

MR. ELSON: It's done by mail now, but I think you should go to court. (they talk about going to court) I think you should each go home and think over what the situation is. I will think it over too. I won't write to you, but I will send you a little memorandum and see if there are any loose ends. And you have to remember all my imperatives about your legal questions. If you want to check it out with a lawyer, you should.

The transcript starts on an emotional note. David and Kate are arguing about whether Kate has a right to a part of David's pension, and David is outraged. Mr. Elson acknowledges David's anger, restates what David is saying so he knows that his point has been made, but cuts David short when he goes on about how he's not going to bleed. He points out that Kate's reason for wanting a percentage of the pension is a position she has adopted because of her sense of having been too easy to override in the past, and he notes that the division of the house seems to be the real issue. Mr. Elson is helping them see the argument for what it is. Clarifying, restating what David and Kate have said, and checking back with them to make sure they agree; helping them see how they are repeating an old conflict from the marriage, a fight for autonomy; asking questions, telling David that rhetoric isn't appropriate, and preventing Kate from trying to read David's mind—thereby losing the point of the discussion—Mr. Elson keeps the mediation moving forward at a brisk pace.

It's important to Mr. Elson that David and Kate make knowledgeable decisions. Mr. Elson wants Kate to know how much the pension is worth before she gives up her interest. He subtley reprimands David for not doing his homework, and tests the sincerity of Kate's willingness to give up her interest in the pension. David becomes edgy when Mr. Elson quotes figures far higher than he believes the pension to be worth. Kate is forced to defend her position or change her mind. Kate defends her position, saying it isn't worth the trouble of fighting for the pension. She then suggests that the fight might do her good. Mr. Elson equates this statement with David's rhetoric in a humorous way, and with this understanding between them, the atmosphere is lightened. Mr. Elson then returns to trying to determine the value of the pension. Both David and Kate have now made their point. David no longer needs to express his anger through not finding out the value of his pension, and he offers to get the figures as soon as possible. At this point Mr. Elson sums up their positions on the matter and leaves them to think it over.

The next part of the mediation involves talking about specific items that are not in contention but which need to be disposed of in a manner that will not cause future difficulties. They talk about the way in which other people have handled the same issues, note advantages and disadvantages, and then Mr. Elson contributes some thoughts.

The issue of Kate's education had been talked about previously; and the couple had been advised to do some homework on it so that they could talk knowledgeably about the issue during this session. Mr. Elson briefly explains a relevant California case. David asks some questions. This is a bargaining chip for David, just like the pension is a bargaining chip for Kate. Mr. Elson makes this explicit so that they don't waste time jockeying for position. The underlying issue is still how they will split the house. David agrees, and Mr. Elson begins to wrap up the discussion of practical concerns: Do they want a letter summarizing the meeting? What is their time schedule? He suggests that they think over the day's negotiations. At the next session David and Kate will be ready to settle on how they divide the house.

Mr. Elson's style of mediation emphasizes the need for couples to be fully informed about their legal positions and to have a very accurate picture of the trades they are making. If the spouses are about to trade a pension for a pension, something that certainly sounds fair, Mr. Elson will want them to know the value of each pension before they trade. He is not trying to mediate a settlement as quickly as possible, but as thoroughly as possible. He doesn't need or want a decision about something just discussed. Next time will be soon enough. Couples are given time to think about each agreement; they may have questions by the time the next meeting is held. The objective is to draw up a final agreement that is satisfactory to both parties.

VALUE-BASED LAWYERING

The theoretical guidelines of the Center for the Development of Mediation and the Law hold that laws were written to facilitate just settlement of disputes. The center is developing several forms of humanistic legal representation, divorce mediation, business mediation, minor dispute resolution, and nonadversary representation (a form of representation in which certain ground rules are established between lawyers and parties to facilitate a fair resolution of the issues; for example, sharing all relevant facts—on a principled basis—disregarding legal technicalities that may provide unfair advantages). Too often the laws are manipulated by attorneys in a highly complex game that can completely lose sight of the underlying objective of the law—a just resolution of conflicts.

Mediating couples are asked to look for the principles behind the laws and to make their decisions based on what they consider to be fair. For example, a couple discussing child support often want to know what the local court schedule for support payments recommends. The mediator supplies them with this information and encourages the couple to use this knowledge. Couples may treat this advice in much the same way as mother's, friend's or associate's opinions would be considered: as a factor that may affect a couple's feelings as to what they feel is fair. Blindly following the law too often leads to unjust results.

Leslie and Robert were members of a traditional community. Leslie's father gave them \$20,000 as a wedding present, with which to make a downpayment on a house. One year later Leslie and Robert wanted a divorce. When they came to the center, Robert already knew that legally, one half of the money he and Leslie had received from Leslie's father was his; it had been given to them in both of their names. Leslie was furious. After a couple hours of mediation, Robert and Leslie came to a settlement in which Robert gave up any claim to the \$20,000, despite his legal right to it. Essentially, the \$20,000 was a dowry which should be returned upon separation, according to the customs of their community. Robert was more comfortable making no claim to the money, thereby maintaining his own self-respect and his good name in his community.

Gary Friedman is founding director of the center as well as a professor at New College of Law, San Francisco, and a staff member of Mediation Law Offices. He began practicing private mediation as an attorney in California in 1976. Disturbed by the difficulty of honoring personal values in an adversary practice, Mr. Friedman began looking for more acceptable alternatives. He moved to California and took a year off from law practice. In that time he explored the human potential movement and ultimately decided he did not want to choose between the practice of law and his own values, but wanted to practice law in a manner that honored those values.

Because divorce mediation has been accepted more rapidly than other forms of value-based lawyering, Mr. Friedman has gained considerable experience and a substantial reputation as a divorce mediator. He may be the only mediator mentioned in this book who became involved in the field of divorce mediation because of a philosophical commitment to alternative dispute resolution processes rather than as the result of a primary interest in improving the nature of divorce.

Unlike most attorney/mediators, Mr. Friedman and some of his colleagues at the center do not maintain malpractice insurance, use previously designed worksheets, or require clients to sign a consent form. Mr. Friedman has commented that consent forms and malpractice insurance may suggest a lack of trust to the client which is antithetical to the spirit of mediation, which emphasizes trust and fairness.

The center has not yet developed any kind of property or budget list, partially because Mr. Friedman and his colleagues have ambivalent feelings about their usefulness. Lists typically exhibit sexual or social biases. Lists can potentially bring up nonproductive areas of contention. One couple will budget $2000 for Christmas as a necessary item; the next couple, who can't quite figure out how to meet daily living expenses, may be overwhelmed by the idea of putting aside money for holidays. On the other hand, creating an original list with the help of a mediator may be a useful exercise for gaining an understanding of the extent and complexity of the issues about to be addressed.

PROPERTY CONFLICT, SECOND SESSION

The following is a role-play done by Mr. Friedman for a group of attorney/mediators.

Mark and Lauren came to Mr. Friedman quite early in the divorce process. They have each seen lawyers but are not yet committed to an adversary divorce. Both thirty-five years old, Mark and Lauren have been married for twelve years. They have a son, Phil, age eleven.

Mark's peak earnings were in 1979, when he earned $75,000. Since then his earnings have steadily declined to $65,000 in 1980, $50,000 in 1981, and—for the first half of 1982—$22,000. Lauren is presently earning $1000 per month take-home pay. She wants to quit her job and go to design school. They own their home, some land in Sebastopol, and some valuable personal property. They have always spent beyond their means and have accumulated a significant number of large debts.

This is Mr. Friedman's second session with Mark and Lauren. At the first session Mr. Friedman determined that Mark and Lauren appeared to be ready and able to mediate. Ground rules were agreed to. Both have consulted with independent counsel at Mr. Friedman's suggestion, and now they are ready to approach substantive issues from an informed perspective.

MR. FRIEDMAN: Did you each see lawyers? (Both parties indicate that they have seen lawyers.) Any particular order you want to deal with the division of the assets?

MARK: Why don't we start talking about the house, since it's clearly community property?

LAUREN: We don't have any problems with that because it's common knowledge that it's community property.

MR. FRIEDMAN: What does that mean? Community property?

LAUREN: My lawyer told me that we owned the house and it's community property . . . and that there are laws, and therefore it's not an issue . . .

MR. FRIEDMAN: I just wanted to say a word about that. Remember when we contracted we talked a little about the law . . . and calling the house community property is a legal concept which means the division of it by halves. If that seems fair to you, to use that concept, then by all means that's the way we should work it . . . if for some reason one or both of you thinks that it might be fairer to deal with it some other way, that is something we can do here.

MARK: I don't think there is any problem with it. It's community property. We're willing to split it in half.

LAUREN: But I don't understand, there are laws . . .

MR. FRIEDMAN: Right.

LAUREN: Aren't there?

MR. FRIEDMAN: There are laws and we don't need to be controlled by the laws here. If the two of you wanted to agree to do something that was different than what a court would do, then you could do that here and it would be legal. If you wanted to decide the house was something other than community property, or you wanted to divide it unequally and that felt fair to the two of you, you could do that here.

LAUREN: Why that never occurred to me.

MR. FRIEDMAN: What do you think of it? How's it feel? (Lauren emits a low chuckle.) We'll talk about the house and how that will work out. Are there other assets that are community property?

LAUREN: Yes.

MARK: There's some land in Sebastopol.

LAUREN: What!

MARK: I said there's the land in Sebastopol.

LAUREN: I, ah, was just shocked when you said it was community property. I talked to my lawyer and he said it was clearly not community property. I own the land.

MARK: That's not what my attorney told me. (Lauren lets out a sarcastic guffaw.)

MR. FRIEDMAN: Shall we talk about Sebastopol and how we can use your lawyers here?

LAUREN: (asking Mr. Friedman for guidance) You'd better say something.

MR. FRIEDMAN: This is not that unusual. Lawyers can disagree about the laws. I could try to tell you what my understanding of the law is. We can deal with this in the same manner we just talked about. Whether a lawyer says this is the way it is is not as important to this process as whether . . . what the lawyer says is something you think is fair. This is the ultimate reference point for any agreement we make here. Your sense of what's fair. I do think we need to get out the views that each of you have. Views expressed not in terms of what my lawyer said, but rather what you think is fair. I will try to help you clarify how to look at this in relationship to law.

MARK: Well it seems fair to me that it's community property. . . . I mean it certainly jives with what I think is the legal reason it's community property.

MR. FRIEDMAN: I think it has something to do with the way you're seeing the law and the way you're seeing lawyers. I'd like to find a way of talking about it which uses what you think is fair. Shall we talk about that?

(Mr. Friedman looks to them both for assent.)

LAUREN: I'll tell you about the Sebastopol property. Is that what you mean?

MR. FRIEDMAN: Yeah.

LAUREN: I had a car accident. He did not have a car accident. I had a car accident. I got money for the accident. I bought, with part of that money, land in Sebastopol. Which he had no interest in, was not in any way connected to, did not want, did not get involved . . .

MARK: (interrupting) Hey Lauren, who paid the medical bills?

LAUREN: We're not talking about the medical bills.

MARK: I know. But who paid the medical bills?

LAUREN: Part of them were paid by the rest of the money from the settlement.

MARK: I know, and who paid for the rest of the medical bills? Whose salary?

LAUREN: Are we talking about Sebastopol?

MARK: Who's salar. . .

LAUREN: We're not talking about Sebastopol . . .

MARK: I am talking about Sebastopol.

(The couple's voices are rising as they try to overcome the other's arguments with greater volume.)

LAUREN: You're not talking about Sebastopol, you're talking about the medical bills.

MARK: If you'd let me finish, I would be talking about Sebastopol.

MR. FRIEDMAN: What I noticed is you started interrupting her as she started talking . . .

MARK: (interrupting) Well I think she interrupted me!

MR. FRIEDMAN: Well, that's not what I saw. What happened is she said "I'd like to start talking about Sebastopol." She started to talk about it and then you chimed in with "What about the medical bills?"

MARK: OK.

MR. FRIEDMAN: I think it might be helpful just for her to get her view out before you talk. Do you want to do that?

MARK: Yes.

(Pause)

LAUREN: There was $15,000 worth of personal injury recovery, so I got that money. I bought the land and I've been paying the expenses out of my own salary from my own job. I pay the taxes and I pay the mortgage back. I've paid $5,000 of that back with my own money. Now that land, as far as I'm concerned, has nothing to do with him. It's completely . . . it's my thing . . . and I just don't see why he should be given any part.

MR. FRIEDMAN: Lauren, who's name is the land listed in?

LAUREN: I'm not sure. But you're not asking me about the law. I thought . . .

MR. FRIEDMAN: Right. I'm . . .

(Lauren interrupts upon remembering that the property is listed in her name.)

LAUREN: I'm telling you it's in my name. I'm telling you about what I've done on my own, and . . . it's totally separate!

MR. FRIEDMAN: Is that how you've experienced it? During the whole time?

LAUREN: The whole time!

MR. FRIEDMAN: OK. (turns to Mark) How do you see it?

MARK: The way I see it is, first of all, the reason it's in her name was for tax purposes. . . . The way I look at it is, I paid for a portion of those medical bills for the accident. My salary is going to support us. (turning toward Lauren) You've bought the land and you're taking part of your salary to support it. So I'll support us and you take your money and you go buy something. That's fine! That's no fair! Let me tell you!

LAUREN: I can't believe this! I mean, there's a reason I'm not supporting us. Do you want to talk about that?

MARK: Yeah.

LAUREN: The deal we made that you . . .

MARK: Yeah, I'd love to hear it.

MR. FRIEDMAN: (looking at Mark) I'd like to hear more about how you see it.

MARK: The way I see it is, I'm out there earning a living and I take my salary to support us, right? And she's out there with this didly shit part-time job, right? And she takes the money and then she buys this land and the money she's taking from this didly shit job doesn't go to support us—it goes for something just by herself. Right? So . . . that really sucks!

MR. FRIEDMAN: Was this an issue . . . between you when you were together?

MARK: She, she never talked about it in terms of her being reliant.

MR. FRIEDMAN: Was it ever an issue who owned . . . or where money she earned was going into. . . ?

MARK: No.

MR. FRIEDMAN: So it wasn't an issue?

MARK: No, it wasn't an issue.

MR. FRIEDMAN: So was there an understanding between the two of you? About . . .

MARK: (Mark interrupts) I would say there was an understanding.

MR. FRIEDMAN: What would you say your understanding was?

MARK: The understanding was that it was our property. It was an investment that we had made.

MR. FRIEDMAN: And who was responsible for the project. . . . What was the understanding for how responsibility for maintaining . . .

MARK: She was paying it off. That's how I understood it. Just like I'm paying off the house.

MR. FRIEDMAN: Was there a reason for that?

MARK: Not specifically, not that I recall.

MR. FRIEDMAN: Uh-huh. It was just a habit that came about?

MARK: Yeah, I guess.

MR. FRIEDMAN: (turning to Lauren) And how did you understand it?

LAUREN: It changed. In the beginning it sorta wasn't talked about much, except I was really excited that all of a sudden I had all this money, that was separate, and had come to me, and I could do something with it, and you know. . . . As time went on, it was clear we were having more and more trouble. I relied on the property. I felt it was mine and separate.

MARK: What I don't see is how you can say the money you got from your settlement was separate when . . .
(Lauren interrupts)

MARK: Can I finish?

LAUREN: Yes.

MARK: Thank you. Because the money I earned was paying our bills, was going to pay off your medical bills, right? So I was earning all this money that's related to your being hurt, and you get the money from the settlement and all of a sudden that's your separate money.

MR. FRIEDMAN: I think it might be helpful here if we looked at the way the law would look at it. Not to have it take over, but to see whether talking about the legal arguments or the legal way of seeing it . . . could be useful for either of you in terms of understanding the issues. Does that make sense?

MARK: Yeah that's fine, because according to my attorney, it's totally community property.

LAUREN: Well according to mine, it isn't.

MR. FRIEDMAN: I could understand how they can take both positions. You see, your lawyer is looking at it from your position and trying to maximize your legal stance in court, and certainly in court your lawyer would take that stance. . . . I could see how each of your lawyers could take a stance to maximize the interests of what each of you would get in court, and I think it might be helpful if I just played it out and you could add anything that your lawyers said or can clarify anything that your lawyers said. . . . We don't have to decide it just based on the law, but we can see if there is anything in that that fits with what you think is fair. Do you want to do that?

LAUREN: I guess so.

MARK: Yeah.
(Mr. Friedman moves his chair next to Mark and faces Lauren as if she were the judge.)

MR. FRIEDMAN: OK. If I was your lawyer, I would make this argument to the judge. I would say that the personal injury settlement that was received was community property. That it came from money that was from an accident that occurred after you were married, received after you were married, and that it was very clear that the money was money that belonged half to you. The way the world looks at it, the earnings of each of you are earnings of that as a community, you are acting together even when you act separately, so that money either of you would earn or receive—such as the personal injury settlement—would be considered to be community property because it's identical with the community. So I'd look at that first money that went to pay for the land and say that was community property, and as for the fact that it is in your name only . . . I would simply deal with it by saying it was a matter of form only because of the implicit understanding or the assumed understanding on his part that it wouldn't be considered in any other way. He did not intend to make a gift of his half of the personal injury recovery to you. Then look at the money that went into it to furnish the taxes. Simply make the same arguments. That was your salary, and your salary is community property, so half of every dollar you paid into the property was contributed by him. OK. There's probably more there. .

LAUREN: That's enough! (Lauren laughs a bit nervously.)

(Mr. Friedman moves over to sit by Lauren and faces Mark.)

MR. FRIEDMAN: As your lawyer I would say: Wherever the money came from, there was always a very clear understanding that the property was hers, that it was originally put in her name, it was kept in her name, that it was always the intention of both of you that it be considered her property, and that if there was ever any community money that went into it, as I would agree that the salary and the personal injury recovery were community property, that changed its form from community property to separate property, and that was intended by you because you knew the property was in her name, and that's the way the two of you acted in respect to separate property.

(Mr. Friedman moves back to a position halfway between Mark and Lauren.)

Does that help?

(There is a long pause as Mark and Lauren think over all that has been said in the last twenty minutes.)

MARK: (looking at Lauren) Did you really think we had an understanding that that was your property?

LAUREN: I'd hoped that was what it was.

MARK: Was that your understanding?

LAUREN: I'd hoped that that was the way you felt about it.

MARK: I'm asking . . .

LAUREN: (interrupting) I know what you're asking.

MR. FRIEDMAN: We don't need to make a final decision now . . . in terms of characterizing the property, but I think that it's important that you both be able to hear concerns that each of you have as we move toward putting the assets together and finding out what your needs are, and then look to what might be a fair distribution. My suggestion would be, unless you want to go further with this now, that we put it on hold and we look at the . . .

END OF TRANSCRIPT

SUMMARY

Mr. Friedman checks to see that Mark and Lauren have done their homework and are equally prepared to mediate, then hands the ball to them. What assets do they want to deal with? When the house is brought up and disposed of in thirty seconds because "it's the law," Mr. Friedman uses this as an opening to emphasize Mark and Lauren's freedom to disregard the law if they so desire. Soon it becomes apparent that the property in Sebastopol is going to be a bone of contention. Mark and Lauren are clearly on opposite sides of the fence, with their attorneys behind them. Mr. Friedman offers to show them how their attorneys' advice can be used here, and once again emphasizes the concept of finding a fair resolution. Lauren begins to tell about the Sebastopol property, and she and Mark begin bickering. After a minute of listening, Mr. Friedman intervenes so as to get one complete story at a time, and has Mark agree that this would be helpful. When Mr. Friedman asks questions to clarify his understanding, Lauren is adamant. Mr. Friedman remains calm, lets Lauren finish, and gives Mark his turn. Mr. Friedman has to prevent Lauren from interrupting this time, keeping his attention on Mark and asking questions. Once both have had an opportunity to explain their positions and vent their feelings, Mr. Friedman is ready to explain what a lawyer's point of view might be should he or she represent either one of them. Mr. Friedman's technique of moving his chair and literally taking each spouse's side help him make his point even more vividly.

This is only the very beginning of the mediation process, yet a great deal has already been accomplished. Mark and Lauren were listening to each other's concerns toward the end of this session. They got the chance to vent their feelings, and once they had done this, they were free to open their minds to new ideas.

Mr. Friedman dissuaded them from going any further at this point because of the many issues they had yet to address. The heightened understanding of each other's needs and feelings will facilitate a more cooperative attitude when it comes time for them to create a comprehensive settlement. Had they continued and tried to reach a final agreement about this one issue, it is quite likely that they would have begun to bicker. As it is, they are left with a bit more compassion for each other. As their understanding of the complexity of the issues they must decide increases, their willingness to cooperate will also grow. What seemed a simple case of community property in Mark's eyes was clearly separate property in Lauren's eyes. This is a vivid example of the potential couples possess to fight over property—both feeling justified. Taken to court, one of them would "win" and the other would "lose." Here they have more flexibility.

FIVE

MENTAL HEALTH PROFESSIONAL MEDIATION

Some mediators believe that training mental health professionals to mediate is more practical than training lawyers to mediate. While the basic legal information necessary to mediate divorces is not that difficult to learn, the psychological skills mental health professionals have at their disposal take years to master; further, it is not entirely clear as to which of these skills are necessary to mediate. Mental health professionals can get a basic understanding of state divorce law by attending a few classes, reading divorce handbooks, or working with attorneys. This will be enough to alert mediators who are not lawyers to many of the possible legal problems that divorcing couples must overcome. Of course, attorneys interested in acquiring more counseling skills can attend classes, read handbooks, and work with mental health professionals. However, the psychology of divorce isn't confined to a few clearly defined issues, and learning counseling skills is a long-term undertaking.

> . . . even if the couple has not previously been in therapy, the professional helper is still more qualified to help dissolve the marriage because, by virtue of the special training, s/he can elicit the causes for the end of the marriage and use that knowledge to help make the divorce process a productive turning point in the couple's lives.[1]

For example: The first visit with a divorce attorney is often a desperate attempt by one spouse to gain attention. However, the attorney may well accept the couple's presence in her office at face value—that is, she may assume the couple wants a divorce. Thus, such a power play can backfire, resulting in an unwanted divorce. The first visit with a mediator may also be a tactical maneuver intended to draw attention to problems in the marriage. However, when a mediator first meets a couple, he or she has a different set of assumptions. A mediator's first task is to assess the parties' emotional commitment to divorce. The mental health professional/mediator is often more appropriately trained to make these kinds of assessments, knowing when and how to guide couples to marital counseling.

Most professionals feel that when custody is the only issue to be mediated, mental health professionals are better suited to the work. Mediators who are experts in child development are more aware of the children's needs and help parents recognize these needs. For instance, if two parents agree to a joint custody arrangement that involves transferring their two-year-old son from one home to the other on a daily basis, a counselor—believing that this might be too disruptive for the child—would tell the parents about any studies that might help them evaluate the situation better themselves, and start a dialogue with the parents about how this might affect their child. An attorney is less likely to feel qualified to evaluate the psychological impact of a decision. Perhaps the attorney would refer the couple to a developmental psychologist or send them to a custody evaluator. Custody issues are an aspect of divorce mediation with which some attorneys are not comfortable, just as some mental health professionals prefer to mediate only custody disputes because this is what they feel best qualified to mediate. Support and property issues are separated out to be resolved by the couple and their attorneys.

While some mental health professionals work only with the nonlegal aspects of a divorce, others help couples mediate their entire settlement because it is as difficult to separate custody and visitation from child support, spousal support, and determination of who gets the house. Some mental health professionals have gone on to become members of their state bar so that they can guide couples through the entire divorce process and write up their legal agreement. Clearly, mediating property and support issues requires a certain amount of legal expertise, even if the mediator does not write up the agreement. Though mental health professionals cannot give legal advice, their ability to recognize the legal issues pertinent to the divorce can be sufficient for the purposes of mediation. When legal questions arise, couples consult their attorneys for information with which to continue their negotiations. Couples negotiate a settlement that reflects their understanding of their state's laws and that is acceptable to the court granting the divorce.

The differing responses of insurance companies to the needs of the mental health professional/mediator are indicative of the confusion that exists in the field concerning the most appropriate role of the mediator. Malpractice insurance available through the Academy of Family Mediators covers all aspects of mediation. On the other hand, the American Professional Agency will write malpractice insurance covering only those therapist/mediators who work within their "proper province," mental health issues. Legal and financial issues are believed to be the province of lawyers and accountants.

Couples in marital counseling frequently prefer to have the counselor they are working with mediate their divorce, since the mediator is familiar with them and their situation. The transition into mediation can be gradual, and often the couple want the mediator to continue to act as a therapist as well as a mediator.

Some mental health professional/mediators feel that therapy and mediation should be done by separate counselors. For this reason, if couples with whom they are doing marital counseling decide to divorce, they refer these couples to independent mediators. Likewise, if they are mediating and the couples need therapy, they will refer them to an independent therapist.

Whether mental health professionals do therapy in mediation or not, more and more are incorporating mediation as an option in their counseling practice. Very few mediators have practices that rely exclusively on mediation. Those who do have spent years building up their clientele and reputation. It is not difficult to understand why so few have practices largely devoted to mediation. Though this is changing in more and more communities across the country, the majority of the mental health professionals who offer mediation services see mediation as but one facet of their practice. They typically have one or two mediations in progress at any given time, fitting these into the family counseling and therapy that comprise the bulk of their practice.

Various mediation styles are described below. All these mental health professionals work with attorneys, use individual caucusing to some extent, and have a therapeutic attitude. Two tend to avoid property and support issues, concentrating instead on custody issues. It is difficult to make generalizations about mental health professionals' mediation styles; there are no comprehensive studies to refer to, and there is tremendous variation in individual styles. An intuitive evaluation of the mental health professional/mediator suggests that he or she is careful to avoid giving legal advice, but may at times give "legal information," particularly when a proposed agreement is far from the norm. At this juncture the mediator can suggest that attorneys be consulted. The limited participation of the spouses' attorneys is often welcomed. Mental health professionals seem more likely than other mediators to do individual caucusing. This may be because individual sessions frequently address parties' separate needs. Also, attorneys may be more careful about conflict-of-interest issues because of their professional training. Further, attorneys may feel less equipped to work with individuals' feelings about the divorce, particularly in a therapeutic fashion.

COMPREHENSIVE MEDIATION

Comprehensive mediation is characterized by a strong focus on an individual's adjustment after the divorce, as well as a preference to mediate entire divorce settlements. John Haynes, Ph.D., practices and teaches a comprehensive form of divorce mediation. He is the first president of the Academy of Family Mediators and has written a book about his particular style of mediation.[2] Professor Haynes's conflict resolution skills are derived from the field of labor mediation, and his divorce mediation techniques reflect the labor mediator's approach to conflict resolution. He helps parties prepare to negotiate, working with spouses to define their own needs and anticipate their spouses' needs.

Professor Haynes outlines the procedure for twelve hours of mediation for the typical mediating couple. As with all mediation styles, a couple's initial session is spent becoming familiar with mediation and making a commitment to the process. In the second and third session, the couple begin to define the issues, jointly work on their budgets, and establish parameters for their agreement. The spouses then meet with Professor Haynes separately to define their short- and long-term goals, needs, and strategy. During individual sessions sensitive issues such as the individual spouse's fears—of the unknown, of being alone, of being without money, of reentering the dating scene, of losing the children, of being replaced by a new spouse—are worked on. If ignored, these fears tend to block the progress of the mediation. (In the last few years, Professor Haynes's style of mediation has evolved. He no longer does individual caucusing as a matter of course.) Professor Haynes also uses this opportunity to continue to evaluate how to orchestrate the mediation so that the couple may best recognize their common goals and meet each other's needs. As they move into the negotiation phase, areas of agreement and disagreement are clearly defined. Bargaining and decision making become simpler under these conditions. The easier issues are addressed first. Children are usually the last issue negotiated.

Many parents have a general idea of how they want to arrange custody and visitation when they enter Professor Haynes's office. In this case parents are helped to articulate their ideas so that they both have a clear picture of their rights and responsibilities regarding the children. Very flexible or very detailed schedules can be worked out as necessary. When the issues of custody and visitation are still unsettled, Professor Haynes works with the parents alone and then, if it is appropriate, brings in the children. Unless parents believe the children's participation will be good for the whole family, children are not included in the mediation sessions until decisions about the divorce are near resolution. This spares the children witnessing many of their parents' conflicts. The parents have the opportunity to prepare themselves for the inclusion of the children in a session designed to allay the children's fears.

The last few hours of mediation are spent translating agreements into a legally binding contract. The couple consult with their attorneys and then return to mediation. Professor Haynes reviews the attorneys' work with the couple to ascertain that the attorneys have adequately followed the spouses' instructions.

On occasion, when it becomes apparent that a couple need counseling time, Professor Haynes steps back into the therapist role. He calls this a "time out," and it is always done with the couple's explicit permission: "The mediation was facilitated by removing major roadblocks that could not have been negotiated away, and the integrity of the mediator was maintained because the couple knew when I was acting as mediator and when as therapist."[3] Professor Haynes describes Pete and Pam, who had come to him after a few sessions in marital counseling. They both claimed to want to divorce, but Pete did not think they made enough money for them to live apart. Professor Haynes suggested a time-out to look at their marriage when it became clear that Pete was going to stick to that position. Pete was receptive to the idea. Pam objected for fear that this would be another attempt to keep them together. Professor Haynes explained that they would be looking at why they were now talking about divorce: "I pointed out that if they did not know and share what it was they did not get out of the marriage, they would probably also have trouble knowing what they wanted to get out of divorce."[4] They both consented once the purpose and scope of the time-out were defined. They scheduled one session to look at Pete's perspective, one session to look at Pam's perspective, and a final session in which to look at the implications of those two sessions.

The first session was not very productive. Pete had a hard time identifying what he did not get out of the marriage. In the second session Professor Haynes used Pam's responses to help Pete recognize what he had missed in the marriage. Finally both Pete and Pam were able to see that they had entered the marriage with very different expectations, and that neither of them had been satisfied in the marriage. Pete was now ready to work out the money issue, understanding that his own goal would be to maintain his relationship with their two children. This therapeutic intervention made it easier for Pam and Pete to go forward. The mediator's integrity was maintained, because the couple had consented to this specific intervention.

CHILD CUSTODY MEDIATION

Mediators that work primarily on custody issues frequently help their clients develop a whole new set of parenting skills. Isolina Ricci is a child and family counselor who has developed a style of mediation she calls "confluent mediation," an approach she developed along with parenting agreements. Confluent mediation includes education and counseling for long-term positive effects for the family. Parents not only develop a parenting agreement but also reduce hostilities and ambiguities about their roles and about day-to-day ground rules as parents. Ricci has been teaching these skills to other professionals since 1975 and has written the book *Mom's House, Dad's House* for parents and professionals.[5]

When clients walk into Ms. Ricci's offices, they are given choices. Clients receive a handout entitled "Mediation: How It Works in Our Office." The handout defines Ms. Ricci's role and orientation and the options available to the client. For example, the client may choose "simple" mediation or "confluent" mediation. Simple mediation focuses on coming to mutual agreements but lacks most of the counseling and educational components of confluent mediation. For couples who regard these additional services as intrusive or unnecessary, simple mediation may be the preferred option.

Ms. Ricci sees parents and children both separately and together depending upon which approach is more useful. She helps couples write agreements about parenting rights and responsibilities, which will then be reviewed by counsel. When clients begin mediation, she requests permission to contact their attorneys so that professional efforts to help the couple with the divorce are coordinated. Ms. Ricci works closely with attorneys whenever she works with couples on support and property issues. Any such agreements are ultimately drafted by attorneys.

TRADED ASSURANCES

Karen and Gary were referred to Ms. Ricci by their attorneys so that they might work out their custody and visitation agreement in a nonadversarial setting.

> The process of traded assurances allows the mediator to diagnose the couple's communication process and dispute resolution patterns. In addition, it gives the mediator an opportunity to determine how capable the couple may be of transforming their past hurts and experiences into concrete action plans in a mediation meeting. The Traded Assurances process can reveal hidden agendas, resistances and help decide the suitability of mediation as a dispute resolution mode.
>
> The objectives of the process are to clarify components of distrust and fear that the couple have around one another and about the mediation itself. Once clarified, behavioral aspects are identified and negotiations are begun on assurances given to one another about these fears. The "trading of assurances" then begins rebuilding their lost mutual trust and can import a sense of hope and order regarding the efficacy of mediation.
>
> The process takes at least fifteen minutes, often longer. It is best initiated at the end of the first joint session where the contract for work is being made. In confluent mediation, the negotiated assurances are put in the mediation contract the couple makes with one another. This contract identifies their goals, objectives and ground rules for mediation.[6]

MS. RICCI: I'm going to ask you each the same set of questions, questions that will give me a better understanding of your situation. Why don't I begin by asking Karen the first question and then you, Gary. What might Gary do that would undermine mediation for you?

KAREN: He'll agree to something, then say that it's not what he said or not what he meant. In the end, the agreement we had is worthless and I'm left holding the bag.

MS. RICCI: Can you give me an example?

KAREN: Yeah, he agreed to joint custody for the children before we separated, only now he says that I have to go along with him living in the house before he'll agree to it. The house had nothing to do with the custody thing. Now he says that if I don't let him have the house, he'll go for sole custody of the kids.

MS. RICCI: Gary, is this news to you?

GARY: I have a better situation for our children than she does. I can afford to keep the house and she can't.

MS. RICCI: Well Gary, let me ask you the same question I've asked Karen. What might she do that would undermine mediation for you?

GARY: She'll have a hard time making decisions or she won't be clear to me what she's thinking. I'll look at her or listen to her and I'll think we have some arrangement for the weekend with the kids, or how to pay some bill, and then she'll drop the bomb on me that she wasn't thinking that at all. It drives me crazy.

MS. RICCI: Karen is this news to you, what Gary is saying?

KAREN: I know I have a hard time making decisions, but he is so dominating that I don't know what I'm thinking when he's around. That scares me about being in mediation with him. How can I know I'm making the right decision for me?

(Ms. Ricci nods in understanding and then turns to Karen.)

MS. RICCI: Karen, what might Gary do in today's meeting to make you fear that he was going to agree to something and then say it wasn't what he meant?

KAREN: He could give me that "look" he has that says, "God are you stupid. . . ." Then if I tell him, "You said such and such," he'll give me that look and say, "That's not what I said,"

(Ms. Ricci nods in understanding and says "OK"; then turns to Gary.)

MS. RICCI: Gary, it's your turn now. What might Karen do today in this meeting that would show you that she was doing the same thing here that you feared she might do?

GARY: She'll act like she wants to try mediation and I'll start believing that maybe this is going to work, and as soon as we leave here, or you go out of the room, she could just tell me that she's not so sure mediation is going to work.

MS. RICCI: I'm beginning to understand. Can you tell me more? For example, Gary, what could Karen do or agree to do that would let you feel you could trust her about this?

GARY: If she would just tell me right away what she's thinking without hiding her thoughts or pretending, then I wouldn't be so worried.

MS. RICCI: What's happened since you arrived here at this meeting that would be a good example?

GARY: Well, I don't know how she feels yet about stopping our attorneys from negotiating about the property while we are mediating custody and visitation here. She nodded her head when we came to that part of the contract, but I can't trust that.

MS. RICCI: Would it help if you could ask her a direct question about it and got a straight "yes," "no," or "maybe"?

GARY: Yes! What a relief that would be.

KAREN: Yes, and the answer is yes. I do plan to stop my attorney, does he?

GARY: Yes.

MS. RICCI: Excellent, you now have your first agreement. You've agreed to instruct your attorneys to put their negotiations on hold. Let's go a step further. Karen, would you be willing to answer Gary's questions in these sessions with a "yes," "no," or "maybe" when he was feeling unsure of your position?

KAREN: Yes.

MS. RICCI: Thank you, Karen. Congratulations to both of you for reaching two agreements. (They both smile) Karen, now it is your turn. What could Gary do to assure you in your fear that he won't see an agreement the same way you do?

KAREN: I want it all in writing. I want everything spelled out in writing, no end runs. And, I don't want him to pressure me to sign anything until I have had my lawyer look over the agreement.

MS. RICCI: Gary, would you be willing to have a highly specific agreement where everything is spelled out in writing?

GARY: Yes, it would be a relief.

MS. RICCI: And, would you agree on attorney review?

GARY: Yes, as long as I can get the same from her.

MS. RICCI: Karen, how does that sound to you?

KAREN: Very good, if he'll just stick to it.

(Ms. Ricci looks at Karen, Karen smiles sheepishly and then shrugs as if to say, "I couldn't help that dig.")

MS. RICCI: Let me be your secretary and you tell me how to write this down in your mediation contract. Gary, how do you want yours worded? "Karen agrees that . . ."

GARY: . . . that when I am unsure about her position on an issue, that she will answer my question about it with a "yes," "no," or "maybe."

MS. RICCI: OK. Good. Karen?

KAREN: Gary agrees that our agreement will be detailed and all in writing and reviewed by our attorneys before final signing.

MS. RICCI: OK. Good. Would both of you look at what I've written in this section of our contract for mediation; and if I've put it down right, we can then go ahead and sign it as part of our agreement to work together.

(Gary and Karen read over the written agreement and all three sign the contract.)

MS. RICCI: Congratulations![7]

Ms. Ricci exercises a great deal of control in the traded assurances process. This is a fairly foolproof technique for further assessing the couple's communication style and making one of their first mediated agreements. The logic of the process is hard to dispute. The mediator lets Karen and Gary know her intentions right off: "I'm going to ask you each the same set of questions." Then she asks Karen how Gary could undermine the mediation. Once Karen has made a general answer, she asks for a specific answer, gets it, and finds out if Gary is aware of Karen's feelings. However, she doesn't explore this avenue in detail; rather, she turns to Gary and asks what Karen might do to undermine the mediation for him. Once both Karen and Gary are giving specific examples—and thus can see what is causing their own and each other's misgivings—she gets them to start thinking of solutions. As they think of options, Ms. Ricci is generous with her praise. She encourages them to be clear about how they could alleviate these fears, having them mutually agree on specific procedures.

The following are step-by-step instructions for having couples trade assurances.

TRADED ASSURANCES:
Step-by-step

1. Ask each parent: What would the other person do to undermine their trust, these mediation meetings, their agreement. (Use your judgment regarding which term will elicit the most important response.) Sometimes it works best to ask, "What is it that you are fearful might happen with him/her in mediation?"
2. Ask for an example of what they mean and when something like this last happened to him/her.

3. Ask the other parent: "Is this news to you?" (sometimes it is) "Would you rephrase how you hear what he/she is saying about you in your own words?"
4. Ask each parent: "What could he/she do today that would bring you to feel he/she was doing this again or "what has he/she done since coming here to this meeting that proves your point (or) that shows nothing is changing for the better?"
5. Ask each parent for an example of what type of concrete behavior might assure him/her that their fear/problem/uneasiness was being given attention and/or that mediation would not be seriously affected by it. (This must be observable, measurable behavior. An attitude or a feeling will not do at this juncture.)
6. Ask each parent if he or she would be willing to do this action to reassure the other parent that they were negotiating in good faith. "Would you be willing to do ____________ ?" (the assurance)
7. Negotiate the balance of traded assurances.
8. Obtain their statements of what they have agreed to do, put these statements in the "Mediation Rules" contract.[8]

THE EFFECTIVE USE OF INDIVIDUAL CAUCUSING

Many mental health professionals find that individual caucusing permits them to help individuals overcome emotional blocks that probably could not be overcome in a joint mediation session. (See pros and cons of individual caucusing, page 47-48.) Some mediators remain very goal oriented when doing individual caucusing, focusing exclusively on the issues at hand; others may do a significant amount of therapy in an individual session. The style of individual caucusing depends upon the type of mediation the couple have contracted for and the mediator's personal style.

Post Divorce Custody Issue

John and Jennie were sent to a mediator to resolve a custody problem they were having concerning their small son, Rick. They had been divorced for two years and their co-parenting arrangement was somewhat unusual. John cared for Rick in the daytime, and Jennie cared for Rick at night. They agreed to this because John's work allowed him to spend most of his days with Rick. At that time Jennie had a nine-to-five job.

Now, two years later, Jennie was remarried and no longer worked all day. Jennie was distressed because it looked as if her new husband was being transferred a few hundred miles away, and she was afraid that John would want to keep Rick. Also, she wanted to spend some days with Rick now that she had free time in the day. Coincidentally, John was at the point where he wanted some evenings with Rick.

Jennie had gone to her attorney and stated her wishes three months before she and John went to see the mediator. Jennie and John's negotiations through attorneys failed to produce any agreement and aroused a great deal of anxiety in both parties. The attorneys suggested that they try to mediate a custody agreement.

Jennie and John agreed, because it was apparent that otherwise they would have to go to court.

The mediator they chose was a woman psychologist with twenty-five years of experience working with families. She explained in the beginning that she draws strongly from her psychological expertise. When necessary, she works on the underlying psychological experiences blocking a mediation. She explained that some of this work might be carried out in separate sessions. Also, she noted that as a custody mediator, she consults with the couple's attorneys, therapists, and any other relevant parties.

The first meeting with the mediator was a joint session. She helped the couple agree to the principles they would use in deciding how to rearrange custody. She then had them write down on separate cards the minimum number of consecutive days they would like to have Rick stay at either home and maximum number of days they would be willing to have Rick stay at the other home.[9] It turned out that they both thought two days would be optimal, and they would not want to be separated from Rick for more than five days. (This technique is useful to find out parties' true feelings. Often negotiating parties unconsciously or consciously react to the other party's suggestions rather than searching for their real needs.) Despite what seemed to be a fundamental underlying agreement, John and Jennie were not close to creating a workable custody arrangement.

The mediator decided that she would be most effective working with John and Jennie separately in the next few sessions, defining their needs, discovering what kind of arrangement they would be amenable to, and preparing them to do some cooperative problem solving for Rick's sake. John was fearful that Jennie would somehow become sole custodial parent and was jealously guarding his time with Rick so that any court would see how involved in Rick's life he really was. Jennie, for her part, seemed to underestimate the value of John's parenting. The mediator wanted to help each of them see how the other parent could be important to Rick and at the same time not threatening to their own relationship with Rick.

Jennie's individual session started much like a therapy session. The mediator had reason to believe that the relationship Jennie and her brother had with their own father was relevant to her concept of her son's needs and of the kind of relationship Rick should have with his father. Jennie talked about her childhood—her relationship with her parents. The mediator asked questions such as How did you feel? When did you notice? How did he respond to. . . ? She then made summary statements which Jennie could either agree to or deny.

MEDIATOR: You mentioned that you and your brother were very close as children, your concept of men was derived from him more than your father. How much did you see of your father when you were Rick's age?

JENNIE: He was very busy. He worked most of the time, and when he got home, we were under strict instructions not to disturb him. When I turned four, he got a job as a salesman and then we never saw him. . . . I think my parents were having marital difficulties. I don't know. I was too young, my mother rarely talks about him. He died when I was eight.

MEDIATOR: So you were four and your brother was five when you stopped seeing your father on a regular basis?

JENNIE: Yes.

MEDIATOR: Did you miss your father?

JENNIE: Well, I really don't remember ever saying to myself, "I wish daddy were here." I was pretty independent, and with school and my household chores, I never had much time to think about those things.

MEDIATOR: How would you describe your childhood overall? Were you happy, withdrawn, irritable . . . ?

JENNIE: Oh, I got along with people all right, but I wasn't very happy, either. I never tried to commit suicide or anything stupid like that, but I didn't have a lot of fun like some of the kids I knew. It seemed like there was always stuff to do.

MEDIATOR: So you feel there was something missing in your childhood?

JENNIE: Well sure, but that's true of everybody, isn't it?

MEDIATOR: Of course.

The mediator is the responsive, intent listener helping Jennie remember her childhood. She makes sure Jennie knows why she is helping her review this. The mediator has Jennie take it from there. After Jennie has talked about the similarities she sees between her own and her brother's childhood and what is happening to Rick now, the mediator adds some insights she has perceived. While Jennie denies much of what the mediator says, the seeds for thought have been planted.

Jennie is encouraged to think of the relationship she would have wanted with her own father. The mediator asks Jennie to imagine a situation in which she is a judge deciding the custody issue and whether she would trust her neutrality considering her experiences. Jennie doesn't agree with much of what the mediator suggests. The mediator continues to ask leading questions but doesn't push her ideas beyond this point. If she pushes the issue, she'll probably cause Jennie to resist her more strongly; and then Jennie might never be able to consider the suggestions in a relatively unhindered manner.

As the individual session continues, Jennie and the mediator begin to broach the situation at hand on a more concrete level. Jennie describes the different arrangements they've had for Rick. The mediator asks if Rick was a burden when Jennie had him most of the time, hoping to help Jennie view John's interest in Rick as more of an asset. Jennie isn't about to do that yet. Perhaps Rick really wasn't a burden; if he was, Jennie may think about it on her own.

Jennie has a negative reaction when the mediator suggests compromise. Jennie felt pushed around in her marriage as well as pressured to agree to the first mediated settlement. The mediator tries to reassure Jennie that this mediation will not be like that.

Near the end of the session, Jennie talks about her present husband, Dave. The mediator suggests that Dave be included in the next joint session because he is a part of any settlement they agree to. Finally, the mediator wraps things up, summarizing, planning where to go from there with Jennie's participation, outlining the effort still required from everyone, and providing lots of praise and reassurance.

Individual caucusing can also be done in a less therapeutic fashion. Juan and Maria live in Montreal, Canada. After four years of marriage and a few sessions in marital counseling, they have decided they want a divorce. Both Juan and Maria have a strong sense of family which, once explored, will form the basis for a caring, ultimately uncompetitive parenting effort. They have a one-year-old daughter, Terisa, and Maria has a six-year-old from a previous marriage. They have come to see Ms. Bruce-Davis at the recommendation of their marital counselor.[10] Juan is scared that he will lose Terisa. Terisa is his first child, proof of his manhood, and evidence that he has not wasted these last few years. He does not want this divorce and does not feel he should suffer as a consequence. Furthermore, Maria already has a daughter. Maria is scared that somehow Juan will take Terisa. She has told him the children should be together and that Terisa is too young to be away from her for long.

After the second meeting with Ms. Bruce-Davis, it becomes clear that Juan and Maria are not about to budge from their positions. Ms. Bruce-Davis decides to have an individual session with each of them. This first session with Juan is to help him become more attuned to the needs of each family member, starting with Terisa. In a one-on-one situation, Juan does not feel as much need to maintain his strong defensive posture. He can explore new ideas without being concerned that Maria will take advantage of any "liberal" ideas he may voice. The individual session is "safe."

<table>
<tr><td>MS. BRUCE-DAVIS:</td><td>Last Friday we agreed to talk about specific fears and needs that you have identified, and possible solutions as you saw them. What are your thoughts?</td></tr>
<tr><td>JUAN:</td><td>I'd get Terisa and find an apartment. She's more my daughter and I need her more. (pause) But everything is so scary.</td></tr>
<tr><td>MS. BRUCE-DAVIS:</td><td>How do you mean scary?</td></tr>
<tr><td>JUAN:</td><td>Well, how could I look after Terisa?</td></tr>
<tr><td>MS. BRUCE-DAVIS:</td><td>That's what we're here to talk about. Let's go through it, one thing at a time.</td></tr>
<tr><td>JUAN:</td><td>There are lots of day-care facilities available. I'll sign her up.</td></tr>
<tr><td>MS. BRUCE-DAVIS:</td><td>OK. You may want to start looking immediately, to test out this assumption and see about the cost. How about weekends?</td></tr>
<tr><td>JUAN:</td><td>I'll look after Terisa.</td></tr>
<tr><td>MS. BRUCE-DAVIS:</td><td>What would you like the next ten years to look like for you?</td></tr>
<tr><td>JUAN:</td><td>I want to remarry, have more children.</td></tr>
<tr><td>MS. BRUCE-DAVIS:</td><td>Do you think you'll be able to do all this if you spend all your free time caring for Terisa?</td></tr>
<tr><td>JUAN:</td><td>I've got friends, they can look after Terisa sometimes, and Maria will want to see her some.</td></tr>
<tr><td>MS. BRUCE-DAVIS:</td><td>Let's talk about that some more. What would be best for Terisa?</td></tr>
</table>

Ms. Bruce-Davis is helping Juan look ahead in a tangible fashion. She poses questions, provides some structure, and allows him to think through and feel through all the issues. She is orchestrating the motivation to divorce and will help him to face the realities required by the decision. Juan may ultimately convince himself that co-parenting with Maria could be the best solution for both Terisa and himself.

The individual caucusing sessions with Jennie and Juan illustrate the variation possible in individual caucusing styles. Ms. Bruce-Davis is goal oriented and avoids doing therapy, unless a (time-limited) contract is made to take time out to do therapy with a particular spouse concerning a particular issue. At all times she deals with practical, here-and-now issues. Therapy is an integral part of the first mediator's style of mediation. In many ways she is quite directive: She has no qualms about delving into Jennie's past in an attempt to have her reevaluate old prejudices that may be affecting her reaction to the present situation.

The appropriateness of doing therapy in mediation is debated by many mediators. Some mediators regard it as but another tool to be used freely to help a couple resolve their differences. Others prefer to have any therapy done by someone other than the mediator. Couples and mediators would do well to clarify their preferences at the start of mediation. Mediation done by mental health professionals is extremely varied. The term *mental health professional* covers a broad spectrum of personnel: marriage, child, and family counselors; social workers; psychologists; psychiatrists; pastoral counselors; and so on. These people may be trained to do Freudian analysis, crisis intervention, or neurolinguistic programming. This does not mean that a mediator's style will reflect his or her training directly, but it will be important if the mediator does do therapy in mediation and the couple has strong feelings about the sort of input the mediator should make.

As with any life situation, the mediating couple needs to have some knowledge of what they want, or else they must be willing to accept the services they receive. Couples should consider whether they want—or will be able—to do individual caucusing; whether they need more than custody mediated; or whether they want therapy/counseling during mediation. It is quite easy to find out if the mediator works only with custody issues, never does individual caucusing, or does a certain amount of therapy when mediating.

FOOTNOTES

[1] John Haynes, *Divorce Mediation: A Handbook for Counselors and Therapists,* (New York: Springer Publishing Co., 1981), p. 4.

[2] Ibid., pp. 1–193.

[3] Ibid., p. 139.

[4] Ibid., p. 138.

[5] Isolina Ricci, *Mom's House, Dad's House: Making Shared Custody Work* (New York: Macmillan Publishing Co., 1980).

[6] Isolina Ricci, *The Confluent Mediation Handbook*, to be published.

[7] Isolina Ricci, "Traded Assurances," from *The Confluent Mediation Handbook*, to be published.

[8] Isolina Ricci, Mediation Transcript #2, from *The Confluent Mediation Handbook*, to be published.

[9] This is a technique often used by mediator Art Bodin.

[10] Ms. Bruce-Davis is one of the first mediators to write a master's thesis about mediation.

SIX

PUBLIC MEDIATION/ CONCILIATION COURT MEDIATION

Public divorce mediation is court connected and typically a service of the family or conciliation court. Though only some jurisdictions offer divorce mediation services, those that do generally charge nothing or only a minimal fee. Often it is only one of many services these courts provide. Other services include marriage and family counseling, where the possibility of reconciliation exists; divorce counseling, to assist families with postdivorce adjustment; mediation of family conflicts (parent/teenager or husband/wife); preparing evaluations for judges when families are unable to resolve custody or visitation issues; seminars for families in the process of divorce; premarital consent evaluations for couples under the age of eighteen; and restraining orders and counseling as regards domestic violence.

Following World War I Michigan was the first of several states to set up conciliation court services. The primary function of these early court services was to help couples reevaluate and improve their marriage in order to avoid a divorce. In the mid 1970s some court services began doing divorce mediation as well because of concern for the families who do not reconcile. Statistics revealed that court custody battles were rising quickly, and many court systems were not equipped to deal with the problems presented by these cases. In 1960 American courts decided over 400,000 custody cases. By 1970 that number had more than doubled.[1] Psychologists were linking childhood disturbances and delinquency to divorce and disturbed family situations. In many states the conciliation or family court services were recruited to provide vital information and guidance to divorcing couples as well as to couples considering reconciliation.

CONCILIATION COURT MEDIATION—NATIONAL OVERVIEW

Unfortunately, very little data about court mediation have been collected. Interested clients and counselors must still find out about type and availability of services in their locality by contacting the family court or county clerk. (See chart, Chapter 11, pp. 225-26). There is no national list of counties that provide mediation. There are few descriptions of the various procedures used by the different counties. There are few statistics on the success of mediation. One study conducted by Stephen Bahr of Brigham Young University, published in 1981, involving California, Connecticut, Minnesota, Canada, and Australia, concludes:

> All available evidence indicates that a court mediation service would save substantial amounts of money and improve the quality of dispute resolution at the time of divorce. Although the data have limitations, their strength is that mediation has been successful under a variety of conditions in several different states and counties. Whether mediation is very brief (2 hours) or rather lengthy (12 hours), it is economically efficient, resolves some disputes that would otherwise go to trial, and appears to improve post-divorce adjustment and compliance with settlements. Therefore, it is recommended that a court mediation service be established in all states.[2]

Many court systems have already taken Professor Bahr's advice.

It is difficult to determine how many court mediation services there are now. Though a few state legislatures encourage mediation, it tends to grow on a county-by-county basis.[3] Counties may introduce mediation services after hearing about mediation through conciliation court conferences or publications. Often a pilot project is approved for six months or a year. The project ultimately becomes another of the court services offered in the county. Judges, court counselors, or even court service directors can encourage mediation services in their counties. Sometimes one or two conciliation court counselors begin mediating on their own initiative. They are encouraged by their results and court policy eventually catches up with them. The result of this ad hoc process is a broad spectrum of mediation and referral policies: Mediators are entitled to work with different issues; they are allotted different amounts of time to mediate; and they differ in their ability to make recommendations to the court.

Portland, Maine, initiated a mediation project for its small claims courts in 1976. The program was initiated by the Cumberland County Bar Association, which solicited the help of the Maine Labor Relations Board and Maine Control for the Humanities and Public Policy. Three district judges agreed to work with the program. About twenty humanists (many of whom were college teachers who had completed a seminar on community conflict resolution) and a number of part-time mediators from the Labor Relations Board acted as mediators. Mediators were paid a fee as well as expenses. Before the end of the second year of the program, judges in both the superior and the district courts were recommending mediation to divorcing couples. Though the overall mediation success rate was 65 percent, success with divorce mediation was 90 percent (success being defined as reaching an out-of-court settlement).[4]

Today the mediation program is supported by the judiciary budget. Mediators are still laypeople. In divorce cases counsel is usually present during the mediation, though the mediator does speak to the parties and the lawyers separately if he or she thinks it will be useful. In general, the lawyer for the plaintiff is asked to sum up areas of disagreement. The lawyer for the defendant is then asked to amend the list until there is general accord on what matters are in dispute. The parties then decide on the order of significance of these matters. The mediator now has an outline for a systematic approach to resolving the issues and often has some good bargaining material when parties have different priorities. It is quite possible to have a divorce mediated during the morning and to have the results acted upon by the court in a brief hearing during the afternoon.

Dade County, Wisconsin, has an approach to mediation which it calls the family self-determination model. The mediation is done by counselors in seven or eight sessions. The purpose of the model is to help the family evaluate the pros and cons of potential living arrangements. Meeting the needs of the children is a primary focus. The mediator facilitates the parents' planning, and the attorneys play a relatively passive role—possibly writing up a formalized legal stipulation to be presented to the judge at the time of the divorce hearing. In 1978 informal figures showed that only 10.5 percent of the families who participated in the mediation process returned to court for modification of their agreement, compared to 34.3 percent of those parents who had a counselor make a recommendation to a judge, who then determined custody.[5]

The mediation program in Ramsey County, Minnesota, was initiated in 1977. Mediated settlements averaged twelve hours and took six weeks to complete. In 1979, 294 couples attempted to mediate, and 59 percent of them reached a voluntary settlement. A study of the costs of mediation as compared to the costs of court investigations which took place prior to 1977 indicates that mediation is much less expensive.[6]

In Toronto, Canada, mediation is a very brief process that averages two hours. A counselor helps the couple mediate using traditional conflict resolution techniques. A study done by Howard Irving showed that even under these comparatively rushed conditions, almost three times as many mediating clients as nonmediating ones, reached agreements with their spouses (22 percent).[7]

Perhaps because the results would be obsolete before the survey could be published—due to the rapid spread of mediation services in both the private and the public sector—no one has as yet conducted a comprehensive survey of counties that offer mediation services. One study of conciliation court mediation reports that the following states have local conciliation court mediation services: Alaska, Arizona, California, Connecticut, Delaware, Florida, Hawaii, Illinois, Indiana, Maine,

Michigan, Nevada (perhaps), New Jersey (perhaps), New York, Ohio, Oregon, Pennsylvania (perhaps), Washington, and Wisconsin.[8] The Divorce Mediation Project Directory reported additional court-connected services in Colorado, Kentucky, Massachusetts, Minnesota, Missouri, Montana, Nebraska, Oklahoma, Texas, and Virginia.[9]

Court mediation services are voluntary, though there may be significant pressures or incentives to mediate. (In California mediation is mandatory in contested custody cases.) Further, they are staffed by mental health professionals, free of charge, and restricted to custody and visitation issues. Child support and possession of the house are issues that are sometimes mediated along with custody and visitation, when they cannot be separated out. With few exceptions, issues that do not directly involve the children, such as spousal support and property division, are not mediated in the public sector. The courts hold that it is their duty to see to the best interests of the children of divorce. Other property issues are the divorcing couple's private affair. Furthermore, many court mediators already complain of a lack of sufficient time to work with custody and visitation issues, and few feel equipped to handle the legal aspects of mediating property and support issues. However, it would be rash to assume all conciliation courts do not mediate support or property—Delaware state policy is to mediate property settlements.[10]

Because the conciliation courts have broadened their role, many counties have found it useful to change the name of the court service so that couples who have no interest in reconciliation are not put off by it. Increasingly popular names for conciliation court services that now also provide mediation include Family or Domestic Relations Division, Family Counseling, Child Custody Mediation, Family Relations Mediation and Investigation, Family Court Services, and Court Mediation Services.

STATE-REQUIRED DIVORCE MEDIATION

As with no-fault divorce, California is testing new territory in the field of divorce. After years of experience with individual counties' mediation programs, and responding to public and private pressure, on January 1, 1981, California became the first state to require mediation of custody and visitation disputes. All California counties must now be able to provide divorcing couples with some sort of mediation services. If California's experiment is a success, more and more states will initiate similar programs, and within ten years the vast majority of the states may offer mediation services to divorcing couples.

States and counties initiating mediation services can take advantage of California's experience with mediation to determine their own needs.

1. Do they want all custody and visitation disputes to be mediated as a matter of policy? Would they prefer to have judges refer appropriate cases to mediators? Or would they provide mediators only to couples who mutually request it? Assuming the last approach, how much would the court system want to promote mediation through educational films, talks, and pamphlets? Perhaps rather than requiring

all couples to mediate or having judges direct disputing couples to mediate, every couple that files for a divorce should get a brochure about the benefits of mediation before they have established antagonistic positions.

2. Should there be uniform qualifications for mediators? Standards must at least reflect the human resources available in a given area.

3. How much influence should the mediator be given over the resolution of the conflict? A mediation policy requiring mediators to make recommendations to the court may attract fewer couples. Attorneys would be less likely to suggest that their clients mediate. Couples would be understandably nervous about volunteering to mediate. This is an important consideration if the county is proposing a voluntary mediation program. Directive mediation (mediation with recommendations) seems far more feasible in a mandatory mediation system.

4. What time limitations will be put upon the mediators? Funding to pay the mediators often restricts counties ability to have enough mediators on hand and is probably the factor affecting this policy consideration.

5. Will the mediators help couples with property and support issues as well as with custody and visitation? This may depend a great deal upon how much time mediators have to work with couples.

Essentially, public mediation can be designed along the same lines as private mediation, or it may be significantly more directive or restricted. California is a good starting point for gathering information. There are significant differences reflected in the styles of mediation practiced in various counties; certain counties have been practicing mediation for over a decade. It would be useful to compare the differences among couples and among success rates in those counties that were providing mediation before it was mandated, and those counties providing it later.

California had one of the first public mediation programs to receive national attention. In 1973 Judge Markey of Los Angeles County began referring highly contested custody and visitation issues to the Los Angeles County Conciliation Court for mediation. By 1976 Judge Markey was referring all contested custody and visitation issues to the conciliation court before trial. He found that mediation saved money for both the court and the couples involved. He also found that mediation was in keeping with goals of the conciliation court. Hugh McIsaac, director of the Family Conciliation Court of Los Angeles County, describes the goals of that court.

1. [To] provide a non-adversarial means of settling conflict within the Superior Court, maximizing participation of the parties involved and giving them maximum responsibility for their own individual and collective lives.
2. [To] help families reconcile and divert from the divorce process.
3. [To] help families going through the divorce process handle the crisis of dissolution effectively and settle their differences amicably.
4. [To] make recommendations regarding underage couples applying for marriage.
5. [To] review public and private policy and programs to make recommendations for the strengthening of family life, both inside and outside the Court system.[11]

While Judge Markey was instituting his policy in Los Angeles, Judge King of San Francisco was putting a similar one into effect. With mediation referral, Judge

King heard fewer custody cases in a year than he had heard in one day before the policy change. San Francisco and Los Angeles Counties' successes with mediation were an inspiration; more and more California counties followed suit. Overall, California counties have reported successful out-of-court resolutions in 55 to 85 percent of their mediation cases.

California Senate Bill 961 was the first major mandatory family mediation legislation in the United Sates. First proposed in 1978, it was not approved until 1980.

> Senate Bill 961 was held up in committees for almost three years, with Governor Brown threatening to veto the bill. However, the bill received considerable community and judicial support. The most persuasive argument was made to the governor's office by a person who had personally participated in the court mediation process during his own divorce. He explained that he and his wife had spent $38,000 in their custody action for attorney's fees and trial costs without mediation. He pointed out that he and his wife had achieved a custody agreement through the Conciliation Court in nine to ten hours at no cost to themselves and only a minimal cost to the county. He concluded that increased divorce filing fees were a minimal burden when balanced against the hardship for divorcing couples if mediation was not available at all. The bill was passed and signed into law March 27, 1980.[12]

On January 1, 1981, the bill went into effect. Now couples must attempt to mediate a custody and visitation settlement before any such dispute goes before a judge.

THREE COUNTIES, THREE MEDIATION POLICIES

The California mediation bill included general professional qualifications for mediators, but left the counties a free hand in determining how to implement the bill. Perhaps this was because the type of mediation offered in California already varied from county to county. Mediators came from a variety of professions, ranging from attorneys, to probation officers, to social workers. Further, each county faces differing policy and economic considerations. Some underpopulated counties have made contractual arrangements with private mediators to handle mediation cases when they come in. Counties such as Los Angeles and San Francisco require large staffs of full-time mediators to work with the many divorcing couples they see every month.

California's lack of comprehensive guidelines can also be attributed to the general lack of data about what makes mediation effective in a court mediation program. There is no clear indication of what would be the best public mediation policy any more than there is one accepted mediation style for mediators. There is active debate over ethical considerations—such as how much influence a court mediator should be allowed and how much pressure to mediate is acceptable. There is also debate over the possibility that couples are being denied their right to representation and a fair trial when they are diverted into a mediation program that gives the mediator decision-making power. The courts have found a process that saves the court time and money, increases couples' postdivorce adjustment, and reduces the likelihood of future litigation. However, the process is not yet refined. Long-term examination of the different processes may someday indicate a preferred system. As yet, most conciliation courts are testing the waters, learning from their own and others' experiences.

In San Francisco couples who cannot offer the court a custody and visitation plan are referred to the Office of Family Court Services. Each couple is shown a twenty-minute film explaining the process and benefits of mediation. Both the couple and their attorneys are asked to sign an agreement to mediate. The couple must also sign an authorization form so that the mediator can get information about the children from their school or doctors if needed. Then the mediator meets with the couple's attorneys in order to see what areas of agreement and disagreement exist between the spouses. At this point the mediator meets with the couple. The mediator may meet with each spouse separately, with the couple together, or with the children as well, depending upon the situation. Should the couple fail to reach an agreement, the mediator will make a recommendation regarding temporary custody. If the couple ultimately require a permanent custody recommendation, they have the option of having the mediator do the custody investigation and make a recommendation, or they may request a new, unbiased investigator.

San Francisco mediators have a great deal of control and influence. In 99 percent of the cases, any recommendation made by a mediator is followed, and both attorneys and couples are aware of this. Over 4500 petitions for dissolution are filed each year in San Francisco Superior Court. Permanent custody hearings occur no more than once or twice a month. In the last six months of 1979, the court had one hearing involving temporary custody, whereas similar courts elsewhere have ten to twenty each week.

The Los Angeles County Conciliation Court shows couples a videotape similar to that shown in San Francisco. The tape talks about how parents can assist their children through the divorce process, and instructs parents on the developmental needs of their children. Unlike the San Francisco program, however, the mediation session here is strictly confidential. Not even a temporary custody recommendation is made to the judge if the parties do not reach an agreement; nor does the mediator do the custody investigation for any upcoming trial.

The Los Angeles Conciliation Court reports that 54.5 percent of its cases are resolved through mediation. Of the other cases (those that are referred on for psychiatric evaluations or custody investigations), less than 2 percent go to trial.

Marin is a small county near San Francisco and has only one court mediator. She will meet with the parents and children one by one over the course of a few weeks. Agreements are passed on to the judge. When couples do not settle, she talks with the attorneys and refers the case to the probation department for investigation. The confidentiality of the mediation session is protected, and spouses cannot subpoena her to testify. (One case in another California county is currently testing the mediator confidentiality privilege.) This mediator has an 80 to 90 percent success rate.

COMPARISON OF PUBLIC MEDIATION AND PRIVATE MEDIATION

As with private mediators, there is considerable variation in the mediation styles of public mediators. In part, this is determined by the differing policies of each county. The type of issues that can be addressed, the social and financial backgrounds of the clients, time limitations, and the influence of the mediator vary greatly from county to county.

Court mediators see a broader segment of the population than do private mediators. Public mediation clients have a wider range of financial backgrounds; typically, they have not heard of mediation, they are almost all parents, and most of them are in conflict over the children. Court mediators see few couples who come to the court mediation services purely on their own initiative. The vast majority of court mediation cases involve couples who have been sent to mediate by their lawyers or by a judge and who have already engaged in heated adversarial negotiation or litigation.[13] Often parents have firmly established antagonistic positions regarding who should have custody of the children and how visitation should be arranged. Public mediators get hotly contested cases because those couples amenable to private mediation or negotiating a settlement through their lawyers do so without requiring the court to intervene. In the cases that come to court, the additional authority of the public mediator is sometimes necessary to get the parents to work out custody agreements. Understandably, pressuring couples to mediate results in a different clientele and atmosphere, and perhaps even a different process, than that encountered in private mediation.

Private mediation is an entirely voluntary process which attracts a large number of well-educated, relatively affluent, and progressive clients. This may be explained by the newness of the field, the advantages of money and education, and the added incentive to save money by mediating when there is a significant amount to save. Many of these couples have been referred by mental health professionals or attorneys. Couples who find private mediators have already accepted that mediation offers them benefits worth paying for. They have demonstrated their ability to cooperate by the act of consulting a mediator together. Even couples who seek private mediation after having engaged in extensive litigation are more committed to mediate than the average couple using public mediation. They have spent their time and money in court, found the process unsatisfactory, and are admittedly ready to try mediation.

There are a wide range of possible differences in the ability of the mediator to maintain the confidentiality of the mediation session. Mediators may maintain strict confidentiality, as do private mediators or mediators in Los Angeles and Marin;

they may be authorized to make a limited recommendation to the court, as in San Francisco; they may have no limitation upon the recommendations they make; they may be required to make recommendations; or they make recommendations only at their discretion. To whom the mediator makes the recommendation is another variable. The recommendations may be made to the judge, to the custody investigator who makes a recommendation to the judge, and/or to the couple's attorneys.

There are advantages to giving the mediator the power to make recommendations. The mediator is privy to a very intimate view of the couple, acquiring a fairly clear idea of their wants and needs. Thus, the mediator is in a good position to make an informed recommendation as to what kind of arrangement would be most acceptable and fair. A fringe benefit of this is that the court has saved the time and expense of doing a totally separate custody investigation. If the couple are aware of the mediator's power, if they know 99 percent of the mediator's recommendations are followed, they may feel less like taking the issue to court. The mediator may choose to drop a hint to (or indeed actually tell) the couple what kind of recommendation he or she will make, thereby pressuring the couple to "mediate" the final agreement then and there. Perhaps the greater influence of the San Francisco mediator as compared to the Los Angeles mediator accounts for the higher percentage of mediated agreements reported by San Francisco.

There are also many disadvantages to allowing mediators to make recommendations. How a couple see mediation may be altered by their perception of the mediator's powers. When the mediator is able to make recommendations to the court, as in San Francisco, the couple may try to use the mediator as a surrogate judge—presenting their case to the mediator, trying to win him or her over—rather than focusing on their own ability to resolve the problem. When this happens, many of the advantages of mediation are lost.

Given the ability to make custody recommendations, it is easy for mediators to perceive themselves more as arbitrators or judges. It is tempting for a mediator with this power to begin evaluating the situation and directing the couple before it is clear that the couple themselves cannot resolve the conflict by relying on their own sense of what is best for the children. Many a mediator on a tight time schedule has had to coax or persuade a couple to accept an agreement. It is true that the couple might ultimately come to the very same agreement under more relaxed circumstances. It is also true that they may be less satisfied with the same agreement: They may say afterwards that they felt pressured or rushed or that the mediator had too much of a role in the agreement.

Attorney/mediator Gary Friedman tells of a lengthy mediation he did with a couple who had been haggling with each other in court, and with attorneys out of court, for over a year. The couple had technically resolved their differences. They had a valid court order, but they were still dissatisfied. After mediating an agreement with the help of Mr. Friedman, their final agreement was no more than $50 off the court-imposed settlement. It cost them in the neighborhood of $1000 to mediate the agreement, as compared to the many thousands of dollars spent on legal fees before going to Mr. Friedman—and they were satisfied with this agreement. The extra time and money was worth it to them because they had finally been given the opportunity to vent their feelings and clear the air. Quite probably, Mr. Friedman's services saved them from more litigation and more expenses.

In San Francisco, when couples can't reach a temporary custody agreement, the mediator makes a recommendation for temporary custody. Couples are then given the choice of having the mediator do the permanent custody investigation and recommendation or having a different court counselor do the custody investigation. It is possible that the disadvantages of allowing mediators to make recommendations can be eliminated if either spouse can say, "No, I don't want the mediator to make any recommendation. I want all my conversations with the mediator to remain confidential." This removes any judgelike authority the mediator might have, assures spouses that what they say in mediation cannot be used against them if the mediation does not result in an agreement, and makes it pointless for either spouse to try to win the mediator over to his or her point of view—the other spouse can simply disqualify the mediator as a custody investigator. When the mediator succeeds in gaining the trust and respect of both, they are pleased to have the mediator do the custody investigation and make the recommendation; it will mean much less disruption of and intrusion into their lives. The decision will be made by a professional whom they have already spent time getting to know. It is reassuring to note that in San Francisco most couples opt for the mediator's recommendation. This implies that these couples do trust and respect the mediators provided by the court.

A private mediator, unlike a public mediator, never makes recommendations to the court, except at a couple's request. If a private mediator is subpoenaed, the mediator may refuse to testify, claiming any number of confidentiality privileges: contractual agreement, settlement negotiation, attorney-client, mental health professional-client, or mediator privileges. Should a court be unwilling to recognize any of these claims, some mediators will still refuse to testify in court. The role of the private mediator is being defined by the couples themselves, by the mediators, and by the laws governing them. Concerned couples should talk this over with their mediator.

One drawback of court mediation programs is the timing and time limitations imposed upon mediators. Some mediators may have as little as one hour to mediate custody issues immediately prior to the court hearing, while others may have as many as twelve hours spread out over a few weeks. Private mediators have no time restraints other than those created by the couple themselves.

A second drawback of many court mediation programs is the emphasis on custody mediation. Many court mediators are restricted to mediating only visitation and custody issues. This means that the couple can continue legal battles for property, child support, and alimony. The mediator's ability to reduce parents' hostility toward one another for the children's sake is sabotaged when the parents continue to fight over other issues. It is possible, but difficult, to separate parenting responsibilities from the rest of the divorce when parties are actively fighting in court for child support or for the house. Support and property issues are intimately connected to custody and visitation issues. For instance, it is usual for the custodial parent to get the house. If Ken wants the house badly, he may fight just that much harder for custody of the children. If Sally pays for half of the rent with the child support she gets for her son, her fight for custody may be a reflection of more than her love for her son. Individual mediators frequently slip in necessary property and support agreements along with the mediated custody and visitation agreements, simply because it is impossible to separate the issues. More and more judges impressed with the results of custody mediations are directing couples to mediate other areas of their divorce; very often court mediators do the mediation regardless of the official county policy. County mediation policies are responding to the judges' encouragement and to the mediators' need for flexibility as to the areas in which they can mediate.

In California, when there is a custody dispute which will require the parents to use court mediators, couples sometimes hire private custody mediators, to avoid the court mediation system. Attorneys who want the mediation to be confidential may suggest this if the county they are in allows court mediators to make recommendations. Or they may know the local mediators and believe that the court mediators have a bias that will affect their client unfavorably. The couple may choose to employ a private mediator because they want to mediate property and support issues along with the custody issues, they want more time than their county mediator can provide, or they desire a different style of mediation than that offered by their county. When couples use private mediators in order to avoid the public mediation system, it can be argued that private mediation is less voluntary—but only slightly so.

So far, court mediation programs have been impressively successful. Court systems that provide mediators have drastically reduced the number of contested custody cases that are heard before their judges. Ideally, mediation is an entirely voluntary process. However, legislative requirements that couples mediate, and judicial pressure for couples to consult mediators, has benefited parents (and their children) who would never have gone to a mediator without these incentives. As with private mediation, there are, of course, some couples who cannot mediate, even with the pressure of mandatory mediation. There are also areas where a mediator simply cannot mediate. For instance, suppose a father has strong religious beliefs and his church requires a certain way of bringing up his children. A court order may be the only way the father can justify not raising his children following the teachings of his church after the divorce. Fortunately, most couples can compromise. The average couple is happy to find out about and learn appropriate cooperative parenting for themselves and their children.

Despite the greater pressures of public mediation, agreements that couples mediate are still more apt to be honored; and mediating couples are less likely to return to the courts for further intervention than those who obtained a litigated settlement. At worst, couples who fail to mediate have wasted a few hours with a mediator and have had their case delayed while they were mediating. (To allay the fears of couples who are afraid mediating will slow their divorce, some counties promise couples that are willing to try mediation that their trial will not be delayed should the mediation not result in an agreement.) At best, children and parents are spared untold emotional and financial losses. The risk of mediating is minimal, while the potential gains for society and for the individuals involved are significant.

INVESTIGATING COURT MEDIATION SERVICES

Professional fees can be saved by using court-connected mediation services. Perhaps a court mediator should be the first professional contacted when a couple decide to divorce, particularly if saving money is a primary concern. The only thing spouses risk losing is their time. Sometimes court mediators are able to help couples mediate their entire divorce. If there are issues that can't be settled in the court mediation setting because court mediators don't mediate property or support matters the spouses can contact a private mediator or attorneys for help with these issues. Understandably, most couples prefer to mediate their whole divorce with one mediator; a certain amount of time must be spent establishing a relationship with each mediator, and all the issues of the divorce are at least somewhat interrelated. If custody and property issues are inextricably intertwined, or if the court mediators have time limitations, using two separate mediators may not be practical. Some attorneys, mental health professionals, and mediators inform divorcing clients about the conciliation court's free custody and visitation mediation services so that they are aware that free mediation is available.

Couples who use mediation will be more satisfied if they have a clear idea of their needs; for example, what kind of help, and how much help, is needed?

1. Interested couples should refer to the section on How To Choose a Mediator. What factors are equally relevant when choosing a court mediator? The skill and style of the conciliation court mediators are a result of the requirements of the court system in which they work as well as of professional experience. Besides having degrees in counseling or social work, mediators often work as custody investigators or probation officers. They may or may not have specialized training as mediators.

Many court mediators regard themselves as advocates for the child or children, particularly those who are custody investigators as well. Judges and court personnel try to resolve custody and visitation issues in accordance with the best interests of the child. Many states empower judges to appoint a lawyer, called the guardian ad litum, to protect a child's interests when it appears that parents have lost sight of their children's needs. Judges and mediators want children to have better—or at least equivalent—protection in a mediated setting. In other words, if parents agree to a custody arrangement that will be disruptive for the children, the mediator will most probably persuade them to negotiate another arrangement that is better for the children. If parents should persist in wanting this particular custody arrangement, the mediator would submit his or her objections to the court and the judge would not allow the agreement, unless convinced otherwise by the parents.

Couples may not have the option of choosing a court mediator, but they can find out the qualifications of mediators available, and a request may be honored. Remember, a mediator's biases may have a profound effect upon negotiations.

2. Are there time limitations? The mediator may have unlimited time or only one hour to spend with the couple.

3. Is the mediation confidential? If not, who could the mediator disclose information to?

a. Mediator may make an automatic recommendation to the court.
b. Mediator may make a recommendation only if the judge requests it.
c. Mediator may make a recommendation only if the couple request it beforehand.
d. Mediator may make a recommendation only if the couple request it after the mediation is over, with no agreement having been reached.
e. Mediator may not make recommendation but can be subpoenaed to testify as to his or her professional opinion.

4. What areas of the divorce can the mediators assist with?
5. What kind of training and what kind of professional reputation do the mediators have?
6. Do the mediators work with the couple's attorneys? If so, how?

If the only unsettled issue of a divorce revolves around a couple's twelve-year-old son, court-connected mediation might be appropriate. If complicated tax and property issues are a couple's primary concern, a consultation with a private mediator/attorney would be more suitable. Couples should consider their needs, evaluate their resources, and choose accordingly.

FOOTNOTES

[1] Nathanial Gozasky, "Court-Ordered Investigation in Child Custody Cases," *Willamette Law Journal*, Vol. 12, pp. 511–526, Summer.

[2] Stephen J. Bahr, "An Evaluation of Court Mediation: A Comparison in Divorce Cases with Children," *Journal of Family Issues*, Vol. 2, No. 1, March 1981, pp. 55–56.

[3] Elizabeth A. Comeaux, J. D. *A Guide to Implementing Divorce Mediation Services in the Public Sector* (n.p., The Divorce Mediation Research Project, March 1983). The first detailed analysis of how divorce mediation services are and can be initiated in the public sector.

[4] A. L. Greason, "Humanists as Mediators: An Experiment in the Courts of Maine," *American Bar Association Law Journal*, Vol. 66, May 1980, p. 579.

[5] Anne Milne, "Custody of Children in a Divorce Process: A Family Self-Determination Model," *Conciliation Courts Review*, Vol. 16, No. 2, September 1978.

[6] Bahr, "An Evaluation of Court Mediation," p. 49.

[7] Bahr, "An Evaluation of Court Mediation," p. 49.

[8] Linda Bahr, "Conciliation Court Mediation" (unpublished article, Golden Gate Law School, 1982).

[9] Jessica Pearson, *The Divorce Mediation Project Directory*, (n.p., The Divorce Mediation Research Project, 1982).

[10] Linda Bahr, "Conciliation Court Mediation."

[11] Reprinted with the permission of the L. A. Conciliation Court.

[12] Linda Bahr, "Conciliation Court Mediation."

[13] J. Pearson, M. Ring, and A. Milne, "A Portrait of Divorce Mediation Services in the Public and Private Sector," *Conciliation Courts Review*, Vol. 21, No. 1, June 1983, pp. 1–24.

SEVEN

CO-MEDIATION

Co-mediation is performed by a pair of mediators working together with a couple. Often in the case of divorce mediation, this team is composed of a male and a female, in order to alleviate either spouse's fears that a single mediator will identify with or be biased in favor of the spouse of the same or opposite sex. Pairing a lawyer with a mental health professional provides the additional advantage of having both legal and therapeutic expertise available at all times during the couple's negotiations. Sometimes a man and wife will form a mediation team. However, co-mediators form teams of every combination of background and gender.

Though the male-female, lawyer-mental health professional team would appear to be the ideal combination, there are occasions when different combinations are equally or more useful. In a turbulent child custody mediation, two mental health professionals might be needed to control the emotional fireworks. A co-mediator/lawyer might feel ill equipped to intervene forcefully. Court mediation teams are almost always composed of mental health professionals. Two lawyers with complementary styles may be ideal for a couple primarily concerned with the legal aspects of their divorce. A couple who distrust mental health professionals or who are already working with a counselor may not want to work with a mental health professional-mediator. Cross-trained lawyer/mental health professional-mediators sometimes do co-mediation as well. While they obviously do not need to work with another professional, they like the other advantages of co-mediation.

Meeting the specific needs of mediating couples is the true objective of any mediator, who should be responsive to the needs of each couple. Teams of like sex can succeed in cases where neither spouse fears sexual bias or where one spouse has an inordinate distrust of the opposite sex. As long as co-mediators are highly compatible, they will probably be effective. Mediation is a skill in itself, drawing in part from counseling and lawyering. While professional mediators acquire a working knowledge of both fields, they remain primarily mediators; that is, they define issues, encourage cooperation, and educate couples.

Some mediators practice co-mediation exclusively, other mediators work with a co-mediator on occasion, while other mediators never work with a co-mediator. Mediators who work with a co-mediator on occasion generally call on a second mediator for the following reasons:

1. One or both clients are overwhelming. Some couples come into the mediation session ready to fight the mediator or unwilling to let the mediator control the negotiation process. The mere presence of a second mediator may be sufficient to get the couple to respond more reasonably.

2. One or both parties have issues to resolve that are outside the mediator's area of expertise. The mental health professional/mediator may help the couple settle custody issues and establish principles for dividing the property and determining the amount of support to be paid. Once this is accomplished, the Mental Health Professional Mediators will bring in an attorney they are familiar with to help the couple work out the details of the property and support issues and possibly to write up the final agreement. If the couple experience difficulties negotiating specific issues, the mental health professional is there to facilitate the negotiation, familiar with their communication patterns and priorities. The attorney/mediator may have helped the couple resolve all the property issues and desire some expert input on how best to resolve the custody issues.

3. Clients have unequal bargaining abilities. In this case it is safer for one of the mediators to provide support and advice to the disadvantaged spouse. The spouse that is not getting support is less apt to feel ganged up on and, if necessary, can get extra support from the other mediator.

4. The spouses are extremely sensitive to sexual biases. In this case the couple is reassured by a male/female balance.

A COMPARATIVE LOOK AT SOLO MEDIATION AND CO-MEDIATION

Mediators work with partners for many different reasons:

1. Often the stress level for each individual mediator is lower when there is a second mediator to rely on. If the active mediator becomes frustrated by an impasse or by hostile clients, the other mediator can often provide a new perspective. The unengaged mediator is in a better position to catch subtle cues of the nonactive spouse, to formulate alternate strategies, and to listen for possible agreements that may not be noticed in the excitement of any given moment. Some couples overwhelm a lone mediator. Lawyers and mental health professionals beginning to practice mediation sometimes work with co-mediators in order to gain greater insight into each other's professions. Alameda conciliation court mediators typically

do solo mediation. However, co-mediation is sometimes employed in particularly troublesome cases.

2. Co-mediators can model appropriate behavior for couples. They show respect and honesty when dealing with each other, and the nonactive mediator's attentive listening is helpful in modeling these qualities for the nonactive spouse.

For example: Divorcing couple John and Julie do not listen to each other; they are too intent upon what they themselves have to say. Mediators Herb and Anne ask John and Julie to relax while they discuss what has been happening in the last fifteen minutes. In addition to clarifying the difficulty that is preventing John and Julie from reaching agreements, Herb and Anne have the opportunity to model good communication between a couple working on a mutual problem.

3. It is possible to have both a male and a female mediator, creating a sexual balance and providing visible assurance to couples concerned about sexual bias.

4. During mediation it is convenient to have the expertise of both an attorney and a mental health professional available.

5. The nonactive mediator can attend to the spouse who is not speaking. Depending upon the demands of the situation, this may take the form of moral support, assurance that he or she will also get a chance to speak, or disapproval if that spouse interferes with the other spouse's time to talk.

For example: John is more likely to feel ignored when Anne is doing solo mediation. If she works exclusively with Julie for five minutes, John may get bored, anxious, angry, or paranoid. When Herb is co-mediating, his nonverbal attention (eye contact, body position, and so on) makes John feel attended to. Herb's attention to the conversation (modeling) provides a second nonactive party to the mediation and encourages John's continued interest in the process.

6. The introduction of a fourth party in the mediation session provides an opportunity to try different seating arrangements and to use team mediation techniques. For instance, if John and Julie are arguing and refuse to be directed toward more useful discussion, Herb and Anne may begin their own conversation. Their calm, low-key discussion will typically attract John and Julie's attention.

HERB: I don't know what to do. Our suggestions aren't working; I can hear their pain but I don't think it is doing either of them any good.

ANNE: The way I see it, we have three options: (1) Sit here until they blow off their anger, (2) stop them and tell them we will work at it again next week and terminate if that doesn't work, or (3) try to secure their commitment to go back to work now.

John and Julie will probably find it hard to argue while this quiet conversation is going on and may well agree to continue their discussion in a nonblaming manner.

7. Co-mediation supplies a more reliable system of checks and balances. If one of the mediators becomes involved in a couple's emotional issues because of some strong personal feelings, the co-mediator is available to bring everyone back into focus.

For example: John and Julie are mediating a custody proposal. They want their five-year-old son Billy to live with John and visit Julie on alternate weekends. Herb is concerned that Billy will not be getting sufficient mothering. Herb begins to ask questions about Julie's housing situation as well as about her time and transportation arrangements. Julie seems to be getting defensive. Anne believes that Julie may be experiencing Herb's questions as pressuring or disapproving, so she refocuses the conversation on Billy's best interests. After John and Julie have left, Herb and Anne discuss Herb's feelings to see if they arise from his professional expertise or from memories of losing his own mother when he was six. If they believe the discussion would be helpful for John and Julie, they will talk in their presence.

8. At times, mediators find it expedient to be tough on one or the other party. When a second mediator is present to provide support for the recipient, the "tough" mediator can be more direct than might be possible in solo mediation.

9. Some co-mediators claim co-mediation is twice as efficient as solo mediation; thus the couple spend half the time mediating and pay the same amount of money. Doubtless this depends upon the couple in question.

Prior to the first session, co-mediators frequently consult with each other to share their knowledge of the couple and their ideas on how to proceed. In order to work effectively together, they must be able to communicate verbally and nonverbally throughout the mediation. After the couple leave, most co-mediators assess their work and plan for the next session.

The primary advantage of co-mediation is in providing additional assurances to clients. Nervous, distrustful, and volatile clients receive the attention of two professionals, as well as two opinions. Mediation teams are capable of different and powerful interventions. If the mediators are calm and feel equal to all challenges, the couple will sense it and respond in kind.

Many pioneers in the field of mediation began practicing mediation alone and have continued to do so out of habit or preference. Reasons to practice solo mediation include the following:

1. A single mediator can direct the mediation and develop strategies without worrying about a partner's intentions. When two mediators' styles are not harmonious, energies are wasted in fighting or in attempting to coordinate efforts.

2. Though the concept of co-mediation is quite appealing, it takes time to find a suitable co-mediator, and it is time-consuming to work out good team responses.

3. The hourly cost of mediation is lower for one professional than for two. Attorneys who charge $100 per hour are reluctant to add another $40 to $100 to that fee. Those who do try co-mediation often lower their typical hourly fee. If the mediation takes less time with two professionals than with one (a point that is in debate), there may be no actual added expense; however, even if co-mediation takes half the time of solo mediation, some couples are put off by the higher hourly fee.

4. Scheduling time is frequently cumbersome for two professionals, particularly when they are active in separate practices.

5. Some mediators who have tried both co-mediation and solo mediation prefer the greater demands and excitement of solo mediation.

6. Some clients feel that the protections and possibilities that co-mediation provide are wasted on them.

DIFFERENT CO-MEDIATION STYLES

Co-mediation is done by mediators who work together regularly or occasionally. Mediators who work with numerous co-mediators tend to choose them according to the perceived needs of a particular couple. An older couple might be more comfortable working with at least one older mediator. When emotional problems are a block, a therapist/mediator may call in a co-therapist because he or she feels the emotional dynamics would be most effectively handled in that manner. If the couple need legal information, an attorney is called in. Attorneys sometimes work with a number of marital counselors, who call them in when couples decide to divorce. Many regular practitioners of co-mediation find a permanent partner and develop an understanding of their partner's style. The ability to work well with a co-mediator increases with experience. Knowledge of each other's cues and orientation facilitates the mediation.

Families in Transition, a San Francisco-based mediation center, is a good example of one of the infinite number of possible approaches to co-mediation. Psychologists Matthew McKay and Peter Rogers conduct the initial orientation session together. Based on the information they accumulate in this first session, they decide which of the two is best suited to mediate the divorce. All future mediation sessions are co-mediated with one of a number of women attorneys they work with. The other psychologist remains available to work with the children or the spouses separately.

Mediation teams cope with the intricacies of co-mediation in a variety of ways. The newly formed lawyer/therapist team often agrees to a division of labor along professional lines. Therapists address the couple's emotional blocks and facilitate custody decisions. Lawyers provide legal information concerning what is possible for the couple to do and what might happen in court, give tax advice, and sometimes write the marital settlement agreement. Mediation teams that have a specific agenda may split duties. For instance, in an initial mediation session, mediator A may agree to take responsibility for going over the consent form and explaining possible custody arrangements. Mediator B could then concentrate on establishing the procedures to be used in the mediation and explaining the mediation process.

As partners gain familiarity with each other, the more subtle interventions possible in co-mediation develop. The lawyer-therapist division of roles becomes less and less clear. The attorney learns to do active listening and to encourage cooperative problem solving. The therapist learns to explain the meaning of joint custody—perhaps more clearly than the lawyer because of his or her lack of legal terminology. Though the lawyer or the mental health professional would not be confident making the interventions or explaining terminology in the absence of the other, together they are able to move freely between their fields of expertise.

MEDIATION ORIENTATION AND NEGOTIATIONS

The following mediation is an educational role-play by the Northwest Mediation Service of Seattle, Washington—a small group of lawyers and mental health professionals who work with each other on a regular basis. The director, Ms. Nancy Kaplan, pairs the mediators for each case. Consideration is given to the personalities of the mediators, how they work with each other, and how a certain team may fit with clients. Usually teams are rotated, but because of the small number of mediators, teams work together on a repeated basis.

Mediators at the Northwest Mediation Service have done over one hundred cases. Cases tend to average five to six hours, with two weeks between sessions. Clients are often college educated, and many have already consulted lawyers and counselors. Ms. Kaplan, a M.S.W. who has practiced mediation for five years, and Howard Bartlett, a lawyer who has practiced mediation for one and one-half years, are the mediators in the following case.

Mike and Sue are both forty years old and have been married for twenty years. They have two children: John, age fifteen, and Abby, age eight. Sue has never worked outside the home. Mike earns $38,000 a year working for a local airplane manufacturer.

THE INITIAL INTERVIEW

MS. KAPLAN: You've received the packet of information we sent you with our rules and the contract?

MIKE: Yes.

SUE: Yes.

MS. KAPLAN: Are there any questions you have about the rules or the way we operate?

SUE: I showed it to my attorney this morning and he didn't think I should do this.

MR. BARTLETT: Did he give you a reason for that?

SUE: He said I could get more if I went to court . . .

MR. BARTLETT: Than you could get here?

SUE: Yes.

MR. BARTLETT: What about you, Mike?

MIKE: I showed it to my attorney too. He advised me that it might not be that great an idea for me to be here either, because he seemed to think that there would be more protections offered to me by court law and a judge than there are in this kind of situation.

MS. KAPLAN: Can you give an idea of why you decided to mediate? Obviously, both of you have some questions about the adversary process versus doing a mediated divorce with us.

MIKE: I'm here for two reasons. I'd like this to be as easy as possible on our two children, and the other concern is cost. If we go through a full-blown court proceeding, it is going to be extremely expensive in terms of attorneys' fees.

SUE: He agreed to pay for it, so what could I say?

MR. BARTLETT: Mike, you seemed to indicate that you or your attorney thought that you couldn't have the same protection here that you could through the court system. Do you have a feeling that you need some protection that you don't think we can give you through this process?

MIKE: Yes. Seems to me it would be very easy for people to point the finger at me and call me the bad guy here. I know that Sue is angry at me for some things that I have done over the last few months, and it seems to me that as mediators, you people may not take into account and consider my reasons for what I've done. You'll just look at the results of my actions and make unfair judgments against me.

MR. BARTLETT: Let me explain a little bit about mediation and maybe respond to that concern. As you are aware, I'm a lawyer and Ms. Kaplan is a mental health worker. It is our hope and our intention, as much as is humanly possible, to be totally neutral to whatever your situation might be, to be impartial, not to take sides. Obviously, everyone has a certain degree of bias within them, but it is our intention to put that aside as we would with any client with whom we are working. Hopefully, we can help the two of you come to an agreement that you believe is reasonable and fair to each other and to your children, and that is in keeping with the laws and rules of our court system in this state. Even though you have some concerns about your behavior, it is certainly not our intention to judge that behavior or to do anything that would make you look bad or help us feel somehow that you shouldn't get what you are entitled to within our laws.

MS. KAPLAN: I think it is important for both of you to realize the difference between mediation and arbitration or the court system, the adversary process. The difference is that nobody is making judgments here. We're not going to tell you what to do. We can give you some suggestions. We can try to help you reach an agreement, but we are not going to judge you. You have control of whatever agreements you make. Both of you would have to agree that this is what you want to do. No one is going to impose a decision on you. Mike, I understand what you're saying about the ease for the children, and I think for yourself also, in reaching an agreement rather than having one imposed on you. You have children, one of whom is eight years old, is that right?

SUE: Yes.

MS. KAPLAN: You two are going to have to cooperate with each other to some degree for several years for the sake of these children. It is important that you learn some of that communication and cooperation now.

MIKE: OK, it sounds like we can both get a fair deal.

MR. BARTLETT: Sue, one of the concerns that you had was that you thought you could get more in court, and I guess there is a trade-off that you have to consider in deciding whether to mediate or go through court. It may or may not be that in going to court you would end up with more material possessions. You have to weigh that against the cost of litigation, going through the court process in terms of the fees involved, the emotional impact upon you and Mike and upon the children. There will be an emotional cost to them. And also just the time involved.

Right now in King County it takes at least a year, and maybe even a year and a half, for a case to go to trial. You live with the process for that length of time. It is our hope that through mediation, by setting up a series of meetings, we can resolve these issues in five or ten hours at most. This will result in a substantial, not only cost, savings, but time and emotional savings.

SUE: But what happens if we make some agreement and then decide to change it later?

MR. BARTLETT: You have the right to do that. What we are asking here is that you enter into the mediation in a spirit of cooperation. It doesn't mean you have to be friends with each other. We just ask that you attempt to cooperate to resolve the problems in a fair and open manner.

MS. KAPLAN: The other thing that I would like to say is that if at some point in the mediation either of you feels that you would like to share the potential decisions with your attorney, run these ideas by him and come back and share whatever input they have with us, that is fine. We encourage you to do that.

MIKE: Well, what if our attorneys say we shouldn't enter into an agreement, or we shouldn't enter into a part of the agreement that is at issue?

MS. KAPLAN: Then I think you should discuss with your attorney why he or she said that. I think you should always remember that your attorney is your employee. Your attorney should not have the power to tell you what to do. You are hiring that person, this is your life.

MR. BARTLETT: It is our hope that we can provide you with some legal information that will help you make decisions here. However, it is very likely that issues will come up for which you will need extra expert advice. Such as valuing your home. You may have to hire an appraiser to do that. For evaluating other assets you may have to hire an accountant. There may be legal issues that come up about which you will want to consult your attorney, and if those issues come up, we'll do our best to identify those for you so that you can go out and get extra legal advice. We're not here to try to be an advocate for either side, but to give you information from which you can then negotiate a settlement cooperatively. Do you have any other questions about the mediation process?

SUE: Is this like a court order at all?

MR. BARTLETT: What we will do is hopefully come to agreements. And we ask that whatever agreement we come to, and this is part of the rules, that you will stick with it.

MIKE: Is it like a contract that one side can enforce if the other side breaks a promise in the agreement?

MR. BARTLETT: We do not specifically prepare a contract for you at the end of your mediation. What we will do is when the mediation has been completed and the agreements have been reached, we will prepare a letter for each of you which outlines what we believe to be the agreements that the two of you have reached. You may then take that to an attorney or handle it yourself, preparing the final agreement yourself. It will be up to the two of you to see that a contract is prepared in a fashion that you are comfortable with, see that the final dissolution documents are prepared, and have those presented to the court. We do not prepare the contract or any of the dissolution documents for you, and we do not review them once they have been prepared.

MS. KAPLAN: Do you have any other questions, or should we proceed to discuss which issues you need to mediate?

This orientation flows well. No one person dominates the session. Mike and Sue have already been given an information packet and now the mediators are ready to answer questions. They encourage Mike and Sue to state their doubts now. When Sue voices her insecurity about mediating, reflecting her attorney's skepticism, Mr. Bartlett has Mike also reveal his doubts and his attorney's advice. In some ways the fact that both clients' attorneys are afraid that their clients will get a bad deal in mediation is reassuring. Neither of them feels they are at a predictable disadvantage.

Ms. Kaplan gets Mike to tell her why he wants to mediate, allowing him to sell himself on mediation. Both Mr. Bartlett and Ms. Kaplan ask questions intended to cause Sue and Mike to voice their concerns so that they can be resolved or so that the couple will find out now that mediation won't work for them. Ms. Kaplan spends a considerable amount of time explaining what mediation is. Mr. Bartlett talks about the price of going to court as one who knows. By the end of the orientation, Mike and Sue have a fair idea of what mediation will entail.

Mr. Bartlett, an attorney, is able to help Mike and Sue explore their fears about foregoing adversarial representation. The couple's questions and doubts about mediation are common concerns. Many lawyers distrust the mediation process due to lack of information, and they instill this distrust in their clients. As a lawyer, Mr. Bartlett addresses Mike and Sue's legal concerns and allows them to make their decision to proceed. Mr. Bartlett's directness and knowledgeable demeanor instill confidence and trust. Mike and Sue now have a second legal opinion to consider.

DISCUSSING THE CHILDREN

MR. BARTLETT: The next issue that we have decided to talk about for awhile is the issue of your children. There are custody and visitation arrangements that obviously need to be dealt with. When we have children involved, we have to deal with living arrangements, how the two of you are going to interact with them, whether or not any support is going to be required and if so, how much, and finally how long that support may last and what fashion it is going to take.

You have two children, John who is fifteen and Abby who is eight. Have the two of you come to any agreement with regard to the children?

SUE: No. I want them to live with me and he wants them to live with him.

MIKE: I want John to live with me. John is 15 years old and he needs a father. I definitely want John to live with me.

SUE: Well you can't split them up.

MIKE: Well then I would like both John and Abby to live with me.

SUE: No! Then I don't have either of them.

MS. KAPLAN: Have you talked to the children about this at all?

MIKE: We've tried to keep this far away from the children's lives at this point. They know what's going on, but we really haven't discussed with them what parent each of them is going to live with or whatever.

SUE: You haven't kept it away from the kids, they know about the girlfriend you're living with!

MIKE: Well they know that we are having problems, yes, but and they . . .

SUE: You don't expect that they know what is going on at night, with you not home for dinner . . .

MIKE: Well I didn't say that they were totally in the dark about our problems, but we haven't discussed who they are going to live with.

SUE: You think I want them living with your girlfriend?

MS. KAPLAN: You're saying Sue that you have some concern about the children living with their dad or seeing their dad with his girlfriend?

SUE: What kind of life is that for them?

MIKE: In my estimation she would be a better mother than you've been for the last few years.

MS. KAPLAN: I don't think we should get into accusing each other of how you've been for the last twenty years of your marriage. Right now, we're here to deal with some really specific issues, and one of them is the custody of the children. Frankly, I don't even like that word. I like to talk about sharing time and responsibilities for the children rather than living with you and custody with you and visitation. I can also understand what you are saying Sue. It sounds like you have some real anger about your husband's relationship with this lady, and it's probably hard for you to concentrate on being fair as far as the children are concerned. Possibly your anger is getting in the way here.

SUE: How would you feel if some woman comes along and takes your husband away from you? All of a sudden you're the fifth wheel.

MS. KAPLAN: I'd feel pretty angry, I would think that is a pretty normal reaction, and it's hard to concentrate and think about what would be best for the children.

MR. BARTLETT: You may also be feeling that she's trying to take the children away from you too. Is that part of your concern?

SUE: Yes.

MR. BARTLETT: Let me ask a question this way. That would be for each of you to think what the other might have to offer the children. That is, Mike, what do you think that Sue has to offer that you don't have to offer?

MIKE: Well, Sue has been a good mother. Sue I apologize for saying what I did. You've done your best for the kids, I know you love them and I know that you watch over them and that you are interested in their well-being. But you are a woman, and I don't think you can provide them with what I think John particularly, and also Abby to a certain extent, need in terms of a father figure.

SUE: But you haven't been there. For the last three months you haven't been there.

MIKE: Three months is a short period of time. I'm still alive and available.

MS. KAPLAN: What do you think Sue? Are there some advantages you think Mike could give the children that possibly you couldn't?

SUE: Probably. John is at an age when he needs a father around the house. I can't be mother and father both.

MS. KAPLAN: Have you considered some kind of shared custody arrangement? Do you know what that is?

SUE: No. Can you explain it?

MS. KAPLAN: (turning to Mr. Bartlett) Would you like to explain it?

MR. BARTLETT: There are a number of different types of custody. Unfortunately, in our legal language we tend to talk in terms of winning and losing. You are awarded custody or not awarded custody. You are awarded the house. We tend to think of the children as another chattel, another piece of property that is awarded to one person or the other. I think that is unfortunate language, because what we can do is talk about the children in terms of what their needs are and what is best for them and what the two of you might have to offer to them.

MS. KAPLAN: Plus the fact that just because you are getting divorced does not mean that one of you is ending his or her parenthood.

MR. BARTLETT: There are a number of possible custody arrangements. The standard that you often hear about is where custody is awarded to one party or the other, the other party has visitation rights every other weekend, some holidays, and some extended time during the year. Alot of people are rethinking whether that is best for the children and best for the parents. This leads into the concept of joint custody. One type is joint legal custody and the other is residential care. Joint legal custody is the language which says that both parties are proper parents and the court doesn't cut off either parent's rights. This still allows you access to school and medical records, to make joint decisions about the children and their well-being in terms of health, education, religious upbringing, and the general decisions about their well-being, and it requires a degree of cooperation. The second issue is residential care. Where the children will reside and at what time. These decisions you can do pretty much what you want with. You can fashion it to your own needs and to the needs of the children.

MS. KAPLAN: I think that that's one of the beauties of mediation versus the court process. In the court you have decisions imposed upon you by a judge who does not have the same knowledge of your children or knowledge of human behavior. Even if you have a mental health professional tell you what to do, that person has probably only seen you for a few hours. It seems to me to be a strange situation where people who have been married for twenty years and who have had children for fifteen years are allowing a professional person to usurp their position as parents. Mediation will allow you to maintain your control. You can do whatever you want with regard to how often or how much you see your children.

MR. BARTLETT: I think it is important if you are considering joint custody to look at what the other parent has to offer. What I have here is a list of some books and articles on joint custody that I would like you to read. Some are favorable and some are unfavorable. You may also want to talk to your own attorney about it. I suggest that we then come back and talk about joint custody at our next session. Is that agreeable?

SUE: Does that mean the kids are going to be bounced from house to house?

MR. BARTLETT: Not necessarily. Again, this gives you the flexibility to do what is best for you. You'll have a better idea of what that might be after reading those books and articles.

MS. KAPLAN: I would also suggest, having children as old as your children are, that you discuss with them the kinds of contact that they would like to have with each of you. Not that you need to put them in a position of deciding, but I think it is important for you to get some input, at least from your fifteen-year-old.

After summarizing his perception of what must be accomplished in terms of arrangements for the children, Mr. Bartlett asks Sue and Mike whether they have come to any agreements about the children already. This sets off an argument which Mike and Sue have obviously had before. Mr. Bartlett and Ms. Kaplan listen for a short while and get a feel for the situation. Ms. Kaplan asks whether the kids have been consulted and probes an obviously tender spot and potential stumbling block to the mediation, Mike's girlfriend. Mike's defensiveness and Sue's hostile reaction elicit both empathy and directive intervention.

Ms. Kaplan makes it clear that she has strong feelings about co-parenting after divorce. In some ways she is an advocate for the children. She talks about Sue being "fair" to the kids and wants Sue to think about what a fair situation would be. Mr. Bartlett, aware of common fears of divorcing parents, checks to see if Sue feels as if

Mike's girlfriend might also take her children. Mike gains some insight from this, becoming more understanding, and Sue has less need to act out her fears. Mike even apologizes for his disparagement of Sue's mothering. The whole tone of the mediation has changed, though Sue is still reluctant to bury the hatchet altogether.

Mike and Sue are now more able to think of what the other has to offer the children—they are ready to hear about options. When Ms. Kaplan asks if they know what shared custody is, Sue asks for an explanation. This is an opening for Mr. Bartlett and Ms. Kaplan to talk about different custody arrangements, something they have done on many occasions. There is no doubt that both Mr. Bartlett and Ms. Kaplan feel that shared custody is best for most children. This is a common bias of many mediators.

DISCUSSING THE PENSION

MR. BARTLETT: Mike I know that you have worked for fifteen years and your company has a pension program. I think it is important that we discuss that as well as all the other issues.

MIKE: You mean my pension has to be divided too?

MR. BARTLETT: In dividing things the pension may not necessarily be divided between the two of you, but it has to be disclosed and valued and disposed of. So yes, it is an item that has to be dealt with.

MIKE: Well I consider it to be mine. I don't think Sue has any claim on it. I mean I've worked there, and I've gotten up every morning and . . .

SUE: And I haven't done a thing! I've just been sitting around watching soap operas at home! What about the kids?

MIKE: What am I going to live on when I become old?

SUE: Yeah, but you've been working all this time and had time to build up a pension, and I haven't.

MIKE: I'm not even going to get any of this money till I'm sixty-two or sixty-five or something, and I don't want you in my life until then. I want to be done with this now. I don't think it is fair to divide this up and give you money that I'm not going to receive for fifteen or more years or maybe never receive. If I die tomorrow, I'm not going to get a dime of this.

MR. BARTLETT: Let me interrupt here because I think the direction we're going here isn't going to solve the problem, and I think I have to be fairly direct with you, Mike. You may want to discuss this with your own attorney.

MIKE: I think I will . . .

MR. BARTLETT: To get his advice. But I think it's important, and I'll be, as I said, fairly direct about it. A pension under the laws of Washington is an asset, and that asset can be valued by actuarial determination; and the courts then treat it as an asset to be disposed of. The only issue that we are going to have here is what is its value and how is it going to be disposed of. That doesn't mean that when the two of you are done it is going to be divided in some mathematical formula. Hopefully, all of the property will be considered and we will come to a reasonable resolution.

MIKE: This whole thing about my pension goes back and supports my original concern about coming into this mediation process. It seems to me that you people are ganging up on me and trying to get something over on me. I need a lawyer to help me with this.

MS. KAPLAN: I hear your concern. It sounds like the two of us are coming down hard on this. Actually, what we are doing is informing you that a pension is a piece of property that does need to be divided up.

MIKE: But I don't even know that I'm going to get anything out of this pension.

MS. KAPLAN: I understand what you are saying, but I think it is important for you to realize that this is part of the law and it is not that we are trying to impose something on you. We do encourage you to consult your attorney.

MR. BARTLETT: There is another issue that I think you should be aware of. If an asset is not divided, it becomes an asset that is held jointly. If it is not divided now, ten years from now Sue could ask for half of your pension. I think underlying this whole thing is a need for you to talk to your attorney about this issue and get advice from him as to whether or not it is a divisable asset, and how it is valued. It seems that you should do that between now and our next session so that we can talk about this in a productive way. We're certainly not trying to gang up on either of you. We're trying to get full disclosure of what assets there are so that everything is on the table, so that we can deal with it in a fair and open manner.

It is appropriate for Mr. Bartlett to open the pension issue as a man and as an attorney. Pensions are a sensitive political issue for both men and women. Mike doesn't like hearing Mr. Bartlett say that he will have to share his pension, and this reopens Mike's desire for "legal protection." Mr. Bartlett encourages Mike to see his attorney, secure in the knowledge that he has presented the facts–Mike must learn to live with them. After Mr. Bartlett presents the legal facts, Ms. Kaplan is in a better position to reassure Mike.

This particular co-mediation did not involve a particularly difficult type of mediation case. Sue and Mike are an average couple. The mediation is relatively straightforward, and the transcript is not terribly different than it might be had a single cross-trained mediator done the mediation. However, there are not many cross-trained mediators in practice, and some of those who do exist prefer to practice co-mediation for the reasons stated at the beginning of this chapter. It might be that Mike and Sue had been unable to agree upon a mediator because Sue wanted a woman and Mike wanted a man; thus, regardless of how manageable they were in the mediation session, it required a team to get them to come in. It is hard to evaluate relative effects of the added attention to each party, modeling, dual expertise, sexual balance, and the sheer calming weight of two mediators as opposed to one.

Highly emotional couples, and couples with substantial custody, property, alimony, and child-support issues to decide, should consider the advantages of co-mediation.

EIGHT
STRUCTURED MEDIATION

Structured mediation is a family mediation model taught nationally by the Family Mediation Association. Originally taught by O. J. Coogler, who is referred to by many mediators as the father of divorce mediation, structured mediation training was the first widely publicized and attended mediation training. (See chart, pp. 225-26, which reports the number of mediators who have taken the structured mediation training.) The training was first available to lawyers and mental health professionals in the mid-1970s.

Inspired by twenty years of legal practice in Atlanta, Georgia, and having personally undergone a hostile divorce, O. J. Coogler developed structured mediation. He was convinced that there should be a more civilized means of separating available to couples who were willing to work together and did not want attorneys to fight for them about the details of their divorce. After obtaining training in marital therapy, and after years of research and practice with his model of family mediation, he began to lecture, write, and train other professionals in mediation techniques. He founded the Family Mediation Association in 1974, and served as its president until his death in 1982.

The training is based on a set of guidelines for family mediators developed and described by O. J. Coogler in *Structured Mediation in Divorce Settlement*, the first professional book about divorce mediation. Coogler realized that lawyers and mental health professionals across the country would want to offer their clients the benefits of mediation, yet there were no trained mediators professionals could refer clients to. Mr. Coogler developed a five-day intensive training program for lawyers and mental health professionals with advanced degrees. The course included extensive readings on divorce and conflict resolution prior to the training. Many professionals travel thousands of miles to receive this training. Presently the Family Mediation Association has four training modules—a one-day overview and introduction, a one-and-a-half-day session focusing on the theoretical underpinnings of mediation, a three-and-a-half-day session on structured mediation based on O. J. Coogler's original five-day course, and a one-day course of individualized assessment and discussion of the practical considerations involved in setting up a mediation practice, for graduates of the three-and-a-half-day course.

Short-term training, no matter how intense, can't provide participants with all the understanding of a practiced mediator. For this reason, trainees have been encouraged to complete a 250-hour supervised practicum in which they have the opportunity to discuss their cases and receive further instruction from more experienced mediators. Some have paired themselves with mediators from a complementary profession and of the opposite sex so that they might benefit from each other's expertise.

Mediators who practice structured mediation use a set of mediation rules, which are designed to protect mediators and clients and facilitate the mediation process. (Structured mediation rules follow this chapter.) Sara Grebe, a therapist/mediator and director of training for the Family Mediation Association, explains:

> Most couples have next to no experience in formal negotiation. To expect them to be aware of all the unwritten rules of bargaining that a labor negotiator learns on the job is unrealistic. The rules provide a common ground for the couple to begin—everyone knowing what is expected, what isn't allowed and how to proceed. People are much less fearful when they know the rules of the game. If they constantly have to guess where they are going it heightens the anxiety in an already anxious situation.

The rules provide mediators and clients with a formula for approaching the issues of divorce, overcoming obstacles in mediation, and defining their relationship. For example, mediators are required to maintain strict confidentiality so that couples are assured of a safe environment in which they can negotiate freely. The content of a mediation must not be revealed to attorneys or courts. Neither the mediator nor the advisory attorney is permitted to represent either party separately should any legal proceedings be initiated.

If a couple fail to reach a mutually acceptable agreement with the help of a mediator, arbitration is provided. Impasse is defined in Section 32, and arbitration procedures are outlined in Section 33. In actuality, arbitration is rarely—if ever—needed.

Section 4 of the mediation rules requires that mediation teams maintain a male-female balance. This is to ensure that no spouse feels overwhelmed.

The mediator is required to disclose any possible taint upon his or her neutrality. For example, if the mediator recognizes that one spouse was on the PTA with her five years ago, the mediator must disclose this information. The spouses can then decide whether they think it might create a bias in the mediation and whether they would prefer to use a different mediator.

Mediators are instructed not to do individual caucusing, since it may taint their neutrality. An individual session might reveal information more appropriately heard by everyone, or the unincluded spouse might fear some sort of conspiracy. In addition, a mediator who has separate knowledge acquires greater decision-making powers. (See pros and cons of individual caucusing, pp. 47-48.) In structured mediation each party is assured of inclusion in every aspect of the negotiation process. Mediators and advisory attorneys are required to refrain from any sort of contact with parties outside of mediation sessions.

Couples are given homework at the first session. This speeds the mediation process by providing relevant information and starting the couple thinking about relevant issues. Preparation of budgets and full disclosure of income tax returns are required. Most couples are asked to fill out a personal data and information form, a financial information and income statement, a monthly expense budget—which includes an emergencies and future goal schedule, a seasonal expense schedule, and an installment debt payment schedule—and an analysis of family expenditures. In order to encourage prompt completion of forms and more efficient, well-researched agreements, couples who fail to fill out necessary forms risk suspension of mediation.

The forms are useful in the problem-solving stages of mediation. For example, the monthly expense budgets cannot exceed the couples' joint monthly income. When this happens, couples need to work cooperatively to bring the two into line. Often flip charts or chalkboards are used to help the couple visualize what they need to do and what they have done.

The rules provide guidelines for division of property (Section 19), spousal maintenance (Section 20), and child support and child custody (Sections 21 and 22). The rights of the custodial parent, the noncustodial parent, and joint custodial parents are defined (Sections 23, 24, and 25). These rules are based on a model code and on more advanced states' divorce laws.

Third parties who have a direct involvement (for example, the children, or grandparents who take care of the children on a regular basis) may be included in the mediation when the mediator considers this beneficial. For an agreement to be solid, all adult participants in an agreement should take part in the negotiation of that agreement.

The use of an advisory attorney is a distinguishing aspect of structured mediation. In contrast to numerous other mediation styles, neither party is permitted to consult outside counsel while mediating. All legal questions are to be directed to the advisory attorney, whose role is to provide legal information and write up the couple's final agreement in an unbiased manner. The attorney acts as a legal consultant to the family. He or she does not represent either party. Arrangements for the appointment of an "advisory attorney" are described in detail (see Sections 29 and 30a-k) as are his or her duties. This minimizes the possibility of spouses getting inflammatory or conflicting legal advice.

Before couples begin to mediate, they must agree to abide by the forty structured mediation rules. The mediator often spends the entire orientation session getting to know the couple while going over the mediation rules, and in this manner gains the couple's commitment to the process.

In addition to the rules that so closely delineate the mediator's role, there are quite a few rules that require a significant commitment from the couple. For instance, upon signing the agreement to mediate, they are required to provide a ten-hour retainer for the mediator's fees, and should they "fail or refuse to proceed with mediation and/or arbitration after ten days written notice has been mailed to them, all deposits remaining are forfeited by the parties" (Section 8d). Unless there are special circumstances, couples are expected to mediate on a weekly basis. They agree to arbitrate, should they reach an impasse in mediation. Agreement to abide by the mediation rules indicates that a couple is committed to the process, and the mediator can be fairly confident that they are ready to mediate.

At first glance, the structured mediation rules may be intimidating. However, most couples see the rules for the first time at their orientation session, where the mediator can answer questions and explain the value of clearly delineated rules. Many people gain confidence from the predictability and structure of detailed rules. They know that once they have agreed to mediate, they are committed to the process and cannot consult outside attorneys or file court actions. They have agreed to do their best to try to meet each other's needs. The divorce process cannot linger on interminably. They have committed themselves to a time schedule. No one will be a loser, especially the children. The mediation rules quite effectively single out those couples who can mediate successfully. Couples who turn away are often not yet ready for mediation.

Hundreds of professionals have added mediation to their practice as a result of structured mediation training. Many modify their mediation methods as they gain experience and practical understanding of the dynamics of mediation. Some have no choice but to modify the structured mediation rules. For example, using a single advisory attorney to impartially advise clients and draw up settlements is actively frowned upon by some states' bar associations, unless separate attorneys are also employed to look over any documents. Though using one attorney does reduce the likelihood of a couple getting inflammatory adversarial advice from separate attorneys, many attorneys and mental health professionals who essentially practice structured mediation consider the benefits of separate legal advice to be greater than any possible detriment. Any spouse who is not fully aware of his or her rights when agreeing to a mediated agreement may later become dissatisfied with the agreement. In other words, if Mary decides she wants no part of her husband's pension—even though she has the right to one-half of it—that is fine, so long as she chooses to give up her rights knowledgeably. Furthermore, if separate attorneys double-check an agreement, they are more likely to catch any oversights.

Mediators who have been trained under the structured mediation format may choose to deviate from the model in other respects. Some write up settlement agreements and have separate counsel review the agreement; or they try individual caucusing to surmount an impasse. Structured mediation is the basis from which many mediators have developed their styles.

A CASE STUDY IN STRUCTURED MEDIATION

Cathy and Matt met in college. They married a few months after graduation and moved to Philadelphia, where Matt had a job at a bank. Now, eight years and one child later, Cathy and Matt have decided to separate. Cathy is thinking about moving to Washington, D.C. to find a job in which she can use her political science degree. Matt's career has been a steady progression of minor promotions. He now earns $40,000 a year and has no desire to leave Philadelphia. He would rather that Cathy stay in the marriage, but he has finally accepted her decision to leave.

Brian, their four-year-old son, is their biggest concern. In principle, Matt and Cathy are prepared to sell their house and split the profit, divide the personal property, and divide their debts on a 50/50 basis. So far, their discussions have been strained and have not resolved much. Brian is always at the back of their thoughts, an issue so charged with emotion that neither of them brings it up.

A friend recently suggested to Cathy that she contact the local Family Mediation Center. After a phone call, Cathy received a pamphlet briefly describing the mediation process and what the center had to offer. Cathy thought it sounded like a good idea and left the pamphlet for Matt to look at. A week later they made an appointment for a two hour orientation interview at the mediation center.

At the orientation session Cathy and Matt each received a package of materials for them to read and work on. The first item in the packet was a detailed description of mediation and the adversary system, with an empathetic acknowledgement of the stress they were currently experiencing and a statement on the underlying tenets of structured mediation. The latter were reassuring: Each party's needs must be met to as great an extent as resources permit. Each party is entitled to respect, and must take responsibility for him- or herself. Each party is assured of the opportunity to consider all relevant information pertinent to making the agreement, before making the agreement. Decisions are to be made on a cooperative, as compared to competitive, basis, and each party is assured of the opportunity to be heard.

Mediation was also briefly compared to the adversary system. The cost of mediation was described as consisting of a $500 advance deposit for ten hours of mediation (any unused time to be refunded upon completion of mediation); and couples must also employ an advisory attorney—at the rate of $50 per hour—for two to six hours, depending upon the couple's needs.

The second and third items in the packet were an explanation of the Marital Mediation Rules and a copy of the rules themselves. As Cathy and Matt read this section, the mediator went over the more important rules and procedures, clarifying and elaborating.

MEDIATOR: I want you to be aware that I am going to be taping all of our sessions together. This serves a number of purposes. There may be a time when it is helpful to go back and listen to a conversation in order to clarify what had been agreed upon. Also, having a record of the mediation makes it possible to go back if there is any question about whether the mediation rules have been followed. The release I would like you to sign allows me to analyze our mediation with my colleagues and attempt to improve our mediation methods. Your names will not be available to my colleagues unless you specifically authorize me to reveal them. In all other cases the tapes are strictly confidential.

We have found that two-hour appointments every week are the most effective way to mediate a divorce. When there is a lot of lag time in between sessions, it takes longer to reach an agreement. This session and signing of the mediation contract is to clarify for you what you will have to do to mediate your divorce and is designed to obtain a commitment from you to do so. If you do reach an impasse in mediation, you will have agreed to have that issue arbitrated under the mediation rules. The arbitrator, a neutral third party, will rule on the issue in controversy. This center has never had to resort to arbitration. Thus far, the process of defining the issue in controversy has resulted in a mediated agreement in each case. If you do turn to arbitration, your money will be refunded, as it will if you reconcile or become disabled, or naturally if you complete your settlement in under ten hours. If you simply quit, you forfeit your deposit.

MATT: I want to know a bit more about what you mean by full disclosure.

MEDIATOR: The effectiveness of this process is contingent upon your honesty with each other in mediation. For you to make the best decisions for yourselves, you will both need to share all the relevant information you have for making intelligent choices. If one of you were to withhold information from the other, it might invalidate the agreement. The requirement that you both bring in budgets relies on this same principle. To make the best agreement, we need all the information available, and if you fail to bring in homework, I may have to cancel the session.

CATHY: Are we going to have to bring Brian in?

MEDIATOR: That depends on you and Brian. We'll certainly talk about it. If it appears that it would be helpful to you and Brian, we will. I think that is an issue we will have to deal with in detail later on.

MATT: I'm not sure I can follow this rule about third-party involvement. I talk over all my problems with my best friend and it helps me to get things out.

MEDIATOR: It may seem a bit hard to do at times, but it prevents you from receiving inappropriate advice. It is impossible for you to relate all that is going on in a mediation session in an unbiased manner. We've found it best to have parties leave the issues for mediation in mediation. It is better for you to not even discuss the issues between yourselves unless it is part of an assigned task that I believe you are ready for.

CATHY: Actually, I kinda like that rule. I've been getting all kinds of advice from everybody, and it's getting to be too much.

MEDIATOR: Now next session we're going to be agreeing on temporary custody and support issues, making agreements regarding any jointly held assets like charge, checking, and savings accounts, and taking care of any other immediate needs. Neither of you is to transfer any property during the mediation. Basically, you should be maintaining the status quo. Now, if there is any controversy over who will have custody of Brian, I'd like to know that now.

CATHY: I think that is our biggest problem.

MEDIATOR: OK, I think Brian is lucky to have two concerned parents. I'm sure you'll find a good arrangement for all of you. In this case, I'm going to be asking you to develop two budgets, one assuming you are the custodial parent and one assuming you are the noncustodial parent. This is so we can mediate property and financial issues before we mediate the custody issue. I dislike it when parents attempt to gain custody of the children simply in order to be awarded the house. The issues are difficult without confusing the motivations. I'm sure you don't want your negotiations about Brian to be influenced by financial or property considerations. You can establish how much it costs to care for Brian and create good custody or visitation principles for the noncustodial parent prior to deciding who the noncustodial parent will be. Essentially, it permits you to cut the cake knowing full well you may end up with either piece. We'll talk about all the choices you have in terms of custody arrangements.

Throughout this process I will be directing your negotiations. I will be contributing very little content, however. You are the experts on your situation. Should you ultimately reach an agreement that I consider fundamentally unfair, I do reserve the right to enter my nonconcurrence on the agreement. This will not affect the legality of the agreement. However, a judge might be a bit more cautious. What normally happens is that parties negotiate a bit more and come to a fairer resolution.

The mediator does her best to let Matt and Cathy know what kind of commitment mediation would entail. Matt and Cathy are reassured by the mediator's straightforward presentation of the duties as well as the benefits of mediation, and they decide they want to mediate their divorce after going through all the rules and discussing the consequences.

Cathy and Matt bring in their completed budget, financial statement, and income forms to the next meeting. At the mediator's suggestion, they have helped each other fill out some of the forms, and the mediator praises them heartily for their cooperative attitude. The temporary settlement is no problem. Cathy has moved out of the house with Brian, and they basically agree to continue doing what they have been doing for Brian.

By the second half of the second session, Cathy and Matt are already working on dividing their marital property. They have little need for the guildelines for division of property, already having a fairly strong sense of what is equitable in their own minds.

During the third session it becomes apparent that the house might be a problem. Cathy fears that Matt will expect to have custody of Brian if he keeps the house. However, they have already discussed selling the house, since keeping it is a bit beyond their means. The mediator has looked at Matt and Cathy's budgets and has determined that the income they receive just barely meets their needs. Thus, she has suggested they think of ways they might contribute to solving this problem. At this session Cathy announces that she has taken a part-time job; and Matt says that he has found a way to trim his budget a bit. Both are quite pleased.

Spousal support and child support are the next issues they negotiate. Cathy wants some help to get on her feet, but after that, all she expects is a fair amount of child support if she gets Brian. Cathy knows she is young, healthy, and educated, and she does not want Matt's support once she has a good job. On the other hand, she has not pursued a career for eight years, first because of the move to Philadelphia and not finding anything appropriate, and then because of Brian. Both she and Matt had decided that she would be a full-time mother. Brian accepts responsibility for his part in that decision and agrees to supplement Cathy's income for two years or until she finds a job that pays her over $20,000 a year.

Matt is relieved to resolve the spousal support issue because he has heard stories from his friends about paying half of their monthly paycheck to divorced spouses and children. He could handle two or three years on a tight budget but would not enjoy many years of budgeting. Now he is concerned about how much support he'll have to pay Cathy for Brian if Cathy is his primary custodian.

MEDIATOR: I hear what you're saying about giving all that money over to Cathy. If we look at what Cathy's expenses are and what her income is, then we see that Cathy by her own income can take care of most of her own expenses, and all she is shy is $150. I don't know if this helps you or not, it doesn't change the way the money flows, but it is a different way of looking at things.

MATT: How can I be sure that that money is going to go to Brian?

MEDIATOR: Why don't you ask her?

CATHY: What else could I do with the money? Do you think I'm going to neglect Brian?

MATT: No.

CATHY: If I know that that is my budget and that is what I have got to have for Brian and me, then that is what I have got to have for Brian and me, and so I will use that money for Brian and me and it will come out the way we arranged.

MEDIATOR: Are you asking if she is going to do something else with it and come back to you and ask for more? We are going to agree to an appropriate figure here.

CATHY: I don't have that much money. If I were to blow the $650, I would have to get it from some place else, and I don't have a someplace else.

MATT: Like she said, you could come back and ask me to pay for it.

CATHY: You don't have that much money. That's all you've got, right?

MATT: Yup.

CATHY: Then how can I get more from you?

MATT: That could suddenly be my responsibility.

CATHY: I've never been really creepy about that sort of thing.

MEDIATOR: Has there been any history of irrational spending? She's been pretty responsible from what you've said in the past.

MATT: Well, her new-found freedom . . .

(Cathy is laughing a bit, and Matt isn't taking himself quite as seriously anymore.)

MEDIATOR: I bet that neither one of you feels very free right now. You're both feeling kinda constricted, aren't you? What do you need to hear from Cathy about the responsibility with which she will handle any money that is transferred back and forth?

The mediator gives Cathy and Matt the necessary time to hear each other's fears and establish an understanding. Together they go over Cathy's budget and do some planning in advance. How can she meet any unexpected expenses? Cathy says she will ask her mother for help if she has to. When Matt hears that, he suggests she ask him first this next year, and if he can help, he will. Ultimately, Matt and Cathy agree on a figure that seems fair to both of them. Cathy agrees to contribute 10 percent of her income to child support if Matt has Brian, and once she has a good job, they can renegotiate that figure. They expect that Cathy's income will increase quite rapidly in the next couple of years whether she actually moves to Washington or not.

Cathy and Matt come to the next session prepared to work on the custody issue. They have both been doing a lot of thinking about it. Both of them still want to be the primary custodian for Brian and are willing to give the other parent very generous visitation rights. Cathy announces that she is not so sure about going to Washington, D.C., now that she has a job of sorts; she is willing to wait awhile on that. The mediator talks about possible custody arrangements. Sole custody is an option that both Matt and Cathy are very aware of. Joint custody has always seemed impractical to them, but now that Cathy plans to stay in Philadelphia for a while, it looks like their best alternative. They agree to a joint custody arrangement for as long as Cathy remains in the area; and they readjust their support arrangements so that Cathy will receive some child support—but not as much as she would receive if she had sole custody. They also agree that Matt will get to claim Brian as a tax deduction as long as he has the higher income. Matt and Cathy work out a very satisfactory joint custody arrangement that will be good for the following year. At the end of that year they will renegotiate, possibly using a mediator, and Cathy might at that time choose to move to Washington, D.C.

The advisory attorney attends the next meeting. Matt and Cathy explain their agreement. The attorney tells them about several ways in which they can save some tax dollars, helps them make one minor alteration in how they are going to sell the house and split the proceeds, and agrees to bring them a marital settlement agreement to sign at the next session.

Matt and Cathy's mediation went extremely smoothly, and the issues were classic. Cathy didn't quite know where she was headed yet professionally, Matt was worried about money, and they were both concerned about parenting Brian. The mediator was quite goal oriented, taking them through the issues in an orderly fashion; yet she made sure they were able to listen to each other and feel heard themselves. The mediator purposefully avoided getting into the custody issue early on in the mediation, because there was too great a chance that Matt and Cathy would get bogged down in their fears about losing Brian. The financial forms they did early on gave them something tangible to work with when they were addressing support issues, and provided the immediate reward of having successfully accomplished the task they set out to do. Also, once Cathy and Matt had worked together on more difficult issues, they had some confidence in their ability to resolve differences. Note that they had already realized that generous visitation would be best if they got custody. Cathy had found some work and no longer felt the same urgency to leave the area. The stage was set for them to negotiate a custody arrangement that was good for Matt, Cathy, and Brian.

A noticeable aspect of this example of structured mediation is its overall similarity to other styles of mediation. Cathy and Matt's mediator had a counseling background. Once she had finished going over the rules with Cathy and Matt, the content of the discussion contained little to indicate that this was structured mediation. Though the rules, the financial forms, the creation of two budgets, the decision to address the custody issue last when the results are unknown, and the use of advisory attorneys are distinctive features of structured mediation, this is not obvious when reading five minutes of transcript. It is far more likely that one would only be able to distinguish a counselor from an attorney when reading a portion of a given mediation.

A couple wishing to mediate their divorce using the structured mediation rules should consider the mediator's background. Are the couple more concerned about their ability to resolve the emotional questions raised by the divorce, or are they worried about the resolution of property issues? If emotional dynamics are a primary concern, it might be helpful to select a mediator with a counseling background. However, if the couple want therapeutic mediation, they should not use structured mediation, which is admittedly a goal-oriented mediation style. Even the mental health professional/structured mediator will refer couples elsewhere for counseling, should he or she recognize the need. Structured mediators tend to limit their role to that of mediator. Likewise, if the couple have numerous property issues to resolve, an attorney mediator may facilitate the mediation more effectively. However, if the couple expect adversarial legal advice from the mediator, they will probably be disappointed. Mediators who practice structured mediation are careful to protect their neutrality and give couples a minimum of advice. It is the advisory attorney's role to give legal advice—the mediator is merely a facilitator. Some couples may prefer co-mediators who practice structured mediation, because of the advantages discussed in the previous chapter. Structured mediation is good for couples who will commit to mediate, who are ready to get to work immediately to get the divorce settled, and who want the security and predictability of detailed rules. With this in mind, they still have the opportunity to select a mediator with particular expertise in law or counseling, a cross-trained mediator, or a mediation team.

The following Marital Mediation Rules are presently used by the Family Mediation Association. While they are essentially the same rules as those that appear in O. J. Coogler's books, they have been somewhat simplified and reordered for greater logical consistency.

MARITAL MEDIATION RULES

SECTION 1: AGREEMENT OF PARTIES TO MEDIATE. The parties shall be deemed to have made these rules a part of their mediation agreement whenever their agreement so provides. These rules and any amendment thereof shall apply in the form obtaining at the time the mediation is initiated. Family Mediation Association is hereinafter referred to as "FMA."

SECTION 2: SCOPE OF MEDIATION. Any mediation process constituted by the parties under these rules, unless otherwise stipulated, shall be related to fostering settlement and resolving controversies between them concerning one or more of the following matters, to wit: division of property, custody of minor children including visitation, spousal maintenance, cost of mediation and arbitration, and attorney's fees.

SECTION 3: MEDIATION SITUATIONS. Mediation under these rules shall be applicable in the following situations:

a. When the parties are husband and wife, have reached a decision to live separately, and either one or both parties have decided on, or are considering the dissolution of their marriage. The decision to dissolve or not dissolve the marriage shall not be an issue for mediation.
b. When the parties are divorced and a controversy exists between them regarding modification of a previous decree of the court and it is contended that there has been a change of circumstances justifying such modification.

SECTION 4: NUMBER OF MEDIATORS. Mediation shall be conducted by a single mediator, unless either party shall request that there be two mediators before the first mediation session. In the event two mediators are requested, one shall be male and the other shall be female.

SECTION 5: QUALIFICATIONS OF MEDIATIORS. Mediators shall be neutral in their relationship to the parties and shall disclose to the parties any circumstances likely to affect their impartiality, including any bias or circumstances likely to create a presumption of bias, or any financial or personal interest in the result of the mediation or any past or present relationships with either of the parties or persons closely related to them.

SECTION 6: COMPENSATIONS OF MEDIATORS. Each mediator shall be compensated at an hourly rate established prior to the commencement of mediation.

SECTION 7: MEDIATION FEE DEPOSIT. Upon signing of the agreement for mediation under these rules (Section 1 or 34), the mediator may require that the parties deposit an amount of money sufficient to cover the following items:

a. Ten hours for mediator's fees.
b. An additional estimated amount to cover administrative costs.

During the mediation process, as the deposit becomes depleted, the mediator may require that the parties make additional deposits so as to maintain adequate funds needed to continue the mediation process without interruption.

SECTION 8: REFUND OF DEPOSIT. The unused portion of deposits provided for in the preceding section shall be refundable to the parties as follows:

a. When settlement has been reached and executed in writing by the parties.
b. If, during mediation, a party becomes permanently disabled or deceased or the parties become reconciled and resume their marital relationship.
c. When impasse has been reached, as provided in Section 32, and the parties are proceeding with arbitration.
d. In the event the parties shall fail or refuse to proceed with mediation and/or arbitration after ten (10) days' written notice has been mailed to them, all deposits remaining are forfeited by the parties.

SECTION 9: ATTENDANCE AT MEDIATION SESSIONS. The parties shall arrange their business and personal affairs so as to provide for attending mediation sessions once each week.

SECTION 10: CANCELLATION OF APPOINTMENTS. Notice of cancellation of mediation appointments must be given by the parties to the mediator not less than 24 hours in advance of the appointment. Otherwise full charge may be made for the appointment not kept.

SECTION 11: CONFIDENTIALITY OF MEDIATION. By undertaking mediation under these rules, the mediator and the parties mutually agree with one another as follows:

a. Mediation is a procedure for reaching settlement of dispute either in litigation or likely to be in litigation between the parties.
b. All communications between the parties and with the mediators related to the dispute shall come within the purview of the rules of evidence which exclude from introduction in evidence by either party against the other disclosure made with a view to settlement.
c. The parties shall be estopped through their adoption of these rules from calling either the mediator or any officer or agent of the mediator as the witness in litigation of any description in which they are called upon to testify as to any matter regarding the mediation proceeding; and the parties shall be estopped from requiring the production in court of any records or documents or tape recordings made by the mediator(s).
d. The foregoing exclusions from evidence and exemptions of the mediators and parties from giving testimony or being called upon to produce documents shall apply in the same manner to arbitration of an impasse.
e. Mediations conducted by a licensed professional shall come within the purview of his professional privilege.

SECTION 12: TAPE RECORDING OF MEDIATION SESSIONS. The mediator may require that mediation sessions be recorded subject to the following conditions:

a. In the absence of written consent of the parties, audio tape recordings will be heard only by the parties, the mediator, and the mediator's supervisor if he is subject to supervision.
b. Mediators shall disclose to the parties at the beginning of mediation whether or not the mediation sesssions will be subject to audio tape supervision.
c. Except as above stated, audio tape recordings are strictly confidential and shall not be used for research, training, or any other purpose without prior written consent of the parties, and then in such a manner as does not disclose the identities of the parties.
d. Video tape recordings shall be made only with the prior written consent of the parties.

SECTION 13: PREPARATION OF BUDGETS. The preparation of budgets by each party, when either spousal maintenance or child support or both are claimed, is an essential part of the mediation process. If either party shall fail or refuse to prepare a budget adequately reflecting his needs, the mediator shall have the duty to suspend mediation of these issues or, at his discretion, delcare an impasse.

SECTION 14: FULL DISCLOSURE. Each party shall fully disclose, in the presence of the other party, all information and writings, such as financial statements, income tax returns, etc., requested by the mediator and all information requested by the opposite party if the mediator finds that the disclosure is appropriate to the mediation process and may aid the parties in reaching settlement.

SECTION 15: TEMPORARY CUSTODY AND SUPPORT AGREEMENT. At the first mediation session the parties will reach agreement, if possible, with regard to temporary custody and temporary support for the minor children, temporary support for the spouse seeking maintenance, attorney's fees, and the cost of mediation and arbitration. In the event the parties shall not reach agreement in whole or in part, the mediators shall declare that the parties are in impasse. Upon determination by the mediator(s) that the parties are in impasse, a single arbitrator will be appointed who will fix a time and place for a hearing not later than seven days after impasse is declared and after hearing from each party who appears, shall render an award fixing temporary spousal maintenance, temporary custody and support of minor children, the cost of mediation, arbitration, and attorney's fees. The agreement reached between the parties, or the award of the arbitrator, and the provisions of Section 16 of these rules may be made an order of the court having jurisdiction upon the petition of either party without further advance notice or service upon the opposite party.

SECTION 16: TRANSFERS OF PROPERTY. During the mediation and arbitration process under these rules, neither party shall transfer, encumber, conceal, or in any other way dispose of any tangible or intangible property except in the usual course of business or for the necessities of life. Proposed transactions by either party in the regular course of business or for any other purpose affecting ten (10) percent or more of the total assets of a party shall be reported to the other party not less than ten days in advance of the transaction contemplated. Transactions made in violation of this rule shall be subject to being declared void and set aside upon the application of the injured party, either in arbitration under these rules or in a court of competent jurisdiction.

SECTION 17: TEMPORARY COURT ORDER. During mediation or arbitration, either party may request a court of competent jurisdiction to issue a temporary injunction without requiring advance notice to the opposite party.

a. Restraining any party from transferring, encumbering, concealing, or in any way disposing of any property except in the usual course of business or for the necessities of life and, if so restrained, requiring him to notify the moving party of any proposed extra-ordinary expenditures and to account to the court for all extra-ordinary expenditures made after the order is issued.
b. Enjoining a party from molesting or disturbing the peace of the other party or of any child.
c. Excluding a party from the family home or from the home of the other party when there is evidence that physical or emotional harm would otherwise result.

SECTION 18: AGREEMENT UPON ISSUES DURING MEDIATION. As agreement is reached upon each issue during mediation, the mediator shall determine that the parties understand the agreement reached. Thereafter, the same issue shall not be reopened for mediation, after a new issue is taken up, without authorization by the mediator. The mediator shall grant authorization to reopen mediation of an issue to the extent needed to correct mistakes or to consider new information which was not reasonably available to one or both parties previously.

SECTION 19: GUIDELINES FOR DIVISION OF PROPERTY. The parties shall reach agreement providing for the division of marital property with the assistance of the mediators, without regard to marital misconduct, in such proportions as is just, after considering all relevant factors, including:

a. The contribution of each spouse to the acquisition of the marital property, including the contribution of a spouse as homemaker.
b. The value of the property to be received or retained by each spouse.
c. The economic circumstances of each spouse at the time the division of property is to become effective, including the desirability of awarding the family home or the right to live therein for reasonable periods to the spouse having custody of any children.
d. Any increases or decreases in the value of the separate property of each spouse during the marriage or the depletion of the separate property for marital purposes.
e. For purposes of this section:
   ACTIVE OWNERSHIP of property is inferred from the owner's making capital improvements, usage, management, and other efforts intended to enhance the value of the property.
   PASSIVE OWNERSHIP is inferred from the absence of factors which would result in an inference of active ownership.

MARITAL PROPERTY means all property acquired by either spouse subsequent to the marriage except:
(1) property acquired by gift, bequest, devise, or descent
(2) property acquired in exchange for property acquired by gift, bequest, devise, or descent
(3) property acquired by a spouse after a decree of legal separation
(4) property excluded by valid agreement of the parties
(5) the increase in value resulting from passive ownership of property acquired prior to the marriage, or after the marriage by gift, bequest, devise, or descent
(6) when increases in value of property acquired prior to the marriage, after the marriage or by gift, bequest, devise, or descent have resulted from both active and passive ownership, a reasonable allocation shall be made so as to exclude increases attributable to passive ownership

f. All property acquired by either spouse after the marriage prior to a decree of legal separation or divorce and all increases in value attributable to active ownership of property whenever or however acquired, are presumed to be marital property regardless of whether title is held individually or by the spouses in some form of coownership, such as joint tenancy, tenancy in common, tenancy by the entirety, and community property. The presumption of marital property shall be overcome by showing that the property or increase in value of property is excluded under the provisions of the preceding subsection.
g. Property shall be valued for purposes of this section as of the date of the first mediation session.

SECTION 20: SPOUSAL MAINTENANCE GUIDELINES. Payment of maintenance by one spouse to the other shall be predicated upon the following considerations as they apply to the spouse seeking maintenance.

a. The spouse lacks sufficient property, including marital property apportioned to him, to provide for his reasonable needs.
b. The spouse is fully or partially unable to support himslf through appropriate employment or is the custodian of a child whose condition or circumstances make it appropriate that the custodian not be required to seek employment outside the home.
c. Maintenance shall be in such amounts and for such periods of time as is just, without regard to marital misconduct and after considering all relevant factors, including the following:
(1) the financial resources of the party seeking maintenance, including marital property apportioned to him, and his ability to meet his needs independently, including the extent to which a provision for support of a child living with the party includes a sum for that party as custodian;
(2) the time necessary to acquire sufficient education or training to enable the party seeking maintenance to find appropriate employment;
(3) the standard of living established during the marriage, reduced by the impact that maintaining two households rather than one may have upon the standard of living of the parties;
(4) the duration of the marriage;
(5) the age and physical and emotional condition of each spouse;
(6) the ability of the spouse from whom maintenance is sought to meet his needs while meeting those of the spouse seeking maintenance.

SECTION 21: CHILD SUPPORT GUIDELINES. Either parent or both parents, according to their ability to do so, shall accept the duty of support for a child of the marriage and contribute an amount reasonably necessary after considering all relevant factors, including:

a. The financial resources of the child;
b. The earning ability and financial resources of each parent;
c. The standard of living the child would have enjoyed had the marriage not been dissolved, reduced by the impact that maintaining two households rather than one may have upon the standard of living of the parties;

d. The physical and emotional condition of the child and his educational needs.

SECTION 22: CHILD CUSTODY GUIDELINES. In reaching agreement regarding custodial arrangements reflecting the best interests of the child, the parties shall consider all relevant factors, including:

a. The wishes of each parent as to the custody of the child;
b. The wishes of the child as to custodial arrangements;
c. The interaction and interrelationship with his parent or parents, his siblings, and any other person who may significantly affect the child's best interests;
d. The child's adjustment to his home, school, and community;
e. The mental and physical health of all individuals involved.

The conduct of a parent that does not demonstrably affect his relationship with the child, or in some other way can be shown to be contrary to the best interests of the child shall not be considered.

SECTION 23: RIGHTS OF THE CUSTODIAL PARENT. The custodial parent may determine the child's upbringing, including his education, health care, and religious training, except as otherwise agreed by the parties. The custodial parent shall have the right to require that the noncustodial parent follow agreed visitation with the children on a consistent and dependable basis.

SECTION 24: RIGHTS OF THE NONCUSTODIAL PARENT. The noncustodial parent of the child shall be entitled to reasonable visitation rights such as do not adversely affect the child's education or physical health or significantly impair his emotional development. The noncustodial parent shall carry out visitation arrangements as a privilege and obligation of parenthood and to share parenting responsibility with the custodial parent.

SECTION 25: RIGHTS OF JOINT CUSTODIAL PARENTS. Joint custodial parents agree to establish a cooperative relationship with each other regarding the exercise of their continuing responsibilities as parents of their children. They accept that each has an equal right to determine the child's upbringing, including his education, health care, and religious training. The child's living arrangements between the two parents shall be such as are in the best interests of the child, using as guidelines the provisions of Section 22 of these rules. Even though joint custody reflects a cooperative attitude on the part of both parents, specific living arrangements shall be included in the settlement agreement. Such arrangements shall be followed except as are otherwise agreed upon by the parents from time to time. The living arrangements contained in the settlement agreement shall not be changed by such subsequent agreements. Either parent on notice to the other may re-establish the arrangements contained in the settlement agreement.

SECTION 26: CONTROVERSY OVER CUSTODY. At the first mediation session, the mediators shall determine whether the parties are in agreement regarding custody of the minor child or children. In the event custody of the children is in controversy, the mediator shall advise the parties that mediation of the custody issue shall be the last item on the agenda after agreement has been reached upon all the following:

a. Division of marital property.
b. Spousal maintenance.
c. Child support.
d. Attorney's fees for the petitioning spouse when the parties contemplate dissolution of their marriage.

The mediator shall further instruct each party to prepare two budgets--one based upon the assumption that he is the custodial parent and a second based upon the assumption that he is the noncustodial parent.

SECTION 27: PARTICIPATION OF CHILDREN AND OTHERS. Children for whom custodial arrangements are being made and other persons having a direct interest in the mediation may participate in mediation sessions related to their interests if the mediator finds that their participation may facilitate settlement.

SECTION 28: THIRD-PARTY INVOLVEMENT. During the mediation process, the parties shall refrain from discussing the matters in mediation with all third parties including friends, relatives, and attorneys, and with each other except as directed by the mediators.

SECTION 29: APPOINTMENT OF ADVISORY ATTORNEY. The parties may select from a panel of attorneys an advisory attorney at law with whom arrangements can be made to provide impartial legal advice needed for reaching settlement. The parties may also select any other attorney mutually acceptable to them, provided he acknowledges in writing appointment as an impartial advisory attorney under these rules and agrees to abide by them in serving the parties. The advisory attorney shall be compensated at an hourly rate acceptable to the parties in advance of appointment. Arrangements for payment to the attorney are the responsibility of the parties and the attorney.

SECTION 30: OBLIGATIONS OF ADVISORY ATTORNEY. The advisory attorney, by accepting appointment, undertakes the following obligations:

a. He will advise the center and the parties of any circumstance which might create a presumption of bias on his part in favor of or against either party.
b. He will under no circumstances accept professional or other employment, or the promise thereof, from either party so long as their marital dispute is unresolved and during a period of one year thereafter. By mutual agreement of the parties, he may represent one of them for the sole purpose of obtaining a decree of separation or divorce which incorporates the settlement agreement reached by the parties under these rules.
c. He will, as fully as possible within the time available, explain to each party in the presence of the other party and the mediators his and her rights and obligations under the law.
d. He will give particular attention to the tax consequences resulting from the various options available to the parties in reaching settlement.
e. He will maintain strict impartiality in his advice to the parties and will refrain from attempting to influence either party toward making a particular decision or settlement.
f. After preparation of a settlement agreement, he will fully and impartially explain its terms to each party in the presence of the other and the mediators, and will answer questions to the best of his professional abilities.
g. He will communicate with the parties only in mediation sessions or through the center or the mediators and in no other manner directly or indirectly. Further, he will immediately report to the mediators any attempt on the part of a party to communicate with him and advise the party of his obligation.
h. He shall make known to the parties and mediators in advance the maximum number of hours of professional time he expects to render outside of mediation sessions for preparation of the settlement contract or legal research.
i. An advisory attorney may spend only the number of professional hours authorized by the parties.
j. He shall have an attorney-client relationship with the parties and will regard all communications and information obtained during mediation as privileged.
k. The motivations of the parties in reaching a decision to separate or to dissolve their marriage are matters to be dealt with by marriage counselors or other properly qualified therapists and od not come within the purview of the mediation and arbitration processes.

SECTION 31: COMMUNICATIONS WITH MEDIATORS AND ADVISORY ATTORNEY. The parties shall not communicate with the mediators or advisory attorney concerning matters in mediation except in the presence of each other during a mediation session. In the event either party shall violate or attempt to violate this rule, the mediator or attorney shall have the duty to ask such party to refrain from such communication. Communications regarding the scheduling of appointments are permitted under this section.

SECTION 32: DETERMINATION OF IMPASSE. Impasse is defined as a situation resulting when the parties and the mediators have examined as fully as appears useful all information and options reasonably available for reaching settlement of an issue and the parties fail to reach an agreement. The failure or refusal of one or both parties to abide by these rules also constitute an impasse when so determined by the mediator. The mediators or a party may declare that an impasse has been reached as follows:

a. By the mediator at any time.
b. By a party with the concurrence of the mediator in advance of completion of ten hours of mediation time.
c. By a party with or without the concurrence of the mediator after completion of ten hours of mediation time.

SECTION 33: ARBITRATION. The parties shall submit to arbitration all controversies which are the subject of mediation under these rules when impasse is reached under Section 32 of these rules. Arbitration shall be conducted under the Marital Arbitration Rules of the FMA and in accordance with applicable statutory arbitration laws of the state in which the arbitration is conducted. The parties accept the jurisdiction of the court competent to handle divorce cases, in the place where the arbitration is conducted for all purposes related to the conduct of the arbitration, such as compelling the attendance of witnesses and production of documents. The parties shall faithfully observe this provision for arbitration and the arbitration rules, so that the award rendered by the arbitrators shall become a part of the settlement agreement reached between the parties, and/or that such award may be entered in and made the judgment of any court having jurisdiction thereof.

SECTION 34: MEDIATION OF FUTURE DISPUTE. A provision for mediation under these rules in either an antenuptial contract or settlement agreement may be initiated in the following manner.

> The initiating party may give notice to the opposite party and to the mediator of his intention to mediate, which notice shall contain a statement setting forth the nature of the dispute including the amount involved, if any, and the remedy sought.

SECTION 35: EXECUTION OF SETTLEMENT AGREEMENT. The advisory attorney shall personally supervise the execution of the settlement agreement reached by the parties during mediation. Such agreement shall be prepared and submitted to the parties when one of the following situations arises:

a. The parties have reached settlement of all issues.
b. The parties have reached setlement of all issues except custody (including visitation) which will require further mediation.
c. The parties have reached settlement of some issues and are in impasse over others, in which case the agreement shall reflect the issues agreed upon and shall clearly specify the position of each party regarding issues in impasse.
d. The parties are in impasse over all issues, in which case the agreement shall clearly specify the position of each party in each issue.
e. The failure or refusal of either party to enter into the agreement provided for in Subsections c and d shall not limit the other's right to proceed with arbitration.
f. A supplemental or revised agreement shall be executed reflecting custodial arrangements agreed upon after further mediation, as provided for in Subsection b above.

SECTION 36: EVALUATION OF SETTLEMENT AGREEMENT. In advance of their execution of the settlement agreement, either party may request that a special evaluation session be scheduled. At such evaluation session, the mediator and the advisory attorney shall offer the parties their opinions as to the overall workability of the proposed agreement, pointing out the advantages and disadvantages to each party. To the best of their ability and on the basis of their previous experience, the mediator and attorney shall indicate whether the agreement is substantially consistent with agreements reached by couples similarly situated.

SECTION 37: CONCURRENCE OF MEDIATORS. The mediators may indicate to the parties their concurrence or nonconcurrence with the settlement agreement reached. A written notation of the mediators' concurrence or nonconcurrence shall be made below the signatures of the parties on the settlement agreement and shall be signed by the mediators. Concurrence indicates the mediator's judgment that the settlement appears to be substantially equitable and fair to each party. Nonconcurrence shall in no way detract from the legal effectiveness of the settlement contract reached between the parties.

SECTION 38: MASCULINE AND FEMININE GENDER. Whenever in these rules the masculine gender is used, it shall be understood to include the feminine unless the context clearly indicates otherwise.

SECTION 39: INTERPRETATION AND APPLICATION OF RULES. The mediator shall interpret and apply these rules. In the event of a controversy between the mediator and the parties regarding interpretation or application of these rules, such questions shall be subject to review by FMA.

SECTION 40: AMENDMENT OF RULES. FMA reserves the right to amend these rules at any time, provided, however, such amendment shall not apply to the rules included in mediation agreements relating to existing controversies. The rules as amended and in force at the time notice of intention to mediate is given under Section 34 shall apply in mediations under agreements to mediate future disputes.

NINE
BROCHURES AND FORMS

This chapter is a collection of materials given to clients interested in mediation. There are brochures designed to explain mediators' processes or help parents understand the needs of their children, and forms to help clients come to terms with the emotional and financial realities of their divorce and define their needs. For some mediators, informational brochures and forms are an integral part of their style of mediation; other mediators rely almost exclusively on themselves to personally convey information and clarify the clients' needs.

Family Law Counseling Services offers clients a style of co-mediation that utilizes numerous informational brochures and forms designed to walk clients through their divorce in a knowledgeable fashion. A couple inquiring about their services is mailed The Family Law Counseling Brochure, Questions People Ask Us, and About Fees. If the couple have children, they may also be mailed Guidelines for a Successful Partnership for Parenting, Bibliography on Divorce, Custody, and Parenting, and Bibliography for Blended and Step-Families. If the parents mention that they are having trouble working with one another, they will also receive Guidelines for Parents When the Other Parent Is Angry, Hostile and Uncooperative. When the holiday season is near, or if parents mention some difficulties with holiday scheduling, they are sent Guidelines for Successful Holidays in Your After-Divorce Family Network. When it appears that the couple are going to want to mediate their divorce, a letter of confirmation is sent along with the Statement of Understanding. Once the mediation is underway, mediators at Family Law Counseling Services have a number of additional brochures to help couples with specific situations, such as spousal support, budgeting, or selling the house.[1]

WHAT IS FAMILY LAW COUNSELING?

Family Law Counseling is designed to help families through hard times. We assist with problems of relationship and divorce, arrangements or rearrangements for children, and plans for marriage or anticipating a birth. We usually work in a man-woman team, one of whom is a counselor and the other an attorney. We use the skills of mediation and conflict management, combining legal and psychological expertise. We provide a couple or a family with an effective way to clarify and resolve situations without the painful and costly court proceedings that have traditionally resulted from domestic conflicts.

You can avoid unnecessary pain and conflict by anticipating the emotional and legal problems, and dealing with them together. The satisfying and creative solutions in which you participate will stand the test of time better than a frustrating adversarial outcome. Families can learn how to manage their own affairs cooperatively, even where angry or hurt feelings persist. In this way, self-reliance is bolstered by success, and continuing assistance from professionals and involvement in court proceedings is no longer needed.

MARITAL TROUBLES?

A FLC team can help you get through to each other to hear in a new way what is really being said. Once the situation is clarified, then we can help you to communicate effectively and decide what to do about your relationship. If "I want a divorce" actually means "I want change", together we can begin to work toward positive changes in your relationship. Or perhaps you want to set up ground rules and have a contract drawn up for your legal protection while you assess your situation. This gives you a chance to reflect on a decision rather than acting in haste. During this time, adjustment to change frequently becomes easier.

NEED A DIVORCE?

A FLC team will work with you to make agreements about division of property and support (whether, how much, and for how long). We will help you as co-parents to make plans about the expenses, residence, and the time of the children. Through our Divorce Assistance Service, the divorce may be processed by mail so that court appearances are not required.

DIVORCED AND STILL FIGHTING?

A FLC team will work with you to get through a dispute about a court order, a budget battle, or disagreements about the residence and time shared with the children. We can process a new agreement through the court resulting in a new court order.

GOING TO BE MARRIED? LIVE TOGETHER?

A FLC team will help you to be clear, in writing, about your expectations and intentions. This provides a solid foundation to the relationship about such issues as obligations, each for the other; previous or expected children; separate property; protection in the event of death; creditors; etc.

ABOUT TO BE PARENTS?

A FLC team can help you make decisions about support, residence, time shared, and other matters about your child or children. We can draft a parenting agreement to reflect your decisions, as well as formulate it into a court order if wanted.

LIVING TOGETHER BUT COMING APART?

A FLC team can help resolve issues between you. We are familiar with the ways in which you situation differs from and is similar to marriage and divorce. We know that these distinctions are important for getting service that meets your needs.

WHAT DOES IT COST?

Fees for each session are collected at the close of that session. There is a standard fee for the Divorce Assistance Service to process papers through court. Drafting of agreements is done outside the session, and fees are charged at an hourly rate. The fee for each member of the team is the same, and is based upon the prevailing local group legal rate for attorneys and the local hourly rate for counselors. The current fee and fee policies are explained in detail on a separate flyer, "About Fees."

FLC, Inc. is a nonprofit, tax exempt corporation for education. We are solely supported by fees generated from services, which are used for office expenses, staff and public education, printing expenses, and, to compensate the professionals rendering services. The team members are efficient, experienced, and have well developed forms to help you save money. Every effort is made to keep expenses down. In case of significant hardship, a FLC team member may be willing to serve at a lower fee. Families wanting such accomodation will be asked to document this need.

Non-Profit Org.
U.S. Postage
PAID
Permit #597
Berkeley, CA

FAMILY LAW COUNSELING, INC.
1600 Shattuck Avenue, Suite 200
Berkeley, California 94709
(415) 548-5551

FAMILY LAW COUNSELING, INC.

A Counseling Approach to Family Law Problems since 1979

North Berkeley Centre
1600 Shattuck Ave. Suite 200
Berkeley, CA 94709

(415) 548-5551

PRINCIPAL STAFF OF FLC, INC. . . .

JAMES B. GARRISON, M.A., is president of Family Law Counseling, Inc. Formerly director of the San Francisco Child Abuse Council, Inc., he received training in clinical psychology at U.C. Berkeley, and is completing a Ph.D. at Saybrook Institute. He has experience with mediation in both public and private contexts. He has also practiced psychotherapy in diverse settings, trained counselors and group leaders, and taught psychology. Jim has been divorced, married again, been a co-parent in a blended family, and is the father of a charming little girl in a nuclear family.

KAREN LAWSON, Ph.D., is a licensed clinical psychologist. She works with individuals and couples in private practice, and with children at Eden Children's Center. She received her formal clinical training at U.C. Berkeley and has studied with several noted practitioners. In her work with children and troubled teenagers for the past ten years, she has seen many whose problems were related to divorces in which their needs were not considered. Her parenting experience includes being a single mother, communal child rearing, co-parenting after divorce, and, currently, being a mother in a nuclear family.

HARRIET WHITMAN LEE, J.D., is a lawyer and is professor of law and psychology at John F. Kennedy University. Formerly the directing attorney at Consumers Group Legal Services, she began her training as a family therapist at Calfiornia Graduate School and is now completing a Ph.D. in psychology at Saybrook Institute. She is divorced and has a cooperative family network with her former husband, their two daughters, and his new family.

FLC, Inc. also maintains consultant relationships with experienced professionals to guarantee appropriate teams or team members.

Please send me information about your services. I am interested in:

- ☐ Clarifying Relationships
- ☐ Separation
- ☐ Divorce
- ☐ Post-divorce
- ☐ Arrangements or Re-arrangements for children
- ☐ Support Issues
- ☐ Premarital
- ☐ Living together
- ☐ Special Relationships
- ☐ About to be Parents
- ☐ Personal or Family Counseling
- ☐ About Fees

Name ____________________

Address ____________________

City ________ State ________ Zip ________

Phone ☐ Day________ Eve________

Family Law Counseling Services

1600 Shattuck Avenue Suite #200
Berkeley, CA 94709
548-5551

QUESTIONS PEOPLE ASK US

HOW LONG HAVE YOU BEEN DOING THIS?

Family Law Counseling Services has been in existence since January 1, 1979. Some Staff members have been with FLCS since its inception; others have joined later. All have experience and training specific to this work.

HOW MANY CASES HAVE YOU HANDLED? WHAT KIND?

As of 1 May 1981,* we had closed 29 Divorce cases and 36 other matters. We had 19 open divorce files and we had some cases "on hold", that is after starting on divorce or structured temporary separation, the couples wanted time to work on their relationship or to think things over.

The closed matters handled by FLCS staff in addition to divorce, included such matters as Family Therapy, After Divorce Disputes about time, parenting, money, etc., Couple Counseling and contracts, separation counseling for people living together and premarital contracts.

HOW MANY SESSIONS DOES IT TAKE FOR DIVORCE OR AFTER DIVORCE PROBLEMS?

The average number of sessions for divorce, in our experience, is between 4 and 6 (actually 5.3). We have helped people do it in 2 sessions; on the other hand, one case in which there was bitter acrimony, a couple used 15 sessions. Occasional difficult cases take more than 6 sessions, rarely more than 9. Actually 70% of them were complete in 5 sessions or less.

For After Divorce disputes, the average is slightly higher (6.5). Again the biggest number ever used was 15 (they had been fighting in court for 7 years). However 60% of the After Divorce disputes were resolved in 4 sessions or less.

HOW MUCH DOES IT COST?

The average cost of divorce with FLCS is $835, for After Divorce Dispute work is $720 and for counseling and contracts of couples, $372.
The most that any clients have ever paid FLCS is $1689. The least that has been paid for a Divorce is $414, the least for After Divorce work is $288.

However, 60% of our Divorce cases cost $500 or less. 50% of our After Divorce cases cost $300 or less.

HOW DO WE PAY?

Our clients pay us each session at the time. They pay for our outside sessions services (like preparation of court papers, drafting of contracts by attorneys, conferring of FLCS Staff, conversational exchanges outside sessions about issues normally to be dealt with in session) at the next session after the service was performed. If there is an issue between you about who is to pay or in what proportions you will share the expense the FLCS team can help you negotiate that.

---

*All data given here is based on figures as of 1 May 1981.

HOW LONG AND HOW OFTEN ARE SESSIONS?

Sessions are normally an hour long but we may go over if we are working well or if we are in the middle of an issue that we need to resolve and time is available. On the other hand we may occasionally have a short session if we have completed possible business in less than an hour and it would be wasteful to extend the session to an hour.

HOW CAN WE REACH YOU BETWEEN SESSIONS?

You can call the FLCS number, 548-5551 and leave a message on the machine. A team member will get back to you as soon as possible. Contact between sessions is normally limited to change of appointment time. Team members will not want to discuss issues outside of sessions and to the extent such discussion happens outside sessions clients will be charged for it. Working on any issues including issues about the service being rendered are best taken up by all participants in the process at one time and in the normal office setting.

HOW CAN WE KEEP THE COST DOWN? WHAT CAN WE DO?

Costs can be kept down by working outside sessions doing "homework", drawing up budgets, coming to agreement as much as possible (saving the problematic issues for sessions) and getting information (for example appraisals, retirement information and the like). In session costs can be kept down by working with FLCS team members to identify and eliminate unproductive communication by setting ground rules for sticking to business. Adherence to one position and unwillingness to explore alternatives will escalate time taken (and therefore cost) and will usually, if there is no change, cause the process to fail altogether.

DO YOU SEE CHILDREN?

We see the children or not depending on your and our perceptions of whether it is needed. Generally in divorce with older children it is very helpful to the whole family to have at least one session together to discuss the changes that are taking place. With after divorce disputes it is important to get older children's input, though occasionally the dispute between the parents is such that the children should not be included because the parents find it hard to separate their issues with each other from their issues about the children. The tendency to mix these causes the children to feel responsible for the bad feelings between their parents.

WHAT CAN WE DO IF THE OTHER PERSON IS UNCOOPERATIVE ABOUT COMING IN?

One of our staff members can call a person to tell them about our service and to give him or her a chance to consider whether the service might be of interest. Persons who are doubtful about FLCS can learn something more about the organization by attending one of our monthly programs (2nd Mondays each month, for information call 548-5551 or 525-3322). If the other person is closed, uncooperative and unwilling to hear about our service you may be interested in meeting with one of our staff members to learn more about what you can do that may make a difference, and you may find helpful our GUIDELINES FOR PARENTS WHEN THE OTHER PARENT IS ANGRY, HOSTILE AND UNCOOPERATIVE and our GUIDELINES FOR PARTNERSHIP IN PARENTING.

Family Law Counseling Services

1600 Shattuck Avenue Suite #200
Berkeley, CA 94709
548-5551

ABOUT FEES

Initial Evaluation: An hour session with a Family Law Counseling team to decide whether our approach is compatible with needs of the clients. Session includes identification of major legal and/or emotional issues, assessment of services needed, costs, and discussion of options.

Divorce and Separation: The team assists the clients to work out the legal, emotional, and economic aspects of the divorce or separation of marital and non-marital partners. Except in special situations, Family Law Counselors work in teams of two during sessions. Each team includes a man and a woman. Outside services may entail legal drafting and consultation with other professionals when needed.

Post-Divorce: All of the services of Family Law Counseling are available to assist parties in resolving custody, visitation, support, and other post-divorce problems.

Contracts for Pre-Marital, Marital and Non-Marital Partners: Counseling and legal drafting for people who wish to formalize their arrangements about property and children.

Individual and Family Counseling: Focus on interpersonal relationships and personal growth. Counselors work individually or in teams of two, depending on client needs.

All of the above @ $60 per hour per Family Law Counselor

Divorce Assistance Service (DAS): Preparation, typing, filing and processing of all necessary divorce papers through all the required steps to complete the legal divorce. This service is available only to clients working with a FLCS team. $180.00 complete.

Court Filing Fees: Each county charges fees for filing the various papers of divorce. These fees are collected separately in advance and paid to the court as the necessary papers are filed.

Phone Calls and Correspondence: We prefer to render services in a way which preserves the concept of working together. Separate phone calls and letters make this awkward if they are about the issues or the provision of services, since these are ordinarily discussed in sessions together. When it becomes necessary to respond to calls or letters outside of our sessions together, a charge is made for the time of the team member(s) at the usual hourly rate.

Typing Services: For written agreements and correspondence arising out of Family Law Counseling. Charged based on our cost.

Copying Costs: 10¢ per page.

We regret that our experience necessitates the following policies:

Lateness: With the exception of emergencies, clients who are late are charged from the time set for the beginning of the appointment. FLCS team members have discretion about working longer than the scheduled time when clients are late.

Cancellation: With the exception of emergencies, clients who cancel with less than 24 hours notice are charged a late cancellation fee of one hour. Whatever the difficulty about getting to an appointment, please call to let us know as soon as possible.

Returned checks: A fee of $25.00 is charged for each returned check to defray processing costs. Work in progress is interrupted until the account is paid in cash, money order or cashiers check.

Family Law Counseling Services

1600 Shattuck Avenue Suite #200
Berkeley, CA 94709
548-5551

GUIDELINES FOR A SUCCESSFUL
PARTNERSHIP FOR PARENTING:

1. What you have as your mutual concern is the raising of your children. Make a conscious decision that you want to create a successful partnership for that project.

2. Be businesslike with your partner; test all of your own behavior against this standard: Was I businesslike? Did I follow these guidelines?

3. Test your partner's behavior not by how you feel; test by the same standard: Was your partner's behavior businesslike? Did it conform to these guidelines?

4. Respect your children's relationship with your partner. Your children did not divorce either parent; don't force them to and do encourage them to get over any feelings of estrangement from the other parent.

5. Make appointments to talk about business. Except for emergencies, call only during business hours or agreed upon times; always ask if the timing is convenient, and if not, make an appointment for a time that is.

6. Be polite; do not use bad language or call names. Do not try to conduct business under the influence of alcohol or other drugs. If you feel yourself getting unbusinesslike, say so and agree to resume the conversation at a later time.

7. Give the benefit of the doubt as to behavior as you would with a stranger. Do not assume anything on past experience without checking out now, at this time, reasons for behavior, what your partner thinks or what your partner has decided.

8. Do not expect approval from your partner; get your personal and emotional needs met elsewhere and with others even if you have to pay. On the other hand, if you are able to acknowledge something positive in word or deed of your partner, do not withhold it. The reward of expressing appreciation, no matter how small, is greater success of the partnership.

9. Do not discuss what is irrelevant to business unless your partner specifically agrees otherwise. Respect your partner's privacy; do not seek to know the details of your partner's life and do not intrude on your partner's territory.

10. Make all agreements explicit and follow up with written confirmation when possible (or make your own written memorandum). Be clear and complete in communications; include time, place, whether children will be fed or not, what clothes they need, etc. Communicate directly; DO NOT ask the children to do your business for you.

11. Keep agreements; do not break appointments; carry through on what you promised. If you can't promise something, make it clear that you can't and say why.

12. Do not make unilateral decisions; consult your partner and the children so that the best, most workable decision can be made.

13. Don't insist on what does not work; on the other hand, commit yourself as much as you are able to being flexible and to experimenting to see what does work.

14. Above all, cultivate good will for the partnership. Keep in mind always the importance of your investment and the expected returns. The investment is what you are willing to do for your children's happiness and success in life. The returns are comfort and security for your children that their

parents care enough to make life work, and smoother and happier times for yourself personally at future events such as birthdays, holidays, graduations, weddings and births of grandchildren. You can make it a good life for yourself personally and for your children.

Family Law Counseling Services

1600 Shattuck Avenue Suite #200
Berkeley, CA 94709
548-5551

BIBLIOGRAPHY ON DIVORCE, CUSTODY, AND PARENTING

The following is a list, neither alphabetical nor in order of importance, of books you may find helpful on issues arising in divorce and custody matters.

The Parents Book About Divorce, by Richard A. Gardner, Doubleday (1977). General advice about problems facing divorcing parents.

Children's Book About Divorce, by Richard A. Gardner, Jason Aronson, Inc. (1970). Directed towards children.

How To Get It Together When Your Parents Are Coming Apart, by Richards and Willis, David McKay (1976). Mainly aimed at teenagers.

Creative Divorce, by Mel Krantzler, M. Evans & Co., Inc. (1973). Popular book describing the "stages" of divorce and how to cope.

Talking About Divorce: A Dialogue Between Parent And Child, Earl A. Grollman, Deakon Press (1975). Written and illustrated for a young child. Provides techniques for communicating between parent and child.

The Custody Handbook, by Persia Woolley, Summit Books (1979). A survey of the area with emphasis on ideas for sharing parenting.

Creative Survival for Single Mothers, by Persia Woolley, Celestial Arts (1975). A discussion of the single mother situation.

Part-Time Father, by Edith Atkin and Estelle Rubin, Van Guard Press (1976). Helpful advice and information for divorced fathers.

Co-Parenting: Sharing Your Child Equally, by Miriam Galper, Philadelphia, Running Press (1978). Survey of specific examples of people who are co-parenting in different ways.

The Disposable Parent: The Case For Joint Custody, Roman and Haddad, Holt, Rinehart & Winston (1978). A thorough critique of the arguments against shared custody and an advocate of co-parenting.

Mom's House, Dad's House, by Isolina Ricci, Macmillan, N.Y. (1979).

The Half Parent, by Brenda Maddox, M. Evans & Co., Inc. (1975). Discusses the step-family experience and its problems.

Step-Parenting, Jean and Beryl Rosenbaum, E.P. Dutton (1977). Treats the step-parent family problems concerning children. Chapters 4, 5, and 6 contain a good simple discussion of child development in relation to divorce and step-parenting issues.

Your Child? I Thought It Was My Child!, by Owen and Nancie Spann, Ward Ritchie Press (1977). A humorous account of the experiences of two families coming together.

TECHNICAL ARTICLES

Abarbanel, Alice, "Shared Parenting after Separation and Divorce: A Study of Joint Custody," American Journal of Orthopsychiatry, Vol. 49, #2, April 1979.

Hetherington, E. Mavix, Martha Cox, and Roger Cox, "The Aftermath of Divorce," in J.H. Stevens, Jr. and Marilyn Matthew (eds.), Mother-Child, Father-Child Relations, Washington, D.C.: NAEYC, 1977.

Keniston, Kenneth and The Carnegie Council on Children, All Our Children: The American Family Under Pressure, Harcourt Brace Jovanovich, New York, 1977.

Mendes, Helen, "Single-Parent Families: A Typology of Life-Styles," Social Work, Vol. 24, #3, May 1979.

Wallerstein, Judith, and Kelly, Joan, "The Effects of Parental Divorce: Experiences of the Child in Early Latency," American Journal of Orthopsychiatry, Vol. 46, #1, January 1976.

Wallerstein, Judith, and Kelly, Joan, "The Effects of Parental Divorce: Experiences of the Child in Later Latency," American Journal of Orthopsychiatry, Vol. 46, #1, 1976.

Wallerstein, Judith, and Kelly, Joan, "The Effects of Parental Divorce: The Adolescent Experience," The Child in His Family: Children at Psychiatric Risk, J. Anthony and C. Koupernik, eds., John Wiley, New York, 1974.

Wallerstein, Judith, and Kelly, Joan, "California's Children of Divorce," Psychology Today, January 1980.

Family Law Counseling Services

1600 Shattuck Avenue Suite #200
Berkeley, CA 94709
548-5551

BIBLIOGRAPHY FOR BLENDED AND STEP-FAMILIES

It's hard to make the adjustments and solve the problems when people remarry and children find themselves in new living arrangements and back and forth between households. Here are some books that help with problems about blended and step-families:

Stepparenting, by Jean and Veryl Rosenbaum, E.P. Dutton, N.Y., 1978.

Step-Families, A Guide to Working with Stepparents & Stepchildren, by Emily and John Visher, Brunner/Mazel, N.Y., 1970.

Your Child? I Thought It Was My Child!, by Owen and Nancie Spann, Ward Ritchie Press, Pasadena, California, 1977.

Peoplemaking (Chapter 12), by Virginia Satir, Science and Behavior Books, Inc., Palo Alto, California, 1972.

Learning to Love Again (Chapter 8), by Mel Krantzler, Thomas Y. Crowell Co., N.Y., 1977.

Here are some books to read about sharing being parents after the end of the marital relationship:

Co-Parenting, by Miriam Galper, Running Press, Philadelphia, 1978.

The Disposable Parent, by Roman and Haddad, Holt, Reinhart & Winston, N.Y., 1978.

The Custody Handbook, by Persia Woolley, Summit Books, N.Y., 1979.

Mom's House, Dad's House, by Isolina Ricci, Macmillan, N.Y., 1980.

Sharing Parenthood After Divorce, by Ciji Ware, Viking Press, N.Y., 1982.

Experts talk about the children:

Surviving the Breakup, Wallerstein & Kelly, Basic Books, N.Y., 1980.

The children talk about it themselves:

Divorced Kids, by Warner Troyer, Harcourt Brace Jovanovich, N.Y., 1979.

The Day the Loving Stopped, by June List, Seaview Books, N.Y., 1980.

Family Law Counseling Services

1600 Shattuck Avenue Suite #200
Berkeley, CA 94709
548-5551

GUIDELINES FOR PARENTS WHEN THE OTHER PARENT IS ANGRY, HOSTILE AND UNCOOPERATIVE

Sometimes we are asked "What can I do? I can't get the other parent to come in for mediation; there is no communication; the children are being kept away from me as much as possible; I can't get a reasonable conversation going."

It is hard to know what is the best course in what seems to be hopeless circumstances. However we have learned some pitfalls to avoid and some long range thinking and planning that help.

1. Develop a long range perspective. Keep in mind that parental efforts often are not appreciated by children for years. Yet eventually children come around to understanding and appreciating the parent who has never given up and never abandoned them even though barriers to communication seemed insurmountable. Keep trying; keep writing; make the most of the opportunities for contact. One day your children will be adult children and if you have never abandoned them, they will probably come looking for you and will be open to establishing a relationship with you.

2. Keep separate your issues with the other parent and your issues with your children.

3. Keep focused on your relationship with your children and make a commitment to direct your efforts toward what is truly in the best interests of the children. Do not allow frustration and anger with the other parent to dictate your actions and attitudes toward your children.

4. Emphasize with the children that you speak only for yourself and cannot speak for the other parent. Do not try to explain the other parent's behavior to the children. Refer them back to the other parent for clarification. Do clarify for children how you see the differences between you and their other parent without evaluation. A simple statement of the issue and the respective parental positions as you understand them will suffice.

5. Do not interfere with your children's relationship with the other parent. Assume that the children want relationship with both parents and will avoid at all cost appearance of disloyalty in the eyes of either parent. Do not place your children in the position of having to choose between parents, do not put them put them in the position of having to show partiality. Research shows that children need both parents.

6. Do not expect reform in behavior of the other parent. Be realistic, accept that this person is not going to change and go about getting the best you can get for you in relation to your children given the other parent's characteristics.

7. Be persistent about negotiating from a position of caring and concern for the children; show sensitivity toward legitimate concerns stated by the other parent and let the other parent know you acknowledge such concerns.

8. Build good will if possible. Be quick to acknowledge reasonableness and cooperation when it occurs.

9. Be fair and expect fairness in return. Be helpful when it is possible and convenient for you to do so. Do not, however, accede to unreasonable demands; do not bend over backwards to be accomodating.

10. Identify and avoid destructive side loops in your communications with the other parent. Exercise self control to stay out of exchanges around issues you know from experience become repetitive and without productive outcome.

11. Be clear and definite in your communications. State your understanding of the other parent's position, make certain you have stated it accurately, ask for confirmation that you have gotten it. State your own position. Then if you feel the exchange becoming an unproductive loop, state your desire to move on to the next topic unless the other parent wants to negotiate change on the issue.

12. Make clear what your objectives are and how you will know when you have achieved them. Do not state less than nor more than what you want about your children. Keep stating what you want and at least twice a year write a letter summarizing how you see things and what you still want.

13. Do not make threats about the legal system.

14. Do make clear that you intend to persevere by whatever reasonable, conciliatory, mediative means you can.

15. Do make clear that you are not going to give up and go away and that your former spouse will have to continue to deal with you.

16. Keep dialogue open about the children. Encourage the other parent to tell you about significant events, idiosyncracies, special toys, relationships, educational problems. If the other parent is withholding about these matters do not retaliate and do continue to tell the other parent about such matters factually without evaluation.

17. If you decide you must take legal action or if the other parent involves you in legal action, give warning before taking each step. If the other parent is going to receive a letter or notice contact him or her and explain why you are taking the action you are taking.

18. Finally, do the best you can to understand the actions of the other parent and what he or she is saying to you. Work at developing your own inner sense of peace. The following thought by Rilke may be comforting:

> "Be patient with all that is unsolved in your heart and love the questions themselves. Do not seek the answers that cannot be given you because you would not be able to live them and the point is to live everything. Live the questions now, perhaps you will gradually, without noticing it, live along some distant day into the answers."
>
> --Rilke

Family Law Counseling Services

A counseling approach to family law problems

548-5551

1600 Shattuck Avenue
Suite #200
Berkeley, CA 94709

GUIDELINES FOR SUCCESSFUL HOLIDAYS
IN YOUR AFTER-DIVORCE FAMILY NETWORK*

1. Make a conscious decision that you want joy for yourself and to bring joy to others through the holidays. Keep in mind that holidays are stressful for everybody. Children get keyed up with excitement and adults often experience blues or depression.

2. Plan ahead, way ahead, if possible. Start talking to your former spouse, your children, your relatives well ahead of Thanksgiving, Christmas, and other holidays and family celebrations.

3. Get an idea of what you want for yourself through the holidays. See how many options you can generate that have attractive features for you and for others in your family network.

4. Accept that the children need to be with their other parent for special holiday celebrations as much as with you. Children need concrete evidence that they still "belong" with each parent.

5. Accept that there is less time available as there are more to share it. Start looking for ways to warp, bend, and shape time to everyone's satisfaction.

6. Invest extra effort to make arrangements that will work for everyone. Your return in your children's happiness and well being will be worth the extra effort. Be willing to compromise. Here are some of the solutions others have used with success:

   Two celebrations - Thanksgiving or Christmas day in one household; second Thanksgiving or Christmas on Sunday or when the children get back from their trip. Hanukkah with one parent and the gifts and candle ritual at another time with the other parent.

   Split celebrations - Christmas Eve with one, Christmas day with the other (be sure to get clear how the transition is to be handled and with whom they will be overnight) or part of the special day in one household, part in the other (again, make sure transition time is specifically agreed upon) or some Hanukkah nights with one and some with the other.

   All together - Some families are able to get together for dinner or part of the day. Care should be taken to avoid kindling hopes for reconciliation in the children and if adults are afraid they can't handle feelings of nostalgia, anger, or regret then this option may pose more problems than benefits.

   One or some children with each - One child with one parent and the other(s) with the other parent. Be sure to take into account whether the children will miss each other and have feelings of loss. Use this one only if there are no issues of favoritism or rejection. When one parent wants only the child he or she gets along with and not the other, it can be devastating. On the other hand, if decided mutually, it can be a relief for a parent and child. This works best if all are working on their ties in other ways or have the perspective that things will be better in time.

7. If you are not going to have child, children, and/or family with you, plan for what you are going to do and how you are going to handle it. Make a definite choice whether you will be alone or with others. Here are some things others have done:

   Special vacation trip - Maybe it is the time to take a vacation cruise,

*Based in part on ideas of Isolina Ricci, author of Mom's House, Dad's House.

go to Mexico, Hawaii, Europe or on a ski trip. Consider how you will feel with vacationers, newly found friends. Will you feel alienated? Homesick? Liberated? Exhilarated?

Change of setting - If finances do not permit an extended or expensive trip, is ther a different setting nearby that would be fun and a welcome change? (Apartment in the city, friend's cabin in the woods, use of camper, etc.?) If you go away by yourself will you feel depressed? Deprived? Bitter? Peaceful? Contented? Joyful in your solitude?

Being host or hostess to others in the same boat - Is this a good time to take in others? You might give much joy by inviting others who are also without their children this year or who have little or no mutually supportive group of non-family adults or will you feel artificial.

Visiting a shut-in - Do you know someone who will be alone and who would welcome your visit? If you don't, senior citizen living centers or hospitals would be delighted with a visit bringing the the spirit of joy and sharing.

"Going home" - Being with your own parents and extended family. Will you feel comforthed or more lonely if you are with your family? How will you feel if you will be seeing other long term relationships that still seem happy and enduring?

The main thing is: Think about whether you need company and if so what kind? What works well for someone else may fit you and your needs. If not, be creative!

8. Do not intrude on your children in other family settings, do not show up at unexpected hours and do not expect to be invited to join in. Remember your children's needs and do not create unpleasantness for them in your dealings with their other parent at the time of picking them up or dropping them off.

9. Be specific about such things as pick up, arrival, and flight times. Be specific and exact about times and dates and who is to provide or pay for transportation. Explain what arrangements there are for an adult to be with them if needed, or who can be called as a back-up, clothing needed, other relatives or new partners who will be involved in the plans, etc. If a new romantic partner will be involved, that information should be shared so that children and the other parent can be prepared rather than surprised.

10. If you are going to have children who are new to you for the holidays, do what you can to get to know them ahead of the time they come into the household. Find out about likes and dislikes, plan for age and plan appropriate gifts and activities. Don't expect instant love or instant feelings of family with persons new to you. Do take things slowly and allow time for adjustment.

11. Plan gift giving. If possible coordinate gift giving with the other parent and other relatives. If not possible then be as informative about your own plans as possible.

12. Discuss rituals and traditions with the children. Plan so that wanted ones are kept in their original forms or altered to suit your current needs and circumstances and so that unwanted ones may be dropped or altered to fit how family members now feel. Take time to re-examine rituals and traditions and to formulate new ones that make sense in your new family formation.

13. Accept and acknowledge feelings of loss. It is inevitable as we grow older that holidays bring back memories of other family occasions and family changes as new families form and elders pass on. Take a moment or two to mourn the passing of other times and other faces; it will help you remember the good things of the past and the good things still possible in the present and future. Christmas, Hanukkah, and New Years

present an opportunity to update your sense of life and the meaning of family in changing times.

Ah, friends, dear friends as years go on
and heads get gray, how fast the
guests do go!
Touch hands, touch hands, with those
that stay.
Strong hands to weak, old hands to
young, around the Christmas board,
touch hands.
The false forget, the foe forgive, for
every guest will go and every fire
burn low and cabin empty stand.
Forget, forgive, for who may say that
Christmas day may every come to host
or guest again.
Touch hands!

from John Norton's Vagabond
by William Henry Harrison
("Adirondack") Murray

HAPPY HOLIDAYS!

Family Law Counseling Services

1600 Shattuck Avenue Suite #200
Berkeley, CA 94709
548-5551

STATEMENT OF UNDERSTANDING

I have read the printed description of the services provided by Family Law Counseling Services (FLCS). In making use of this process, I am choosing not to make use of the adversary process. I understand that when parties resort to litigation and court hearings to resolve issues such as those listed below, they separately retian their own attorneys to negotiate the best result for them or to present their case in the best light to a judge if the issues are not resolved through negotiations. I further understand communications in such a process are limited and are through attorneys and a party need not reveal disadvantageous information except as discovered by attorneys using depositions and other methods characteristic of the conventional legal process. I choose to forego the advantages of the adversary process and we agree to the following:

1. We will be discussing some of all of the following issues:

   We may set aside some of the above issues and we may discover and add issues.

2. Our goal will be to reach agreement if possible, and if not, to identify specifically the nature of our disagreement. The FLCS team will assist us to develop our own problem solving abilities and to recognize our common ground and maximize areas of agreement.

3. The team will assist us as a family network to get the best possible result for all concerned, not necessarily for one alone.

4. The FLCS team will share information with us about the law and how other families have resolved similar issues. However, we understand that our goal is to generate our own agreement to meet our own needs.

5. Neither of us will be represented by any FLCS staff member against any other participant in the process.

6. The FLCS team will not arbitrate, nor judge, nor decide issues between us.

7. This process is confidential and based on trust. We agree to work in a spirit of open and full disclosure, ant that what we say in this process is under penalty of perjury. We agree not to call any FLCS staff member and FLCS staff members agree not to appear as a witness, and we agree not to use any information revealed in this process to the disadvantage of any other participant in the process.

8. We agree to notify all participants in the process if either of us seek the advice and counsel of any attorney outside the process and we agree to give notice to all participants in the process first before taking any legal action.

9. If we insist on an agreement which FLCS staff members feel from experience will be vulnerable to legal attack or deterioration in operation and if after negotiations we continue to want such agreement, then FLCS staff members reserve the right to change the composition of the FLCS team or to withdraw from the process leaving us free to seek other services to formalize our agreement.

10. We understand that we and FLCS staff may negotiate about bringing in more parties or changing the members of the FLCS team or having separate sessions.

11. We agree that if in separate sessions, one party wants to reveal information which is not to be shared, this information will be shared within the FLCS team. If the information is of such a character that to withhold it would endanger the process, we understand FLCS staff members will negotiate with the party making the request for confidentiality to establish conditions under which the information may be shared and will assist us to work through the complications that ensue. If these negotiations fail to produce agreement, FLCS staff members reserve the right to change the composition of the FLCS team or to withdraw from the process leaving us free to seek other services.

12. We agree to participate in periodic candid evaluation of what we are doing together. We agree to communicate about it if either of us feels unsure or uneasy about any aspect of the process or of a proposed resolution of any issue. We agree to state clearly or ask for help in formulating any reservations either of us may have.

13. We agree to pay the stated fee per hour per professional to be paid at each session. We agree to pay the stated fee per hour on receipt of service for any FLCS staff work contracted for us and performed outside sessions such as. but not limited to, drafting papers, arranging for consultant services for appraisal, getting information, doing research, and court appearance including travel and waiting.

14. We agree to pay the fee for Processing Divorce and court filing fees if we elect to have FLCS staff process divorce papers and make arrangements for the interlocutory hearing for us.

15. We agree that no default shall be taken in any legal proceedings between us that are subject of this agreement without first giving written notice allowing 30 days within which to respond.

WE WISH TO MAKE USE OF FAMILY LAW COUNSELING SERVICES AND AGREE TO THE TERMS SET FORTH ABOVE.

__________ Date   __________ Signature   __________ Date   __________ Signature

Family Law Counseling Services

1600 Shattuck Avenue Suite #200
Berkeley, CA 94709
548-5551

BUDGET PACKET
for

____

The Budget Packet is to assist you in working your way through issues about your family budget, now that the family is, or will soon be, rearranged. The packet provides checklists of budget items for parents and children. This is an important time to assess which family members need economic assistance and how long before they can become economically self-sufficient.

Use the Packet to Suit Your Needs. In some cases plans are needed for only for the children and sometimes plans are needed for one of the married partners who cannot realistically be expected to become totally self-sufficient economically. In most cases, family plans are needed for a spouse who has not been working and for minor children.

Use the part of the packet that you need. If you have not worked on the packet, come to your appointment and we will begin from where you are.

Use Your Own Style in Gathering the Necessary Information. Because individuals and families differ in working methods, we want you to feel free to be as detailed or as general as you want in preparing for budget discussions. In fact, you don't have to use this packet at all if another way seems better.

The check lists will help you think of things you might otherwise not have remembered. If you wish, present things in your own way. What is important is that you and your family generate the information that is your own, is agreed on, and that is sufficient for each of you to feel you know what you need to know for resolution of the issues without prying into each other's private lives.

Lawyers and Court Forms. If you each went to a lawyer, your lawyer would enlarge your needs and minimize your resources, including depreciating your ability to earn. You would fill out court forms and your lawyer would do everything possible to discover every last detail about the other's money and to minimize how much the other found out about your money.

Family Law Counseling, Openness and Full Disclosure. In Family Law Counseling, we emphasize realistic appraisal of the resources available and, therefore, we insist on open, honest and full disclosure. At the same time, we make every effort to assist you to develop and use this information respectfully and with dignity. We ask you to avoid picking at information provided by the other and personal attacks.

Separate Budgets for Parents and Children. In order to help you minimize conflict and to get a sense of separateness from one another, we ask that you think in terms of separate budgets for each of you and for the children.

Privacy but not Secrecy. To assure dignity for each of you, we encourage you to allow each other some privacy about your respective budgets (what is one person's necessity is another person's luxury and often these issues were fundamental and divisive ones in the marriage, leaving bitter memories)

On the other hand, secrecy about money which results in advantage taking cannot be tolerated. If one hides information about his or her ability to contribute to legitimate family needs or is unwilling to look at how funds are managed and used to meet the family needs for which they were intended, then the standards of open and honest disclosure necessary for family law counseling are not present. We would need to rectify this situation in order to proceed. We will discuss whether to discontinue the family counseling process should the desire to cooperate be absent.

Support. A family member who has never been on the job market or who does not have current job skills ordinarily needs economic assistance. If you are the wage earner, you may feel uneasy about how much and for how long you are going to be burdened economically. If you are not secure in wage earning abilities, you are probably panicked, or at least anxious, at the thought that you are going to have to be economically self-sufficient and that with all the other problems you are having to deal with at this time you are just not prepared for this yet.

These feelings can sometimes be worse when you feel betrayed or if you blame the other person because he or she asked for the divorce. It can also be hard if the other seems unwilling to assume responsibility in a way that meets your idea of what is fair under the circumstances.

The legal adversary process can considerably exaccerbate these feelings because you must persuade a judge to agree with your viewpoint. You tend to exaggerate your own claims and put down the other's claims. Your lawyer goes about collecting information to prove your claims in ways that are unpleasant and leaves a residue of bitterness and distrust.

Working with the FLCS team will give you an opportunity to express your feelings directly to each other and to come to an agreement based on your feelings rather than submitting to an order imposed on you by the court.

Children Beyond 18. The two of you as parents are naturally concerned about supporting your children through sufficient education or training so that they can become financially independent of you and productive members of society. If you haven't yet done so, you may want at this time to make plans for college education or training beyond high school. What funds are you willing to make available? Perhaps even starting a trust fund for that purpose is appropriate now.

Spouse of Long Marriage. In a few cases when the marriage has been lengthy, the parties are going to continue to be financially connected because one spouse is not going to be able to become totally self-sufficient. Sometimes this makes emotional disengagement harder; however, we can assist you to find ways to set up your financial arrangements to minimize feelings of burden, dependence, and resentment.

Your Budget: Your Agreement. Coming to your own agreement gives you each more control over your lives. You can work responsibly toward a goal you have mutually set which is realistic in the amount of time allowed for gradual adjustment to total disengagement. It provides a solid basis for the best results in rearing your children to adulthood.

Family Law Counseling Services

1600 Shattuck Avenue Suite #200
Berkeley, CA 94709
548-5551

The following issues are frequently raised when couples discuss spousal support:

1. Amount?

2. Frequency of payment (once a month? on the 1st and 15th?)

3. Duration? For how long?

4. Terminability? Will there be a definite cut off date that can not be changed?

5. Will amount, duration, cut off dates, be subject to change? Or will they be nonmodifiable?

6. Will consideration be given to supportee's ability to earn by contrast to actual earnings?

7. Is supportee aiming toward a career?

8. Will consideration be given to what supportee actually earns?

9. Will there be a provision that if supportee earns above a certain amount, support will be reduced? How will supporter know if supportee has earned more than the agreed amount?

10. Is there any special condition (health, age of children, disability, dependent or whatever) that would keep the supportee from working? If so, are there kinds of work possible despite that?

11. What is the ability of the person asked to support to pay?

12. Will there be consideration of effect of income available to supportee from sources other than from assets that are distributed to supportee as a result of the dissolution? (e.g., family wealth, trust funds, etc.)

13. Will there be consideration of the effect of cohabitation by supportee? What if supportee has new partner in life?

14. What will be the method of payment? Will there be arrangements for automatic payments?

15. Will there be security for payment?

16. Will there be insurance on supporter's life?

17. What will be the effect of death of supporter?

18. What will be the effect of new family obligations of supporter?

Family Law Counseling Services

1600 Shattuck Avenue Suite #200
Berkeley, CA 94709
548-5551

ISSUES ABOUT SALE OF THE RESIDENCE

( ) Sell now _____ Later _____

( ) Division of proceeds
( ) equal ( ) unequal
( ) payment to ___ wife ___ husband
for

( ) Whether parties are to have right of first purchase?

( ) Whether it might change as to who occupies it up to time of sale?

( ) When it is to be sold? Deadline?

Can deadline be renegotiated?

( ) Form of ownership: Joint tenancy? Tenancy in Common? What is purpose of ownership? Investment for children?

( ) Who pays for what costs? Major repairs?
Minor repairs? Expenses to prepare for sale?

( ) What credit if any for mortgage payments?

Investment in equity?
Effect of low mortgage payments as benefit on living cost?

( ) How value will be calculated at time of sale, or when one buys the other out?

( ) Use of arbitration if can't agree? Other way to settle?

( ) What will be the tax consequences?
Loss of possibility of deferred capital gains?
Capital gains?
Want to make tax consequence equitable?

Mediation: How It Works in Our Office is an informational brochure Isolina Ricci gives to clients considering mediation.[2] (See Chapter 7 for further description of Ms. Ricci's mediation.)

ISOLINA RICCI, M.A.
LICENSED CHILD AND FAMILY COUNSELOR
210 CALIFORNIA AVENUE, SUITE G
PALO ALTO, CALIFORNIA 94306
(415) 323-3218

MEDIATION: HOW IT WORKS IN OUR OFFICE*

What is the difference between mediation, counseling or arbitration?
Mediation differs from counseling or arbitration in important ways. In arbitration, the third party acts as a mini-judge and renders a decision after hearing both sides of the issue. In counseling, the parties work on their emotional dynamics and the affected issues utilizing the counselor for advice, feedback, consultation, facilitation and as a teacher of interpersonal skills. Counselors or psychotherapists may also give evaluations or recommendations and may testify in court.

Mediation is neither counseling or arbitration. Mediation is a process where the parties deal with specific unresolved issues and, with the aid of the mediator, arrive at mutually acceptable agreements that are formalized in writing.

In our office the mediator aids the parties to 1) decide what the major issues are, 2) agree on mutually acceptable ground rules for resolving these issues, 3) keep the parties on their chosen path during the subsequent negotiations by structuring the meetings, acting as a moderator and monitoring the rules and goals the parties choose for themselves, 4) aid the parties to generate options, alternatives and ideas from which they can choose and/or redesign, and 5) aid the parties in structuring their formal written agreement so that misunderstandings are minimized.

Is mediation limited to custody and visitation matters?
Yes, the central issues are 1) How parents share or divide their rights and responsibilities as parents now that they no longer live together, and 2) how this will work in day-to-day

reality. Occasionally, by request of both attorneys, I also mediate property and support issues. In these cases, I work closely with each attorney.

If negotiations break down, will you take sides or give a recommendation to the court?
I do not take sides or render a decision for the parents at any time. Furthermore, before mediation officially begins, I will ask the parents to sign a stipulation that states that they will not, any any time ask me to take a side for or against a parent regarding any issue nor will I appear or testify in court on behalf of either party. I see all the parties as my clients--not just one client over another. My allegiance is to the family, not to a single family member.

Are the sessions confidential?
Yes, the sessions are confidential. When one party sees me in private, however, what is said is to be open knowledge to the other party. In other words, I will keep no secrets from one parent at the request of the other.

How long does mediation take?
The duration of mediation depends on the family's needs and circumstances. Some families need only one or two session lasting from one to three hours. Other families use three, four or more sessions. When family members do their "homework," mediation proceeds most efficiently and economically.

Will you see us separately or together?
This depends on the situation. Usually the beginning of the first meeting is with both parents, sometimes with children present. For the first 15 minutes or so, everyone has the opportunity to ask questions and to say what they want accomplished in mediation. At the end of this discussion, the children usually leave and I either a) see each parent separately for 20 minutes or more, then see them again together for a brief meeting or b) see the parents together for the remaining time. This first meeting usually takes about one and a half to two hours.

Are the children or other friends and relatives involved?
This depends on the family's needs and circumstances as well as the ages of the children and how important other adults are to the success of both the mediation and the resulting agreement. The parents and I discuss these questions at the beginning. I like to meet the children at least once and whenever appropriate, to involve them in some key way.

Will you want to discuss my case with my attorney?
Yes. I ask the parents for written permission to discuss matters with each of their attorneys. In my experience, these discussions are of great benefit to the final outcome. Ordinarily, I have a brief phone conversation with each attorney before mediation begins and then again at certain points during the course of mediation.

Are there different types of mediation?
Yes. I frequently use "Confluent Mediation," an approach I developed along with Parenting Agreements in 1975. "Confluent Mediation" includes selected educational and counseling components for long-term positive effects for the family. The results are that parents not only develop a parenting agreement but also reduce hostilities and/or ambiguities about their roles and day-to-day ground rules as parents. Simple mediation is focused on coming to a mutual agreement.

What's the difference between private mediation and mediation with the family court services?
Family court services usually provide short-term simple mediation services free of charge. Often, mediation is limited to three meetings or less. The client does not have a choice of mediators. Private mediation, as practiced in our office, includes both simple and confluent mediation and has the additional component of counseling and/or education as needed or desired by the parents. Of course, in private mediation, the choice of mediator is made by the client. This means that the mediator's style, approach, personal training, and agreement format is a known quantity. The number of meetings are determined together by the client and mediator.

Does confluent mediation take more time than ordinary mediation?
Not usually. The goal of mediation is to reach an agreement that is going to work in real life when mediation ends. Confluent mediation does this in specific, practical ways.

When a family uses this approach to work out some unfinished family business from the past, mediation will take more time.

Is confluent mediation better than simple mediation?
There is no one answer. Each family situation is unique and the parents and I will usually reach a mutual agreement on the type of mediation we will use to best suit their needs and aid them in reaching their goals.

Will you write up our parenting agreement?
When the agreement is limited to the issues of parenting rights and responsibilities, I help the parents write their own highly specific agreement. All parents are advised to obtain legal counsel to review the final agreement before signing it. If the agreement includes agreements on support or property issues, I insist that these paragraphs be drafted and reviewed by each attorney.

Parents Are Forever is the Association of Family Conciliation Courts' handout for parents going through divorce. Many family court services throughout the country provide this for parents.[3] (See Chapter 4 for further descriptions of conciliation court mediation.)

DEAR PARENT,

As you know, a divorce or separation decree cannot and does not end your responsibility as a parent. PARENTS ARE FOREVER. Both parents should make every attempt to continue to play a vital part in the lives of their children. Children need the ongoing interest and concern of their parents. Children must feel they have two parents who love them, even though those parents could not live happily with each other.

It is our hope that the information in this pamphlet will assist you in helping your children cope with your divorce or separation with a minimum of hurt. The practical guidelines which follow are based on the many years of experience of court marriage and family counselors.

If you are like most people, you probably have some feelings of isolation, despair, depression, loneliness, grief, guilt, and a loss of self-confidence. You are worried about many things, such as finances, a new social life, employment, fulfillment of sexual needs and the welfare of your children. You can use this present time of difficulty as an opportunity for growth or a surrender to self-pity.

The way you feel about yourself will affect the way your children feel about themselves. The way you cope with your divorce will in large part determine how your children cope with it. Yes, you are at a cross-roads and can choose from alternative routes.

One road leads to self-pity, living in the past, nurturing bitterness and turning the children against your former marriage partner. This is a dead-end road which spells trouble for you and your children.

The other road, and the constructive one, leads to becoming involved with experiences that provide opportunities for you to again feel success, to get to know yourself better, restore your self-confidence, reach out for goals that will make your life productive, satisfying, and meaningful.

The task of all parents, whether or not a marriage continues, is not easy. All parents make mistakes. But if you have a good relationship with your children and they feel your love and acceptance, they will soon forget your mistakes and remember only your goodness.

Reprinted with permission of the Association of Family Conciliation Courts.

<u>American Association of Marriage and Family Therapists</u>

924 W. Ninth Street
Upland, California 91786

Other sources to contact to obtain help in finding a marriage and family counselor includes Family Service Agencies, your family doctor, your minister, priest or rabbi.

Choose a counselor as you would a doctor or lawyer. Ask about credentials, training, and years in practice. Do not head blindly for the yellow pages in the telephone directory. Such listings often include some persons with no training at all, or training that is skimpy or outdated.

The distribution of this pamphlet is made possible by a grant from the Family Law Section of the Los Angeles County Bar Association.

This pamphlet was originally written by the Conciliation Court of Los Angeles County, California. The art work is reproduced with permission by Parents Without Partners, Inc.

This pamphlet is prepared and distributed by the Association of Family Conciliation Courts, an international association of judges, counselors, behavioral scientists and lawyers concerned about marriage and family life, and lessening the pain of divorce.

ASSOCIATION OF FAMILY CONCILIATION COURTS
c/o Nova University Law Center
3100 S.W. Ninth Avenue
Fort Lauderdale, Florida 33315
Telephone (305) 522-2300

PRINTED IN U.S.A.

PARENTS ARE FOREVER

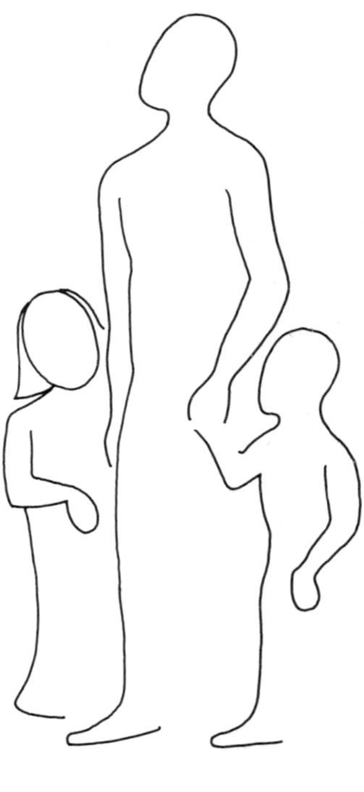

ASSOCIATION OF FAMILY CONCILIATION COURTS

GUIDELINES FOR PARENTS

As we have already indicated, the way you cope with your divorce will in large part determine how your children cope with it. Try to use the experience of divorce as an opportunity for personal growth, not defeat. In this way you can continue to be effective as a parent and to not only effectively meet your children's needs, but just as important, your own needs as a person. Continuing conflict between you and your marriage partner during and after divorce can interfere with your effectiveness as a parent.

1. Allow yourself and your children time for readjustment. Convalescence from an emotional operation such as divorce or separation is essential.

2. Remember the best parts of your marriage. Share them with your children and use them constructively whether or not you have custody.

3. Assure your children that they are not to blame for the breakup and that they are not being rejected or abandoned. Children, especially the young ones, often feel they have done something wrong and believe the problems in the family are the result of their misdeeds. Small children may feel that some action or secret wish of theirs has caused the trouble between their parents.

4. Continuing anger or bitterness toward your former partner can injure your children far more than the divorce or separation itself. The feelings you show are more important than the words you use.

5. Refrain from voicing criticism of the other parent. It is difficult but absolutely necessary for a child's healthy development. It is important that the child respect both parents.

6. Do not force or encourage your children to take sides. To do so encourages frustration, guilt, and resentment.

7. Try not to upset a child's routine too abruptly. Children need a sense of continuity and it is disturbing to them if they must cope with too many changes at once.

8. Divorce or separation often leads to financial pressures on both parents. When there is a financial crisis, the parents' first impulse may be to try to keep the children from realizing it. Often, they would rather make sacrifices themselves than ask the child to do so. The atmosphere is healthier when there is frankness and when children are expected to help.

9. Marriage breakdown is always hard on the children. They may not always show their distress or realize at first what this will mean to them. Parents should be direct and simple in telling children what is happening and why, and in a way a child can understand and digest. This will vary with the circumstances and each child's age and comprehension. The worst course is to try and hush things up and make children feel they must not talk or even think about what they sense is going on. Unpleasant happenings need explanation which should be brief, prompt, direct, and honest.

10. The story of your divorce or separation may have to be retold after the children get older and consider life more maturely. Though it would be unfortunate to present either situation as a tragedy and either parent as a martyr, it would be a pity also to pretend there are no regrets and that the breakdown of a marriage is so common it hardly matters.

11. The guilt parents may feel about the marriage breakdown may interfere in their disciplining the children. A child needs consistent control and direction. Over-permissiveness, or indecisive parents who leave a child at the mercy of every passing whim and impulse interfere with a child's healthy development. Children need and want to know quite clearly what

is expected of them. Children feel more secure when limits are set. They are confused when grown-ups seem to permit behavior which they themselves know to be wrong and are trying to outgrow. Children need leadership and sometimes authority. Parents must be ready to say "NO" when necessary.

VISITATION GUIDELINES

The behavior of parents has a great influence on the emotional adjustment of their children. This is equally true after the breakdown of a marriage. The following visitation guidelines have been found to be helpful in achieving meaningful visits.

1. It is important to try to maintain contact between the child and the parent who has left home. Maintaining some form of contact helps the child deal with his fantasies which are much worse than the reality of what is happening; helps to decrease feelings of rejection; decreases feelings that the divorce happened because he is a bad child; reduce his feelings that he may never see the other parent again.

2. Visits should be pleasant not only for the children but for both parents. Visitation should help your children maintain a positive relationship with their visiting parent. It is important that neither parent verbally or physically attack the other parent in the presence of the children. Children tend to view such attacks as attacks on them.

3. The parent with whom the children live must prepare them physically and emotionally for the visit. The children should be available promptly at the time mutually agreed upon and returned at the time agreed upon.

4. The visits should not take place only in the children's home. The visiting parent may wish the children to visit in his or her home overnight, or may want to plan an enjoyable outing.

5. The question is often asked, "Should the father take the children to the girlfriend's house?" The same question is asked about the mother if she is the noncustodial parent. Visitation is the time for the children and parent to be with each other; to enjoy each other; to maintain positive relationships. Having other people participate may dilute the parent-child experience during visitation. However, it should not be ruled out altogether. Avoid "parades."

6. Visits should be as frequent as practical. Any schedules established should be flexible. Should scheduled visits need to be cancelled (and sometimes they have to be), inform the other parent as soon as possible with a full and honest explanation to the child.

7. You may need to adjust the visitation schedule from time to time according to your children's age, health, and interests.

8. Frequently noncustodial parents ask why they should visit. They are hurt, feel they are no longer needed, the custodial parent has the home and the children. The visit is one of the few times that the noncustodial parent has personal contact with the children and for that reason it should be a meaningful one for both; the noncustodial parent and the children. Even though the parents have not been able to get along, the children still need both parents.

9. Often, the noncustodial parent questions where they should take the children on the visits and what they should plan in the way of amusement for them, particularly if the children are young. Activities may add to the pleasure of the visit, but most important of all is the noncustodial parent's involvement with the children. A giving of self is more important than whatever material things they may get.

10. The visit should not be used to check on the other parent. Children should not be pumped for this kind of information. They should not be used as little spies. Often in the children's perception, the parents hate each other and the children will feel uncomfortable at the time of the visits. In the children's mind, if they do anything to please the visiting parent, they may invite outright rejection by their other parent. They may feel they have already lost one parent and are fearful of losing the other. For these reasons, parents should show mutual respect for each other.

11. The children may be left with many problems following visits and both parents should make every effort to discuss them and to agree on ways to deal with them.

12. Both parents should strive for agreement in decisions pertaining to the children, especially discipline, so that one parent is not undermining the other parent's efforts.

IF YOU NEED HELP

It is unfortunate that many people believe that to ask for help is a sign of weakness, for in reality it is a sign of strength. It takes a great deal of courage for a person to say, "I have a problem which I cannot solve alone and I need help with it."

Asking for help does not mean people are incapable of solving their problems. For in the final analysis, it is the people themselves who solve their problems. Counselors merely guide people and give some direction to their search for solutions. There are a few people who have not needed help at some time in their lives. Those who reach for professional help in times of crisis have a better chance of finding effective and permanent solutions in a shorter time.

Persons with problems often become discouraged which only emphasizes weaknesses. They often overlook strengths still present as well as other alternatives for coping with these problems. A trained counselor may assist in achieving a better understanding fo strngths or weaknesses.

Advice from well-meaning friends and relatives, in many cases, may further aggravate the situation. Friends or relatives usually are not professionally trained to treat problems and they can seldom be objective.

Professional counseling may create an awareness which can assist you in dealing with your and your children's problems at this time.

If you need marriage and family counseling before, during, or after divorce, the following sources are suggested to locate a professional counselor.

Association of Family Conciliation Courts
c/o Nova University Law Center
3100 S.W. Ninth Avenue
Fort Lauderdale, Florida 33315

The following materials are given to potential clients by Families in Transition.

The Spousal Information List provides the mediators with information concerning couples' financial position, living situation, and facts necessary for drawing up a marital settlement agreement.

The Consent Form specifically delineates the role of the attorney in mediation, protecting both the parties and the attorney.[4]

The G M Divorce Awareness Scale is designed to help the couple begin to come to terms with their emotional reaction to the divorce and to deal with it in a constructive manner.[5]

Legal Issues of Dissolution provides a brief explanation of the laws and principles that are going to affect the decisions couples make as they mediate.[4] (Though these laws and principles are only designed for Californians, many states have similar criteria for determining support and property issues.)

SPOUSAL INFORMATION LIST

1. FULL NAME ______________________________
   Home Address ______________________ Home phone ____________
   ____
   Work Address ______________________ Work phone ____________
   ____
   Social Security Number ______________
   Lived at present address since ______________
   All home addresses for past two years: Dates
   ______________________ (From ________ to ________)
   ______________________ (From ________ to ________)

2. MARRIAGE Date ______________ Place ______________
   If you were not married in California, when did you move to California? ______________

3. CHILDREN:

Full Name	Date of Birth	Living With
______________	______________	______________
______________	______________	______________
______________	______________	______________
______________	______________	______________
______________	______________	______________

4. Are you and your spouse living together now? ______________
   If not, state date of separation ______________, and where you were living at the time of the separation ______________
   ______________.

5. Are you employed? ______________
   Name of employer ______________
   Job title ______________ Nature of job ______________
   Employed since ______________ Salary ______________
   (biweekly, monthly or annual)

6. Date of birth:____________________

7. List your prior marriages. (Include name of prior spouse and how, when and where prior marriage terminated.)

____

____

____

8. List names and ages of any your children of any prior marriage and state with whom such children live.

____

____

____

9. Do you desire custody of the children?__________________

10. Do you have a Will?_______ If yes, when was it signed? _______________.

ASSETS

11. Do you own a home?_________ If so, is title to that property in joint tenancy_______ community property_______ other______ Please attach a copy of the grant deed.

What do you estimate is its fair market value?____________

12. Do you own other real property?

Address	Form of Title	Date Acquired	Estimated Current Val.	Cost	Loans Outstanding

Securities. (Attach list if space is inadequate)

Description	Form of Title	Date Acquired	Estimated Current Val.	Cost	Pledged as Collateral?

Cash and deposits with credit unions, banks and money market funds.

Description of Account	Estimated Current Value	Form of Title

Tangible personal property, (personal effect, jewelry, household furnishings, vehicles, boats, collections, etc.)

Description	Estimated Current Value

Debts owed to you.

Business interests. (partnerships, proprietorships, corporations)

Copyrights, patents, mineral rights.

Are you the beneficiary of a trust?

Do you hold any powers of appointment?

Life insurance.

Company	Policy #	Type	Face Val.	Current Value	Owner	Insured	Primary Beneficiary
							Contingent Beneficiary

MONTHLY INCOME

GROSS MONTHLY INCOME	Husband	Wife
1. Salary & wages (include commissions, bonuses and overtime)................	$............	$............

2.	Pensions & retirement....	$............	$............
3.	Social Security..........	$............	$............
4.	Disability & unemployment benefits.................	$............	$............
5.	Public assistance(Welfare AFDC payments, etc.).....	$............	$............
6.	Child/spousal support....	$............	$............
7.	Dividends & interest.....	$............	$............
8.	Rents paid to you........	$............	$............
9.	Contributions to household expenses from other sources..................	$............	$............
10.	Income from all other sources..................	$............	$............
11.	TOTAL GROSS MONTHLY INCOME...........	$............	$............

Death and retirement benefits.

Source of Benefits	Type of Benefits	Percentage Vested	Estimated Current Val	Primary Beneficiary	Contingent Beneficiary

Annuities.

Other:

DEDUCTIONS FROM GROSS INCOME	Husband	Wife
12. State income taxes.......	$............	$............
13. Federal income taxes.....	$............	$............

14. Social Security..........	$............	$............
15. State disability ins.....	$............	$............
16. Medical and other ins....	$............	$............
17. Union and other dues.....	$............	$............
18. Retirement & pension fund	$............	$............
19. Savings plan..............	$............	$............
20. Other deductions (specify)	$............	$............
21. TOTAL DEDUCTIONS..........	$............	$............

---

11. TOTAL GROSS MONTHLY INCOME (from line 11:.....	$............	$............
21. TOTAL DEDUCTIONS (From line 21):...........	$............	$............
22. NET MONTHLY INCOME (line 11 minus line 21)...	$............	$............

---

23. TAX WITHHOLDING INFORMATION
    a. Number of exemptions claimed:
    b. Marital status:

MONTHLY EXPENSES

If you do not anticipate that the children of your present marriage will live with you, complete only the first column. If you anticipate that your children will live with you, complete the second column with your estimated expenses for yourself and your children.

24. List the name, age and relationship of all member of the household whose expenses are included below:

MONTHLY EXPENSES	Yourself	You and children
25. Residence payments		
a. Rent or mortgage......	$............	$............
b. Taxes & ins...........	$............	$............
c. Maintenance...........	$............	$............
26. Food & household supplies	$............	$............
27. Utilities & telephone....	$............	$............
28. Laundry & cleaning.......	$............	$............
29. Clothing.................	$............	$............
30. Medical & dental.........	$............	$............

31. Insurance (life, health accident, etc.)..........	$............	$............
32. Child care...............	$............	$............
33. Child/spousal support (prior marriage).........	$............	$............
34. School...................	$............	$............
35. Entertainment............	$............	$............
36. Incidentals..............	$............	$............
37. Transportataion & auto expenses (insurance, gas, oil repair)..............	$............	$............
38. Installment pmts. (insert total and itemize at 41)	$............	$............
39. Other: (specify).........	$............	$............
40. TOTAL MONTHLY EXPENSES...	$............	$............

41. ITEMIZATION OF INSTALLMENT PAYMENTS OR OTHER DEBTS

Creditor's Name	For	Monthly Pmt.	Balance
		$	$
		$	$
		$	$
		$	$
		$	$
		$	$
		$	$
		$	$
		$	$
		$	$
		$	$

FAMILIES IN TRANSITION
CONSENT FORM

_________________________ and _________________________
desire to mediate the dissolution of their marriage with the aid of Families in Transition. To assist in the resolution of the legal issues related to dissolution, Families in Transition has engaged attorney _________________________ and is solely responsible for her fees.

1. The parties understand and agree that _________________________ will be an independent legal advisor, and not the legal representative of either party.

2. The parties understand and agree that ____________________ shall represent neither party in any court proceeding without the consent of the other.
3. The parties acknowledge that they have been advised to have any marital property agreement, spousal support arrangement or child custody that is prepared as a result of the mediation process reviewed by an attorney of their choosing before signing such agreements.
4. The parties agree to retain the services of an independent assessor or auditor if such services are deemed necessary to an equitable settlement by Families in Transition.
5. Any legal services other than the preparation of the marital settlement agreement will be rendered to either party at the expense of the party in question. ____________________ will decline to render any services that in her opinion would compromise her objectivity in the mediation process.

Date:

____________________	____________________
Husband	(for Families in Transition)
____________________	____________________
Wife	Attorney

G M Divorce Awareness Scale

Directions: **This is a checklist to be used by people who are divorcing or separating from a spouse.** Put an "X" in the box by any items which reflect how you think or feel. When scored, the scale may help you clarify and better understand some of the painful parts of your experience.

- ☐ A 1 What will people think? A lot of people will be upset that I'm divorcing.
- ☐ A 2 I was too good for him/her.
- ☐ A 3 I'll no longer fit into my circle of friends.
- ☐ A 4 I'll always be alone and lonely.

By Matthew McKay, Ph.D. and Richard Gosse, M.A.

- ☐ A 5 I've wasted my life.
- ☐ A 6 I didn't love enough.
- ☐ A 7 I should be turned on to this new freedom more than I am.
- ☐ A 8 I'm a loser because I got divorced.
- ☐ B 1 His/her relatives will hate me. They'll blame me for hurting him/her.
- ☐ B 2 If s/he would have done a little changing, improved and compromised, or been more accepting, things would have turned out differently.
- ☐ B 3 I'm not going to survive financially.
- ☐ B 4 I'll never find anyone else.
- ☐ B 5 I can't stand this loneliness.
- ☐ B 6 If I'd only worked harder at it, I could have kept the marriage together.
- ☐ B 7 I should be going out with a lot of people.
- ☐ B 8 S/he is a bitch, jerk, or __hole.
- ☐ C 1 Secretly, people will look down on me now.
- ☐ C 2 S/he made me miserable and ruined our marriage.
- ☐ C 3 My ex-spouse will fall apart without me.
- ☐ C 4 My relationships will always fail.
- ☐ C 5 I'm overwhelmed by unbearable pain.
- ☐ C 6 I wasn't a good husband/wife.
- ☐ C 7 Even though I don't feel like it, I should be initiating contact. I should be asking people (of the opposite sex) out.
- ☐ C 8 S/he was basically selfish.
- ☐ D 1 My friends won't want to see me.
- ☐ D 2 His/her lack of communication had a lot to do with our divorce.
- ☐ D 3 I'm not going to be able to stand this, I'll fall apart.
- ☐ D 4 Nobody will be attracted enough to me to want a relationship.
- ☐ D 5 The hurt is too great.
- ☐ D 6 If only I hadn't (whatever you think you did), everything would have been all right.
- ☐ D 7 I shouldn't go out at night and abandon my kids.
- ☐ D 8 S/he was stupid, insensitive and/or inconsiderate.
- ☐ E 1 People blame me for the break-up.
- ☐ E 2 His/her hostility ruined things.
- ☐ E 3 My children may be permanently harmed by the divorce.
- ☐ E 4 I'll probably always feel depressed.
- ☐ E 5 I spent my youth on him/her.
- ☐ E 6 I messed up what could have been a good marriage.
- ☐ E 7 I should have stayed married for the kids.
- ☐ E 8 S/he was mean, hostile, and/or sadistic.
- ☐ F 1 People think I'm a failure.
- ☐ F 2 If s/he had worked harder, we could have saved the marriage.
- ☐ F 3 I'm not going to be able to get back into dating, or fit into modern single life.
- ☐ F 4 I'll never feel really close to anyone again.
- ☐ F 5 I'm trapped and powerless.
- ☐ F 6 I keep regretting the way I was, the mistakes I made in the marriage.
- ☐ F 7 I shouldn't have hurt him/her. I should have worked harder to keep us together.
- ☐ F 8 S/he is a liar.
- ☐ G 1 My married friends don't understand. They feel uncomfortable around me.
- ☐ G 2 S/he never had enough time or paid enough attention to me. S/he didn't really care.
- ☐ G 3 I'll have to live the rest of my life alone.
- ☐ G 4 I'm no good at marriage.
- ☐ G 5 I'm utterly confused.
- ☐ G 6 I keep thinking that I'm responsible for the pain s/he is suffering.
- ☐ G 7 I should be closer to people, more outgoing.
- ☐ G 8 S/he was withdrawn, uninvolved, and/or uncaring.
- ☐ H 1 His/her friends secretly don't like me.
- ☐ H 2 I wasn't treated fairly, I was basically "screwed over."
- ☐ H 3 New relationships will fail and I'll be hurt again.
- ☐ H 4 I'll never feel really secure again.
- ☐ H 5 The anxiety and fear is overwhelming. I feel like I'm falling apart.
- ☐ H 6 I wasn't flexible enough, I could have saved the marriage.
- ☐ H 7 I should be independent and comfortable being alone.
- ☐ H 8 S/he was lousy at communicating.

INSTRUCTIONS FOR SCORING THE G M DIVORCE AWARENESS SCALE

This test has eight subscales. All questions with a number one (A1, B1, C1, etc.) comprise subscale 1, all questions with a number two (A2, B2, C2, etc.) comprise subscale 2, etc.

Count the number of marked boxes for all number one questions, all number two questions, all threes, etc. Put the totals in the appropriate space:

Subscale 1 total _______

Subscale 2 total _______

Subscale 3 total _______

Subscale 4 total _______

Subscale 5 total _______

Subscale 6 total _______

Subscale 7 total _______

Subscale 8 total _______

Scores for each of the subscales range between zero and eight. Higher scores on a subscale indicate a tendency toward the cognitive distortion tested by that subscale:

Subscale 1 .... MINDREADING

Higher scores indicate the tendency to make assumptions about the feelings, attitudes and motivations of others—all without any direct confirmation. The divorcing person will often use mindreading to guess the reactions of relatives and friends.

Subscale 2 .... BLAMING OTHERS/EXTERNAL CONTROL FALLACY

Higher scores indicate the tendency to hold others responsible for any pain, loss or failure. The spouse is blamed for the loneliness, hurt and fear that may accompany a divorce. Blaming others has its roots in the belief that one is helpless to provide for his/her emotional needs.

Subscale 3 .... CATASTROPHIZING

Higher scores indicate the tendency to exaggerate potential danger and habitually focus on future scenarios of disaster. The divorcing person may use this distortion to paint a future full of bleak and frightening "possibilities."

Subscale 4 .... OVERGENERALIZING

Higher scores indicate the tendency to make broad, generalized conclusions based on a single case or very little evidence. The Overgeneralizer will make absolute statements that imply immutable laws limiting his/her chances for happiness. Key words are: "all, every, never, always, everybody, none, nobody."

Subscale 5 .... FILTERING

Higher scores indicate the tendency to focus on the worst possible aspects of a situation and ignore everything else. Because Filtering creates a kind of negative tunnel vision, the divorcing person will often magnify and awfulize his/her fears and losses.

Subscale 6 .... SELF-BLAME/OMNIPOTENT CONTROL FALLACY

Higher scores indicate the tendency to exaggerate responsibility for a spouse's pain and the break-up of the marriage. The divorcing person perceives whatever happened as largely his or her fault. There is an inclination toward self-attack for mistakes, insensitivity, failing to work harder, love more, etc.

Subscale 7 .... SHOULDS

Higher scores indicate the tendency to have strict rules governing what are acceptable thoughts, feelings and actions. These rules often contradict what is healthy, natural and needed at a particular stage in the divorcing process.

Subscale 8 .... GLOBAL LABELING

Higher scores indicate the tendency to generalize one or two negative qualities into a global judgment. The label ignores all contrary evidence in favor of a stereotyped, one-dimensional viewpoint.

FAMILIES IN TRANSITION
St. Mary's Medical Center
2166 Hayes Street, Suite 203C
San Francisco, California 94117

All the legal issues in the dissolution of a marriage can be allocated to one of three categories:

°property division (assets and liabilities)

°spousal support

°child custody and support

PROPERTY DIVISION

The issues of property division can be broken down into:

1) Characterization of property as community property or separate property;
2) Valuation of the community property; and
3) Division of the community between the spouses.

Separate property is any property owned before marriage, acquired by gift or inheritance; or earned after separation.

Community property is all property acquired during marriage, except property purchased with the proceeds of separate property. If an asset is bought with some separate property funds and some community property funds, it may be part separate and part community property.

Both spouses are equally liable for debts incurred during the marriage.

Property is valued at the time of trial or the marital settlement agreement.

Califoria law requires that community property be divided equally between the spouses. Separate property must be awarded to the owner spouse. The parties can agree, however, that a spouse who gets a disproportionate share of the community property according to the agreement of the parties will transfer an equalizing amount of separate property to the other spouse.

SPOUSAL SUPPORT

The court can order either spouse to pay for the support of the other spouse in any amount and for any time period that the court finds reasonable. In deciding the amount and duration of the support obligation, the court looks at the following factors:

1. the earning capacity of each spouse
2. the needs of each party
3. the obligations and assets, including separate property, of the spouses
4. the duration of the marriage
5. the needs of dependent children in the custody of the supported spouse
6. the time required by the supported spouse to acquire education, training and employment
7. the age and the health of the parties
8. the living standard of the parties

Unless the parties waive their rights to support, the court may change the amount of spousal support when either party's circumstances change.

CHILD SUPPORT

Both parents are obligated to support their children. The court will fix the amount that the non custodial parent pays for the support of the children in light of the resources of both parents. The court retains the power to make orders regarding the custody and support of a child until the child is eighteen. Whereas a parent may agree to waive support for him or herself or agree to a fixed amount of support regardless of changes in circumstances, the parents may not make such agreements on behalf of their children.

Custody is the sum of parental rights with respect to rearing a child. Custody includes the right to direct the child's activities and to make decisions regarding his care and control, education, health and religion.

The preference of the law is for joint legal custody in which the parents share these rights.

A dissolution is begun by one spouse filing a PETITION for dissolution in the Superior Court for the county in which that spouse lives. The PETITION sets out the grounds for the dissolution, usually irreconcilable differences. (One spouse can get a dissolution even if the other spouse want to preserve the marriage.) The petition sets out the relief that spouse, now called the PETITIONER, seeks from the court concerning property division, spousal support, child custody and support, change of name and attorney's fees.

The petitioner has the petition served on the other spouse, the RESPONDENT. The respondent has 30 days from the time of service to file a RESPONSE. The response addresses the same issues as the petition. Comparing the petition and the response reveals in which areas the couple is in agreement about the issues surrounding dissolution and in which areas they disagree.

At any time after the action is filed, either party may request a hearing on an ORDER TO SHOW CAUSE (OSC). This proceeding allows the judge to make temporary orders concerning spousal and child support, custody of the children and preservation of the community property until a final judgment is entered.

The parties use methods of DISCOVERY to elicit facts from each other concerning the issues in dispute. At the same time, the parties try to establish the value of the community property.

Negotiations seek to get agreement between the parties about the issues in dispute. Agreements are put in the form of stipulations or a MARITAL SETTLEMENT AGREEMENT. At the request of the parties, the court will include the terms of the settlement agreement reached by the parties in its order. The agreement becomes part of the court's judgment and enforceable through the court's contempt powers.

Issues unresolved are the subject of a TRIAL. If all the issues are resolved by agreement, the matter is heard on the uncontested calendar. One party appears to testify to the jurisdictional facts and to present the agreement to the court. An INTERLOCUTORY JUDGMENT is issued by the court.

If, within 60 days after the entry of the interlocutory judgment, no appeal has been filed, and more than six months has passed since the respondent was first served with the petition, the court will enter a FINAL JUDGMENT.

Upon a change in circumstances, either party can request a modification of the court's orders regarding support and custody. Matters concerning property are generally final after the appeal period passes.

• Divorce Mediation • Family Counseling • Support Groups

Attorney Barbara DiFranza uses a questionnaire, much like Families in Transition's Spousal Information List, to assure that she gets a complete picture of her clients' situation. The Confidential Questionnaire for Clients Contemplating Marital Termination also asks clients some questions that a mediator would work with in person, such as question 3.C.: "What support arrangement do you believe would be fair?"

Approaches to Division of Tangible Personal Property is a detailed explanation of different ways in which couples can divide their own property. Couples able to negotiate their own property division can save a significant amount in professional fees. Barbara DiFranza distributes this form to clients inquiring about divorce. Some mediators give clients a similar brochure to speed the mediation. Couples who are knowledgeable about their options require less educating in mediation. Of course, some couples are able to resolve the issues alone, with just this bit of guidance.[6]

CONFIDENTIAL
QUESTIONNAIRE FOR CLIENTS
CONTEMPLATING MARITAL TERMINATION

This questionnaire has been designed to aid our legal staff in advising you of your rights and obligations with respect to a marital termination. All information is covered by attorney-client privilege and will, therefore, be kept in strictest confidence.

Please do your best in filling this form out based upon your knowledge at this time.

Name of Person Filling in Questionnaire________________

Name of Client if Different________________

Date of Completion________________

Note that unless otherwise agreed at the commencement of the consultation, your initial consultation will be charged at the attorney's normal hourly rate and payment must be made at the end of the consultation.

A. INFORMATION ABOUT YOU

1. Name: ________________

2. (a) Telephone: Home - ( ) ______ (b) May we phone you at work?____
   Work - ( ) ______ May we leave a message?____
   Other - ( ) ______

   (c) Note any telephone or mail restrictions with regard to your home or your place of employment:
   ____
   ____

3. (a) In what county do you reside? ______ How long? ______
   (b) Mailing address: ________________
   (c) Residence address (if different from above): ________

4. Birthdate: ____________

5. (a) Former name(s): ________________

(b) Do you wish your former name restored? _______ Now?______ Later?____
Think about it?________ (c) If yes, which name?________________

6. Social Security Number: ____________________

7. (a) Employer: ____________________
(b) Location address: ____________________
(c) Days/Hours at work: ____________________
(d) Pay: Approximate monthly net from employment: ____________
Other monthly net income: ____________________

(Note: There are 4-1/3 weeks per month; to determine "net pay" deduct only SDI, FICA, withholding tax, mandatory retirement contributions. Do not deduct credit union payments, stock or savings plan, etc. Other net income includes that after taxes from investments, rentals, savings, or business.)

(e) Do you have medical and/or dental coverage through your employer?
____________ (f) At what cost to you? ____________
(g) How long have you worked at this place of employment? ____________

8. Do you have any health problems for which special attention is required?
____________ If so, please describe briefly: ____________
____

9. What is the cost of child care enabling you to work? ____________

10. Are you contemplating remarriage at present? ____________

11. If you are currently residing with anyone (other than your spouse or children) state: Name: ____________ Age: ______
Relationship to you: ____________________

12. Also, please describe the monetary arrangements between you and the above person, if any: ____________________
____

B. GENERAL INFORMATION ABOUT YOUR PRESENT MARRIAGE

1. Your name: ____________________
2. Your spouse's name: ____________________
3. Date of marriage: ____________________
4. Place of marriage: (City) ____________ (State)________
5. How long have you lived in Santa Clara County ____________
California ____________

Your spouse: ____________
____

6. Separation date: ____________________

(Note: "Separation date" means the date on which you and your spouse lived in different residences or rooms; or perhaps when one of you definitely communicated to the other that the marriage was over. If there is any doubt, please place a question mark here.)

7. If you have been served with divorce-related papers, date served:

____

8. Which of the parties wishes the dissolution? ______________________

9. Do you desire reconciliation? ___________. If so, are you interested in marital counseling? ____________. Has there been marital counseling in the past? _________________. With whom? ______________.

10. Describe any violence which has recently occurred between you and your spouse or which your spouse might allege has occurred.

____

____

____

C. SUPPORT ARRANGEMENTS BETWEEN YOU AND SPOUSE

1. If you have already separated or discussed separating, detail the financial arrangements you have made:

   (a) Periodic payments (how much, how often, etc.)

   ____

   ____

   ____

   ____

   (b) Direct payment of living expenses (monthly and other) such as mortgage (list items, amounts, and how often paid):

   ____

   ____

   ____

   ____

   ____

   ____

   ____

   (c) Other: ______________________________

   ____

   ____

   ____

   ____

2. Is there an agreement in writing covering support arrangements? ________

____

3. What support arrangement do you believe would be fair? ______________

____

____

____

____

D. INFORMATION ABOUT YOUR SPOUSE

1. Name: ____________________ 2. Telephone: Home - ( )________
   Work - ( )________
3. (a) County of residence ________________
   How long? ________________
   (b) Mailing address: ________________
   (c) Residence address (If different from above): ________________
4. Your spouse's birthdate: ________________
5. Social Security Number: ________________
6. Former names (if any): ________________
7. (a) Employer: ________________
   (b) Address: ________________
   (c) Approximate hire date: ________________
   (d) Approximate monthly net income from employment ________________
   Other: ________________ (See definition, part A)
   (e) Medical/Dental insurance through his/her employer? ________________
   Coverage: You _____ Children _____ Monthly cost to your spouse_______
   Name of plan: ________________
8. Cost of child care enabling your spouse to work: ________________
9. Is your spouse contemplating remarriage at present? ________________
10. If your spouse currently resides with anyone (other than you or the children of this marriage) state:

Name	Age	Relationship to Spouse
________	____	________
________	____	________
________	____	________

11. Describe any monetary arrangements you know of or have reason to suspect your spouse and the persons indicated above have: ________________
    ____
12. Spouse's attorney, if known: Name: ________________
    Address: ________________ Telephone: ________
    If you have not been served, do you know whether your spouse's attorney is in the process of preparing papers? ________________
    ____

E. CHILDREN OF THIS MARRIAGE

1. List children from this marriage, even if over 18 years of age:

Name	Age	Birthdate	Residing with/at
________	____	________	________

__________ ____ ______ __________

__________ ____ ______ __________

__________ ____ ______ __________

2. If any of your dependent children have income, please describe: ________

3. Do you desire sole custody? ________ Shared custody? ________
   Visitation rights? ________

4. If you anticipate any dispute regarding custody, please state the reasons:

5. If you have been separated, describe any custody sharing or visitation arrangements and how it has been working: ________

6. Do you now have or has your spouse ever expressed doubts as to the paternity of the above children? ________

F. INFORMATION ABOUT PREVIOUS MARRIAGES/RELATIONSHIPS (IF APPLICABLE)

1. Your Previous Marriages/Relationships

   (a) When was the marriage terminated? ________ How? ________

   (b) Do you have children from this previous marriage? _____. If so, please list them (include those over 18 years old).

Name	Age	Birthdate	Dependents?*	Residing With

*i.e., are these children dependents of you or your spouse.

   (c) If you have any children from a non-marital relationship, list them:

Name	Age	Birthdate	Dependents?	Residing With

   (d) If you are paying or receiving support, child support, living expenses, school costs, etc., for any of the above children, please supply details (monthly amount owed per child, amount overdue if any, etc.):

____

____

(e) If any of the above children are receiving other income, such as social security, please describe:

____

____

____

2. Your Spouse's Previous Marriages/Relationships

(a) When was the marriage terminated? ____________ How?____________

(b) Does your spouse have children from this previous marriage? ________ If so, please list them (include those over 18 years old):

Name	Age	Birthdate	Dependents?	Residing With

(c) If your spouse has any children from a non-marital relationship, list them:

Name	Age	Birthdate	Dependents?	Residing With

(d) If your spouse is paying or receiving support, child support, living expenses, school costs, etc., for any of the above children, please supply details (monthly amount owed per child, amount overdue if any, etc.):

____

____

____

(e) If any of the above children are receiving other income, such as social security, please describe:

____

____

____

G. ASSETS

1. Residence of Parties:

(a) Address: ____
(number) (street) (county)

(b) Current name(s) in title:

Husband: ______________ Wife:______________ Other:______________

Method of holding title: Not owned by either of us: _____ (If so, go to (j).)

Joint tenancy: _______ Community Property: _______

Tenancy in Common: _______ Other: _______

(c) If there has been a change of title since this property was originally acquired by either of you, give history: ______________________

____

____

____

(d) The downpayment in the amount of $____________ was made

By: (Amounts) Source: (Post/Pre-marital savings, loan, etc.)

Husband: ______________ ______________________

Wife: ______________ ______________________

Other: ______________ ______________________

(e) Monies originally borrowed to purchase house:

	Amount	Balance Then	Balance Now
(1) First Deed of Trust	________	________	________
(2) Second Deed of Trust	________	________	________
(f) Subsequent Deeds of Trust	________	________	________

(g) Home refinanced? ______________

If so, when? ______________

(h) If the house payment during marriage has not been paid from wages of either party, explain source: ______________________

____

(i) If you or your spouse will claim that residence is not "50/50," explain:

____

____

____

(j) Are most of the furniture, furnishings and appliances, and other tangible personal property items (excluding vehicles) still located in the residence? _________ If not, explain: ______________

____

____

____

2. Other Real Estate:

Rental Properties (RR), Unimproved Land (U), Farms (F), Ranches (R), Commercial Properties (C)

Type (RR, U, F, R, or C)	Address	# Dwelling Units	Purchase Price	Current Market Value
(a)				
(b)				
(c)				
(d)				
(e)				
(f)				

	Current Principal Balance of Trust Deeds	Amount/ Source Downpayment	Title In H/W/ Other	Amount of Negative/Positive Cash Flow
(a)				
(b)				
(c)				
(d)				
(e)				
(f)				

3. Automobiles and other vehicles owned by you and/or your spouse:

Registered Owner H/W/ Other	Year/Make/Model	Amount Owed	Approximate Miles	Condition

4. Bank, savings and loan, credit union accounts or money market funds, treasury bills or certificates of deposit held by you and/or your spouse:

Name(s) on Account H/W/Other	Where Held/ Type of Account	Balance At Separation	Balance Now	Maturity Date	Which Party Received Or Controls (H/W/ Other)

5. Individual retirement accounts (IRA) or Keogh accounts held by you and/or your spouse:

Name(s) on Account H/W/Other	Institution and Branch	Type of Account	Approximate Value/ Amount	Maturity Date If applicable

6. Securities: Mutual funds, bonds, limited partnerships, stocks owned by you and/or your spouse:

In Whose Name H/W/ Other	Broker (if any)	Description Including Number of Shares Or Interest At Separation	Approximate Net Value Today

(Note: if any of the above stock is held in a "margin" account, indicate "M" after the Broker's name.)

7. Life Insurance policies held by you and/or your spouse:

Company	Policy #	Face Value	Whole or Term	Beneficiary	Insured

______	______	______	______	______	______
______	______	______	______	______	______
______	______	______	______	______	______

8. Pension, profit sharing or retirement benefits in which you and/or your spouse have an interest, whether vested or not:

Spouse In Plan H or W	Company/Union	Location	Years In Plan	Description/ Amount of Benefits
______	______	______	______	______
	______	______		______
______	______	______	______	______
	______	______		______
______	______	______	______	______
	______	______		______

9. Identify interests held by you or your spouse in any business, professional practice or corporation (with estimated net values):

____

____

____

____

____

____

10. Tax Returns: What was the last tax return year for which you and your spouse filed joint returns? __________. Is there a refund still owing to you both? __________. If so, $__________ from state; $__________ federal. Please also detail any monies you or your spouse owe for previous returns or for returns due to be filed in the next twelve months.

____

____

____

11. Generally describe any antiques, art, jewelry, oriental rugs, collectibles, or other unique personal property owned by you and/or your spouse:

____

____

____

____

____

H. OBLIGATIONS

	CREDITOR	PURPOSE	LIABLE[1] SPOUSE (H/W)	BALANCE TODAY	BALANCE AT SEPARATION
1.					
2.					
3.					
4.					
5.					

Note: You need not include recurring monthly obligations such as PG&E, Pacific Telephone, etc., unless there is an unusually large debt outstanding.

	PORTION OF DEBT INCURRED DURING MARRIAGE AND BEFORE SEPARATION	ANNUAL INTEREST RATE	MONTHLY PAYMENT	DATE TOTAL BALANCE DUE	WRITTEN AGREEMENT (YES/NO)	RECORDS IN POSSESSION OF H/W
1.						
2.						
3.						
4.						
5.						

[1] Which spouse either verbally or in writing is liable for this because of a direct promise to the creditor? For example, wife may have opened a charge account. If husband has never signed a credit statement nor a charge slip, the answer is "W." If husband has signed on the account, the answer is "H/W."

I. SEPARATE PROPERTY

Definition: Separate property or debts are those arising prior to your marriage. After marriage, separate property is that which is received as gifts or inheritance, or debts connected with the separate property or other debts for the purpose of a spouse's education. After the parties separate, monies earned by a spouse are that spouse's separate property.

1. For any property or debts mentioned previously that are all or partially the separate property of you or your spouse, please put an "S" next to it.

2. Please itemize below any other property or debts not already mentioned that you consider to be your separate property or that of your spouse:

Item	How Acquired	From Whom	Whose S/P
____________	____________	________	______
____________	____________	________	______
____________	____________	________	______
____________	____________	________	______
____________	____________	________	______

3. If you or your spouse has a "gambling habit," note here what losses have occurred of community funds:

____

____

____

J. DIVISION OF PROPERTY AND OBLIGATIONS

1. Have you and your spouse discussed the division of property and obligations? ____________. If so, briefly describe here (if the agreement is exhaustive, it may be better to attach separate sheets or discuss with the attorney handling your case):

____

____

____

____

____

____

____

K. WILLS AND JOINT TENANCY PROPERTIES

1. When was the last time you made a will? __________________

2. List the items of your properties placed in joint tenancy (if any) if not already mentioned previously. If you prefer, for those items listed previously, go back and put "JT" next to that item.

____
____
____
____
____
____

L. OTHER

1. List any problems you foresee in dealing with your spouse either directly or through attorneys (e.g., fear, distrust, dishonesty, vindictiveness, use of children, unwillingness to compromise, etc.):

____
____
____
____
____
____
____
____
____
____

2. Please list other issues you wish to explore with the attorney as well as other information which you believe may be helpful:

____
____
____
____
____

APPROACHES TO DIVISION OF TANGIBLE PERSONAL PROPERTY

The division of household furniture, tools, silver, etc., can most economically be resolved by resort to some of the following methods of division:

1. By Professional Personal Property Appraiser. This brings up the following decisions:

(a) The parties may hire their own appraiser.

(b) The parties may hire a joint appraiser.

(c) In the case of the above, one or both parties may bear the cost.

(d) In the case of the joint appraiser, the parties may agree to be bound ahead of time as to the value.

(e) In the case of the joint appraiser, the parties may agree to be bound ahead of time as to which party gets particular items (for example, they may agree that each party will retain the items they currently possess and that they will be bound by the appraiser's valuation of those items.)

2. Division and Equal Value. The parties may get together and agree that they have divided the property into two piles of equal value. By doing this, the use of the appraiser is no longer necessary. A variation on this would be dividing it into two piles of equal value, assigning an appraiser to value a third pile and deciding to divide it according to the method above.

3. Parties as Appraisers. The parties may decide (with permission of both attorneys as required by State Bar ethical opinions) to get together and value each of the items on their own, reaching bottom line debit figures for the possessions assigned to each. In doing this, the parties should keep in mind the law on this subject: the fair market value is what a willing buyer would pay a willing seller for the items, neither of them being under any undue pressure.

4. The Two-Pile System With a Twist. One party gets to divide the property into two piles; the other party gets to choose the property he or she wishes to have. This is a rather drastic resolution. There would have to be a decision as to which party was the chooser -- perhaps by a flip of a coin or the cut of a deck.

5. A third party may be chosen as binding arbitrator to distribute and evaluate the property. This could be the appraiser. We are unlikely to find volunteers to do this on your behalf.

6. Alternate Choice System. Each of the items can be numbered and the parties can make alternate choices of the numbered items. If there was any dispute or feeling that one party did not trust the other in following through with this, a list of priority items could be made so that the ultimate choice would be self-executing. But if worse came

to worse, a stenographic reporter could be present to take down the stipulation of the parties.

A Variation: The choices could be made with values assigned that will be binding on the parties or without any values assigned, such that each party would receive an equal share with a presumed equal valuation. Obviously, this would be unwise where there was one very large item of personal property with a much higher value than any other item.

7. The Wedding Gift Agreement. To complicate the personal property, much of it was received by either of the parties as wedding gifts. The parties may decide to agree that he keeps those items given by his family and friends; she keeps those items given by her family and friends. There is very rarely one friend which is identified as belonging to both of the parties.

8. Sale of the Personal Property. Occasionally, the matter is so frustrating that the entire lot is put up for sale, a very wasteful practice. Sale may be useful where the parties are choosing alternate items and neither wishes to choose an item they feel is over-valued. Before a sale to third parties is thought of, the parties should think about having an auction as between themselves: whoever is going to pay most for the item gets that item. The parties could submit sealed bids on the disputed item, the highest bidder then receives that item.

9. An Item Donation. The parties may decide to jointly donate the item to Goodwill or to one of their children.

10. Special Note Re Children's Items. According to cases under Civil Code §202, the child's property belongs to the child. Therefore, unless there was a Van Gogh painting hanging in one of your children's rooms, it would be best to concede that the children's bedroom sets were owned by them and have them excluded from the personal property division.

11. Gifts to Each Other. These items belong to the recipient as his or her sole and separate property.

12. Family Photographs and Slides. Divide according to what each wishes. Those desired by both will be duplicated at the expense of both.

Therapist/mediator John Haynes distributes the following financial information sheets to divorcing clients. Note that categories are presented in a manner that promotes future planning and realistic evaluation of needs.[7]

Joint Household
Work Sheet I: Fixed Expenses

Household & Taxes	*Past*	*Future*
Rent or mortgage	$	$
Federal income tax[a]		
State income tax[a]		
City income tax		
Property tax		
Telephone		
Gas/electricity		
Water		
Fuel		
Garbage pick-up		
Cable TV		
Other		
Total	$	$
Insurance[b]		
Life	$	$
Auto		
Health & accident		
Hospitalization		
Fire & theft		
Personal property		
Social security		
Other		
Total	$	$
Installment Payments		
Auto	$	$
Furniture/appliances		
Charge accounts		
Credit cards		
Personal loans		
Christmas/Chanukkah club		
Other		
Total	$	$
Education[b]		
Tuition	$	$

[a]Your federal and state taxes will increase when you file individual returns.
[b]Remember to include cost for self and child(ren) if applicable.

	Past	Future
Room & board		
Books		
Other		
Total	$	$
Transportation		
Auto license plates	$	$
Vehicle sticker		
Parking		
Commuting fare(s)		
Other		
Total	$	$
Personal Allowance		
Self	$	$
Child(ren) cash		
Music lessons		
Aging parents		
Other		
Total	$	$
Memberships		
Union	$	$
Professional associations		
Clubs		
Religious		
Other		
Total	$	$
Miscellaneous		
Forthcoming major repairs	$	$
Emergency fund		
Other		
Total	$	$
Total fixed expenses	$	$

Joint Household
Work Sheet IA: Flexible Expenses

	Past	Future
Food		
Meals at home	$	$
Meals out (including school lunches)		
Total	$	$

	Past	Future
Household Supplies		
Cleaning supplies	$	$
Small home items		
First aid		
Total	$	$
Household Assistance		
Babysitter	$	$
Yard care		
House cleaning		
Total	$	$
Clothing		
New clothes	$	$
Self		
Child(ren)		
Laundry	$	$
Dry cleaning		
Repairs		
Total	$	$
Equipment		
New appliances[a]	$	$
New furniture[a]		
Repairs		
Total	$	$
Home Improvement		
Maintenance	$	$
Replacement[a]		
Total	$	$
Transportation		
Gas/oil	$	$
Auto repair upkeep[a]		
Noncommuting bus/train		
Total	$	$
Health (not covered by insurance)		
Medical	$	$
Dental		
Drugs/medication		
Total	$	$

[a]Make note of any expense with high probability in next two years.

	Past	Future
Personal		
Grooming aids	$	$
Barber/beauty aids		
Extra food		
Theatre/movie		
Sports		
Hobbies		
Vacation		
Newspapers		
Magazines		
Stationery/postage		
Alcohol		
Tobacco		
Home entertainment		
Other		
Total	$	$
Gifts		
Birthdays	$	$
Religious celebrations		
Total	$	$
Contributions		
Religious	$	$
Charity		
Schools/colleges		
Other		
Total	$	$
Total flexible expenses	$	$

Work Sheet III
Net Worth Statement

What You Own	
Cash in checking accounts	$
Cash in savings accounts	
Gov't. bonds @ current value	
Cash surrender value of insurance	
Equity in pension	
Current value of annuities	
Equity in real estate	
Market value of securities	
Bonds	

Stocks
Mutual funds
Investment trusts
Other assets
Total $

What You Owe
Current bills outstanding $
Amount owed on installment purchases
Amount owed on personal loans
Amount due on taxes
Federal/state
Real estate
Other liabilities
Total $
Total assets $
Total liabilities $
Net worth $

Property or assets owned prior to the marriage are normally excluded from this calculation as are inheritances of one party during the marriage. However, there is the question of the appreciation of these items during the marriage; if either of these situations prevail, they will need special consideration.

Work Sheet IV
Material Assets Distribution

You have accumulated many assets over the span of your marriage. As you now plan to separate, how will you divide these assets? If you are planning to move from the present home, what will you need to take with you? If you are the party staying, what must you have to maintain the home? In completing this worksheet, first make an inventory of the major items in each room and then fill in the left-hand column with this inventory. There is no need to itemize every possession; just list those that are important furnishings for that room. Then use this inventory and list what you will need in your new arrangement. For example, you may list under autos two cars, a sedan and a station wagon. Under the *needs* column, you would list what you need, for example, wagon.

Inventory *Needs*
Auto(s)
Appliances
Garden equipment
Sports equipment
Hobby equipment

Inventory	*Needs*
Books	
Records	
Pets	
House plants	
TVs	
Radios	
Paintings	
Mementos	
Furnishings:	
Bedroom 1	
Bedroom 2	
Bedroom 3	
Bedroom 4	
Living room	
Dining room	
Kitchen	
Den	
Other	

Art Bodin uses charts and suggestion sheets to help his clients determine custody issues and to sensitize parents to the needs of their children.

The Planning Form for Child's Contact with Each Parent is graphic and specific. It helps parents visualize the custody arrangement they are making. The bottom portion lists birthdays and holidays that parents commonly pay particular attention to. Agreeing to a holiday schedule averts future problems.

The Parental Activities form is a living document that parents add to as they see fit. Dr. Bodin points out that mothers first gave him items for this form; therefore, this particular form contains more mother/child activities.[8] However, the form is open-ended, so that parents can add to it to make it appropriate for their situation. While it is often used for custody evaluations, it can also be used in mediation to help parents look at both the present and the future in a very specific manner. If parents are having a custody dispute, this will bring into focus how much time each parent actually does spend with the child now. Does the parent truly want custody? Is this a departure from the norm? Does the parent want to take on more or less responsibility for the child? Shall the parents continue to do the same activities with the child? Is there a discrepancy between the way in which each parent views his or her relationship with the child and the way in which the other parent views that relationship? In other words, do both parents think that they usually buy Tom his clothes? Do both of Tom's parents think the other parent is going to parent-teacher conferences, when actually no one is going? This provides an opportunity for parents to realize that Tom requires a great deal of attention and there are plenty of activities for each parent to do with him.

DIPLOMATE IN CLINICAL PSYCHOLOGY
AMERICAN BOARD OF PROFESSIONAL PSYCHOLOGY

DIPLOMATE IN FORENSIC PSYCHOLOGY
AMERICAN BOARD OF FORENSIC PSYCHOLOGY

PLANNING FORM
for
CHILD'S CONTACT WITH EACH PARENT

	M	T	W	Th	F	Sa	Su	M	T	W	Th	F	Sa	Sun
DAY														
NIGHT														

	M	T	W	Th	F	Sa	Su	M	T	W	Th	F	Sa	Sun
DAY														
NIGHT														

	M	T	W	Th	F	Sa	Su	M	T	W	Th	F	Sa	Sun
DAY														
NIGHT														

	M	T	W	Th	F	Sa	Su	M	T	W	Th	F	Sa	Sun
DAY														
NIGHT														

	M	T	W	Th	F	Sa	Su	M	T	W	Th	F	Sa	Sun
DAY														
NIGHT														

Thanksgiving ____________

Christmas (Winter Recess) ____________

Easter (Spring Recess) ____________

Other Religious Holidays ____________

Three/four day weekends ____________

Child's Birthday ____________

Mother's Birthday ____________

Father's Birthday ____________

Mother's Day ____________

Father's Day ____________

PARENTAL ACTIVITIES

Arthur M. Bodin, Ph.D.

Name ______________________________

Please use M _and_ F on each line to show activity both of mother _and_ of father.

	Always	Usually	Equally	Seldom	Never
Buy clothes					
Cut hair					
Take to barber					
Do laundry					
Wash hair					
Cook meals					
Pack lunch/lunch money					
Consult with teachers					
Answer birthday invitations					
Buy gifts for parties					
Buy groceries					
Do dishes					
Prepare meals					
Fill out school papers					
Arrange for sitters					
Put to bed					
Make brush teeth					
Arrange birthday parties					
Take trick or treating					
Make bed, fold/hang clothes					
Set play rules					
Go over school work					
Practice school material					
Tend to minor first aid					
Take to dentist					
Take to doctor					

	Always	Usually	Equally	Seldom	Never
Tend when sick					
Maintain medical records					
Take to school first day					
Discipline					
Mend clothes					
Maintain toys					
Pack for trips					
Take to music lessons					
Take to scouting/club meetings					
Take to camp/day care					
Arrange car pools					
Take to religious school/church					
Take to sport activities					
Attend PTA meetings					
Others (please specify)					

FOOTNOTES

[1] Reprinted with permission of Harriet Whitman Lee as Family Law Counseling Services, Berkeley, California.

[2] Isolina Ricci, from the *Confluent Mediation Handbook*, to be published.

[3] Reprinted with permission of the Association of Family and Conciliation Courts.

[4] Reprinted with permission of Families in Transition, San Francisco, California.

[5] New Harbinger Publications, Oakland, California, 1981.

[6] Reprinted with permission of Barbara DiFranza, San Jose, California.

[7] From John M. Haynes, *Divorce Mediation*. Copyright 1981 by John M. Haynes. Published by Springer Publishing Company, Inc., New York. Used by permission.

[8] Reprinted with permission of Art Bodin, Palo Alto, California.

TEN

AGREEMENTS

This chapter includes agreements to mediate, a memorandum of a separation agreement, child custody agreements, and a marital settlement agreement.

The Northwest Mediation Service presents interested clients with a description of their style of mediation. The clients go over the rules with the mediator, and if they choose to mediate, they sign the Contract to Participate in Mediation.[1] (See Chapter 5 for further information about the Northwest Mediation Service.)

Northwest Mediation Service

27-100th N.E., Bellevue, Washington 98004 (206) 455-3989

RULES OF THE NORTHWEST MEDIATION SERVICE
(Revised March 1982)

1. DEFINITION: WHAT IS THE NORTHWEST MEDIATION SERVICE?

Mediation is a process whereby people discuss their areas of differences and reach agreements with the help of trained resource people. The Northwest Mediation Service is a non-profit organization founded for the purpose of assisting couples in settling areas of disagreement pertaining to divorce or separation conflicts. Mediation is not to be confused with arbitration or litigation. With arbitration, the disputing couple or their attorneys present their differences to a third party or panel who makes the decision for them; with litigation, disputes are presented by both parties, or their attorneys, to a judge who then makes a decision for the parties based on their arguments.

Mediator: a person skilled in assisting persons in resolving their own problems. The Northwest Mediation Service contracts with attorneys and mental health professionals as mediators to provide alternatives and help individuals reach agreements.

2. AGREEMENT OF PARTIES TO MEDIATE

The Northwest Mediation Service will agree to provide mediation services if (1) you have made a joint decision to seek mediation; (2) you have agreed to follow these Northwest Mediation Service rules on mediation; and (3) you have agreed not to take any action inconsistent with the mediation process during the time of mediation; i.e., start a legal action without the prior discussion in mediation. The mediation process shall be deemed to have started upon completion of a written mediation contract between the mediators and the persons involved. A copy of this contract is attached to these rules for your review.

3. SCOPE OF MEDIATION

At the beginning of the mediation process, the parties and the mediators will agree as to the issues to be discussed. These may include, but not be limited to: negotiation of property rights; custody or living arrangements of minor children; financial arrangements for family support or spousal maintenance; family decisions regarding care of the children (religious training, education, health care, daycare, social and psychological care); and, payment of the expense of mediation.

4. ROLE OF MEDIATORS

The role of the mediators will be to help facilitate a dialogue, to identify and evaluate various options to solve the areas of disagreement, and to achieve an agreement after both clients understand various options available to them. You can anticipate meeting with co-mediators, one male and one female, one trained in the legal profession, and one trained in the counseling profession.

The mediators will not be serving as individual counselors, therapists, or attorneys.

Neither of the mediators will act as the attorney or mental health worker for either of the clients. The mediators are acting as resource people only.

Clients are free to consult their own therapist or attorney during the mediation process.

5. COMMUNICATIONS WITH MEDIATORS

All communication between the clients and mediators will be made in the presence of both mediators and both clients, with the exception of routine appointment scheduling.

6. ATTENDANCE AT MEDIATION SESSIONS

It is understood that both parties will be present at all mediation sessions scheduled. Except by advance agreement, no other outside parties will be present. Children for whom custodial arrangements are being made, and other persons having a direct interest in the mediation, may participate in mediation sessions related to their interests if the parties agree.

7. CONFIDENTIALITY

The Northwest Mediation Service, the mediators, and the clients mutually agree that:

a) By utilizing the mediation procedure, the clients are attempting to resolve issues which may be in litigation or are likely to be in litigation at a subsequent date.

b) All communications between the clients and the mediators related to the matters at issue shall not be admissable in evidence at any trial.

c) In consideration for the other client entering into the mediation process, they shall not call a mediator, or any officer or agent of the mediator or of the Northwest Mediation Service or any others involved in the mediation process, as a witness in litigation or any action wherein they may be called upon to testify as to the mediation proceeding; and the clients agree that neither shall seek the production in court of any records or documents made in the course of, or by virtue of, the mediation. The only exception to this rule would be in a case where both clients agree to the use in court of a partial settlement or a document such as a real estate appraisal.

8. FULL DISCLOSURE

Each client shall fully disclose all property and debts and all relevant evidence, such as financial statements, income tax returns, etc, requested by the other client. Any non-disclosed property or debts cannot be legally disposed of and both parties will continue to own or owe these items if not disclosed. Therefore, a final settlement can be reached only when a full disclosure has been made.

9. RESPECT FOR RIGHTS OF OTHERS

Each client agrees to respect the other's physical, emotional, and financial integrity as a requirement of the mediation process.

a) Each will refrain from using physical violence or psychological harassment on the persons involved, including children.

b) Each client agrees not to act unilaterally (without the consent of the other) in regard to property and financial transactions.

c) Violation of this respect may lead to termination of mediation.

10. TERMINATION

The mediation process will be terminated when:

a) The parties attain agreement on the issues; and this agreement is presented to them in letter form by the mediators.

b) By the clients after completion of the hours which they have agreed to in the mediation contract.

c) By the mediators when one or both of the clients do not abide by the mediation contract or the Rules of Mediation.

d) When the clients have considered the options and information available and have not reached an agreement.

e) When the clients agree that issues cannot be resolved by mediation and choose arbitration or litigation as a means to deal with them.

The value of mediation in divorce settlement is extremely positive. The Northwest Mediation Service has provided successful mediation to almost all those who have worked with us since 1977. We look forward to working with you in the future.

The Center for the Development of Mediation and the Law creates the following contract with parties that agree to mediate. Often this contract is an oral agreement between the parties, though sometimes it is written. (See Chapter 6 for further information about the Center for the Development of Mediation and the Law.)[2]

CONTRACT TO PARTICIPATE IN MEDIATION

We, ______________________________, agree to abide
(clients)
by the Rules of the Northwest Mediation Service which we have recieved and read. We agree to pay the sum of $__________ per hour for the services of the mediators when the services are performed, plus a $25.00 set up fee. This will be paid by:

(1) the clients in equal shares; (2) all by ____________________;

(3) the clients in these proportions: ____________________

____

We, ______________________________, agree to abide
(mediators)
by the Rules of the Northwest Mediation Service and to use our utmost effort in helping the clinets reach a mutual agreement on the issues before them.

DATED: ____________________

____________________	____________________
Client	Mediator
____________________	____________________
Client	Mediator

ELEMENTS OF MEDIATOR-PARTIES' CONTRACT

The following represent typical "clauses" we use in oral contracts between the parties and mediator at the outset of a mediation. We commence each mediation by ascertaining some background of the parties with respect to their dispute, why they are in mediation, and their understanding of the mediation process. We emphasize those elements of the contract which seem particularly relevant to them.

The following list is not meant to be definitive. Mediators need to choose a contracting process reflective of their own approach and the parties needs; and as the art of mediation evolves, so does the contracting process.

1. Non-representation. A mediator does not represent either party, and therefore does not assume the role of protector of either as would be the case with an adversary lawyer. The mediator's function is to look at the totality of the situation, and facilitate a resolution of conflict responding to each of the parties' needs and sense of fairness.

2. Future Non-participation. The mediator is unavailable to work for either of the parties as a counselor or advocate in connection with any of the matters arising in the mediation at a later time, nor would s/he be a witness for either of them unless both consented and it was consistent with the mediator's view of the parties' interests.

3. Role of Mediator. The mediator's role is to set the tone, facilitate productive communication, surface assumptions, expectations and feelings, define issues, point to guiding principles, help the parties define and assert their needs and develop options, point out legal and other implications, and draft the agreement.

4. Mutuality of Process. The mediator describes the process of mediation as one to be mutually agreed upon by the parties and mediator, including what items are to be discussed and when. The priority is that a process is used which responds to their most normal ways of behaving with each other, and that is productive. This means that the three of us must agree what issues will be discussed and when. It is important to find common principles to which both parties agree as a basis for creating a framework from which a specific agreement can follow.

5. Non-binding Process. Nothing is binding in a mediation until after an agreement has been reached, drafted, reviewed by lawyers, and then signed. Either party is free to leave at any time. The mediator has no power to decide what agreement the parties should reach.

6. Risks of Process. The mediator describes the risks of mediation, including the risk of coming to an agreement for the sake of agreeing rather than standing up for what each believes to be fair.

7. Good Faith Negotiation. The mediator and parties agree that this is a good faith negotiation and that any statements made by either party would be inadmissible as evidence against the other. The basis for this is to create as much willingness on the part of the parties to say whatever they would like with a minimum of consequence for the adversary process.

8. Full Disclosure. Each party promises to fully disclose any and all relevant facts, documents, etc., requested by the other party that have any possible relevance to the mediation.

9. Confidentiality. The mediator holds all matters confidential as to outsiders, but holds nothing confidential between the parties. If the mediator speaks with either of the parties separately, that information is available to the other party. The mediator will not speak with either of the reviewing lawyers about anything that was said in the mediation unless both parties give permission. The parties also agree that they will hold everything said in the process to be confidential.

10. Lawyer Review. The mediator describes the value of lawyer review. It is important that the parties view the lawyers who review the agreement as consultants to them rather than as lawyers who will take over the case from them. We also discuss and agree upon the timing of lawyer involvement.

11. Participation of Others. We agree upon involvement of others in the process, either directly or indirectly, such as children, appraisers, accountants or psychologists.

12. Expression of Opinion by Mediator. The priority is for the parties to reach an agreement that they each believe to be fair and the mediator will not offer any advice or opinion about any particular issue. There are three exceptions: (1) if the mediator believes that one party is taking advantage of the other; (2) that the parties are reaching an agreement that in the mediator's view appears to be sufficiently unfair that it would be a severe miscarriage of justice; or (3) the mediator believes that a court would not accept the agreement.

13. The Role of Law. The mediator can make predictions about what a court would do and what adversary lawyers would say in a given situation. It is important, however, for the mediator to find a balance between keeping law, or predictions about what a court would do, from taking over or being disregarded as irrelevant.

Ideally the law is part of the mix of things which are relevant in mediation, having no greater or lesser strength than other equally important factors.

14. Splitting of Fees. Unless there is a good reason to adopt some other principle, the mediator seeks agreement to the principle that the parties will split the mediation fees equally.

Family Law Counseling Services has clients sign the following agreement. (See Chapter 9 pp. 145-49, for further information.)[3]

Family Law Counseling Services

1600 Shattuck Avenue Suite #200
Berkeley, CA 94709
548-5551

COUNSELING AGREEMENT

We, ____________________ and ____________________, agree to enter into counseling with Family Law Counseling Services (FLCS) for purposes of developing a working relationship for the parenting of our children during or after our dissolution of marriage proceedings. We do this for the betterment of our children in an effort to minimize the difficulties the dissolution of our marriage may have upon our children and also to better exercise our responsibilities as parents. We also jointly recognize that Court proceedings regarding children and custody and visitation matters can be detrimental to the child and to adults, and we therefore have decided to attempt to resolve these questions ourselves using this manner.

We enter this counseling with the following agreement and under the following conditions, and FLCS agrees to conduct such counseling pursuant to and only pursuant to, such agreement and under such circumstances:

1. All communications between us and any employee, agent, or contractor of FLCS shall be confidential and, in the event of litigation regarding custody of or visitation with our children, or any other matters discussed with any such employee, agent, or contractor of FLCS, neither party shall cause or cause anyone else to call such persons as a witness or to subpoena any of the records of FLCS, or of any of its employees, agents, or contractors.

2. In the event either party causes any agent, employee, or contractor of FLCS to be called as a witness, or causes the records of FLCS, or any of its agents, employees, or contractors to be subpoenaed, the party so causing shall be responsible for paying all of the reasonable costs incurred in quashing any such subpoena.

3. We agree that our purpose in entering into this counseling with FLCS is a form of negotiation with its object the settlement and resolution of those issues which divided us. We agree that it is our intention that nothing that any of us say ("us" to include either party and any employee, agent, or contractor of FLCS) shall ever be used in any court of law. We agree that all statements made by either party, and by any agent, employee, or contractor of FLCS, shall be and hereby is deemed to be "conduct or statements made in negotiation" in the attempt to compromise or settle our disagreements and shall be inadmissible as evidence in any court proceeding pursuant to California Evidence Code Section 1152, and pursuant to this agreement.

4. We agree to sign and to abide by the FLCS Statement of Understanding, a copy of which is attached hereto and made a part hereof by this reference.

5. The parties agree that, prior to the commencement of counseling, they and their attorneys shall execute a stipulation in the form attached hereto and shall file the stipulation with the court and obtain an order of the court as set forth in said document and shall provide copies of said stipulation and order to FLCS.

Dated: ______________________ ______________________________

Dated: ______________________ ______________________________

Family Law Counselors:

Dated: ______________________ ______________________________

Dated: ______________________ ______________________________

NOTE: FLCS is

FAMILY LAW COUNSELING SERVICES
1600 Shattuck Avenue, Suite #200
Berkeley, CA 94709

John Haynes helps his clients write up agreements or memorandums of understanding that clearly state all the agreements made in mediation, and which can be used by the clients to have attorneys draw up a formal agreement. He will use formal or informal language depending upon which is more appropriate for the couple in question. Informal agreements often express attitudes and intentions that cannot be enforced by a court order but which couples wish to document nonetheless.[4]

Memorandum of understanding as precursor to separation agreement using formal language

We have arrived at the following agreements in the process of mediation. These agreements represent a total package, carefully balancing our mutual and individual interests. They are the agreements we wish our respective attorneys to incorporate into the Separation Agreement.

Debts. All debts have been paid. Dan carries a number of credit cards and he will continue to carry them and be solely responsible for all charges made on them.

Personal property. Most of the property will stay in the house. Dan has taken what he needs and we have agreed, to our mutual satisfaction, on the distribution of all personal property. Dan will take the 1970 Dart and the savings account at the Island Federal Savings and Loan Association, while Cindy will take the 1977 Mustang.

Real Estate. We jointly own the following properties:

1. 123 Main Street, Midtown, New York, which is the main house. We intend to rent that out for the next year.
2. Hideaway, Lake Loon, Trailways, New York, which we also will try to rent out for the next year. Each of us will move into new apartments and Cindy will manage the rentals. We will open a joint account into which we will put all of the money from the rents, and each year, after all the expenses have been paid, we will share the surplus equally. If there is a deficit we will share that equally.

Joint savings. We hold a long-term savings certificate at the Island Federal Savings and Loan Association. We want to maintain joint ownership of that certificate until it matures and then we will split the proceeds equally.

Alimony. We have agreed that there will be no alimony. Rather, all the support will be in the form of child support.

Custody. Cindy will have custody of Kriss for the next two years. At the end of the two years we will review how this has worked. We have both shared equal parental responsibility in bringing up Kriss and wish to continue to do so. To do this we wish to incorporate the attached parenting clauses into the final agreement. [1]

Child support. Dan will pay Cindy $600 a month in child support. He is paid monthly and will send the $600 to Cindy within three days of his pay day. This $600 is 60 percent of Dan's net take-home pay from his teaching job (gross income, less taxes, social security, disability, medical insurance, and pension contributions). Dan will continue to pay child support equal to 60 percent of his teaching salary until Cindy earns a gross salary of $8,000 a

[1]These clauses are items 7–12 and 14 in the actual separation agreement.

year. When Cindy's gross income exceeds $8,000 a year, Dan's percentage of his net will be reduced as follows:

When Cindy's Gross Income Is:	Dan's Payments For Child Support Shall Be Reduced to This % of His Take-Home Pay:
$ 8,001–9,000	50%
9,001–10,000	40%
10,001–12,000	30%
12,001–14,000	20%
Equal to Dan's	10%

These payments are to continue until Kriss reaches age 21. If Kriss is unmarried and financially dependent after age 21, Dan will provide support directly to Kriss. If Cindy remarries then the child support shall be reduced to 20 percent, regardless of Cindy's income, and to 10 percent if Cindy's income equals Dan's. If, two years from now, we agree to change custody of Kriss from Cindy to Dan, then Dan will not pay any support to Cindy. Dan will continue to cover Cindy and Kriss on his medical insurance at work for as long as he is permitted by his employer.

Income taxes. Dan will claim Kriss as a dependent for federal and state tax purposes. Dan and Cindy will continue to file joint tax returns for as long as it is permitted by law. We will share in any taxes due and any refunds in the same proportion as our respective incomes declared on the tax return.

Life insurance. Dan will maintain life insurance in the amount of $75,000, naming Cindy and Kriss as beneficiaries. He will not revoke them as beneficiaries before Kriss reaches age 21, or completes four years of college. In either event, on Kriss's 22nd birthday he is free to designate any beneficiary he desires.

Savings account for Kriss. Dan and Cindy plan to use the income from the rentals to establish a savings account for Kriss, primarily for her college education. Each year we will decide how much to place into the account and we will contribute equally that amount each year.

Arbitration. Having reached this agreement through mediation, we wish to provide that if we cannot reach agreement on any significant issue regarding Kriss that we agree to submit the dispute to a third person to act as an arbitrator. We will choose the arbitrator from either John M. Haynes (our mediator) or the panel of arbitrators of the Family Dispute Panel of the American Arbitration Association of Nassau County.

Agreement using formal language[2]

AGREEMENT made this 12th day of May, 1978, by and between Cindy Smith, residing at 123 Main Street, Midtown, New York (hereinafter referred to as the "Wife" or "Cindy"), and Daniel Smith, residing at 123 First Street, Midtown, New York (hereinafter referred to as the "Husband" or "Dan").

W I T N E S S E T H

WHEREAS, the Wife and the Husband were married on August 19, 1960, in Queens County, New York, and thereafter lived together in the State of New York; and

WHEREAS, one child, namely, Kriss M. Smith (hereinafter referred to as "Kriss") was born of this marriage on October 28, 1965; and

WHEREAS, in consequence of disputes and irreconcilable differences between them, the parties have separated and are living apart;

NOW, THEREFORE, in view of their intention to live apart for the rest of their lives, and to settle their respective property rights, past, present, and future, the parties promise and agree as follows:

1. *Separation of the Parties*. The Wife and the Husband shall at all times live and continue to live separately and apart from each other and dispose of property as he or she may deem fit, free from control, restraint or interference, directly or indirectly, by the other in all respects as if each were sole and unmarried, except as herein otherwise provided.

2. *Payment of Outstanding Obligations*. All mutual household obligations of the parties have been paid, except those noted in Section 3. It is agreed that all credit cards, accounts, and obligations currently held by

---

[2]This is the full separation agreement drafted by the attorneys. It incorporates the agreements reached in mediation. Those agreements are in sections 2–18, and 25.

Agreement using nonlegal language

This agreement is entered into by Jean   and Jack   out of a deep respect for each other and a shared love for our son Josh.

Although we are no longer living together, we wish to protect our individual and joint concerns for Josh. Jean will shortly leave for Oregon. It is agreed that she will take Josh and be responsible for him from the time she leaves New York until on or about March 31, 1978. During that time she will provide Jack with her location at all times so that he may be in telephone contact and be able to communicate with his son at all times.

It is also understood that by mutual consent, Josh and/or Jean shall return to New York for the period including the Chanukka and Christmas holidays so that Josh can be with his father at these holidays.

On or about March 31, 1978, by mutual consent of Jean and Jack, Josh will return to New York to live with his father for six months. During that time Jack will be responsible for Josh and shall ensure that Josh will be available to Jean for telephone or other form of communication that Jean should want to use.

At the end of those six months, on or about September 30, 1978, by mutual agreement, Josh shall return to wherever Jean is residing to live with her for the following six months. The same conditions will prevail as in the previous custody period.

On or about March 31, 1979, Josh shall return to wherever Jack is residing to live for the following six months with his father. The same conditions of the previous six months shall operate during this custody period.

During the summer of 1979 we will review the experiences of the previous two years and attempt to determine the living arrangement that is best suited for Josh. At that time we will attempt to develop a workable permanent solution that, as in this agreement, recognizes the love and concern each has for Josh.

We anticipate that Josh will enter regular grade school in September 1979. We agree that it will be in Josh's best interest to reside with one parent during the regular school year and with the other parent during the summer months once regular school begins, with holiday visitations arranged as feasible.

We recognize that in order to implement this agreement there is a need to establish a fund to pay the expenses of travel from the East to the West and vice versa. Therefore, we agree to open a joint savings account and to each pay $10 per week into the account. The account shall be opened in our joint names in trust for Josh.

The first payment shall be for the week ending Friday, August 19, 1977, with payments to continue for the life of this agreement. Funds shall be withdrawn from this account only by mutual consent of Jean and Jack for the expenses incurred in traveling under the terms of this agreement.

Therefore, if there are sufficient funds by December 1977, either Josh and/or Jean shall come East to visit with Jack for the holidays or Jack will go West for the holidays.

At the end of each custody period, funds shall be withdrawn by mutual agreement to pay the expenses incurred in getting Josh from one parent to the other.

If either Jean or Jack wishes to visit Josh at any time other than the December holidays at her/his own expense, the other parent agrees to assist in making whatever arrangements are needed locally to accommodate such a visit.

It is recognized and hoped that the expenses incurred in implementing this agreement will not exceed the payments made into the joint account and that there will be a surplus in the account at the end of the two years. Such surplus shall stay in the account in trust for Josh to be given to him on his eighteenth birthday.

We recognize that this is a temporary solution to the problem of custody, and we each agree to work toward a permanent solution that will be based on the experiences of the next two years.

Jean

John

The following sample temporary child custody and visitation agreement was written by Art Bodin. Agreements are written so that attorneys can use them to write more formal temporary or final marital settlement agreements.[5]

OUR PROPOSED AGREEMENT

This agreement is entered into by Mr. and Mrs. Q out of respect for each other and shared love for our son.

Although we no longer live together, we wish to continue exercizing co-parental responsibility through cooperation in dealing with our concerns for our son. We believe that he will be benefitted by frequent and continuing contact with both parents.

To fit our current work schedules, we agree to continue the arrangement we have basically been following since November, 1982, unless and until there may be significant difficulties posed by changes in either of our work schedules. Specifically, as illustrated in the attached Planning Form for Child's Contact with Each Parent, our son will be with his father from Sunday morning at 8:30 am through Tuesday evening at 6:00 pm (Wednesday morning at 8:30 am on alternate weeks, coinciding with mother's Tuesday night work shifts). He will be with his mother from Tuesday evening or Wednesday morning (alternative weeks as explained above) through Sunday morning at 8:30.

If either parent cannot be present during all or part of his or her regular time with the son, that parent agrees that as a first step, he or she will ask the other parent whether he or she wishes or is able to have the son, during that time. Mother's parents would be the next people asked by the parent who will be absent. If they are not available, then the parent who will be absent will be responsible for arranging and paying any costs for child care.

Exceptions in following this schedule may be requested by the other parent, preferably one week in advance, but at any time prior to the actual proposed transition between parents. All such exceptions will be discussed and cleared with the other parent without the son listening, and before any discussion with the son, about what might be done with this newly available time. Reasons may be explained in presenting such proposed exceptions; no reasons need be given for agreeing or not agreeing to the exception requested. The same request may not be made again for that occasion. Refusals shall cover only the occasion in question.

Mother's parents (father's are deceased) will continue to have frequent contact with the son, through joining mother and for some activities and through "babysitting." In addition, father has the option of initiating through his request both these kinds of contact between the son and his grandparents.

Holidays will be arranged as follows: son will spend Christmas eve with mother and Christmas day with father in 1983 and the reverse thereafter. In odd numbered years son will spend Thanksgiving with mother and Easter with father, and vice versa in even numbered years. The parent with whom son spends a particular holiday has the option, if going away, of being with son for the whole holiday weekend or any portion of it.

The child's birthday will be spent with whichever parent he is scheduled to be on that day, with sequential (not simultaneous) sharing by prearrangement between mother and father, following the procedures already outlined for exceptions.

Son, will spend Father's Day with father and Mother's Day with mother. For the latter father will have the option of a compensatory day since Mother's day falls on a Sunday.

Marital settlement agreements can be written in an infinite number of ways, ranging from the very formal to the very informal. Many states now have books for couples who want to do their own divorce, and the books provide one or two examples. California has a number of no-fault-divorce books.

The following marital settlement agreement is reprinted from Nolo Press's *How to Do Your Own Divorce in California.*[6] The agreement contains most of the essential elements for any marital settlement agreement. Certain formal language is geared to specific requirements of the state. Couples should make sure that any agreement they draw up themselves is current, and appropriate for their situation.

SETTLEMENT AGREEMENTS

If you have any trouble at all understanding the contract, or wording it to fit your own circumstances, do not attempt to do your own. Don't try to do your own if you have a big, intricate estate. If you want to have a contract anyway, get help (see A12). Perhaps you can find an attorney who will prepare a contract for you, then you can do the rest yourself.

Many aspects of any marital settlement agreement can have tax consequences. Be sure to review Tax Information Publication #504 (see Chapter A12). Depending upon what property you have, you may save a lot of money by seeing a tax expert before making this agreement.

You will need an original, a copy for Respondent, and three other copies. Attach the original contract to the original Interlocutory Judgment and a copy of the contract to each copy of the Interlocutory Judgment. Take these to court at the time of the hearing. Sacramento County wants a copy of the marital contract attached to the Petition if it is completed at that time.

MARITAL SETTLEMENT AGREEMENT

I, _______________, Husband, and I, _______________, Wife, agree as follows:

I. GENERALLY: We are now husband and wife. We were married on __________, 19__, and separated on __________, 19__. We make this agreement with reference to the following facts:

A. Children: There are
(a) no children
(b) the following minor children of the parties (list by full name and give birth date of each).

B. Unhappy and irreconcilable differences have arisen between us which have caused the irremediable breakdown of our marriage. We now desire and agree to completely settle all of our mutual rights and duties by this agreement.

II. SEPARATION: We agree to live separately and apart, and, except for the duties and obligations imposed and assumed under this agreement, each shall be free from interference and control of the other as fully as if he or she were single. We agree not to molest, interfere with, or harass the other.

III. CUSTODY OF CHILDREN:
(a) The Wife
(b) The Husband
(c) Husband and Wife, jointly
(d) _____(other)_____

shall have the care, custody and control of the minor child(ren) of the parties, subject to the right of the other spouse to visit said child(ren)
(a) at reasonable times and places
(b) as follows: ______________________________

IV. SUPPORT OF CHILDREN: Subject to the power of the court to modify the same, _______ shall pay to _______, as and for child support, the sum of $_____ per month per child, a total of $_____ per month, payable on the ___ day of each month, beginning on the ___ day of ________, 19__, and continuing for each child until said child dies, marries, becomes self-supporting, or reaches the age of _____, whichever occurs first.

Optional: In addition, during the term of the support obligation for each child, _______________ shall

(a) carry and maintain medical and hospital insurance for the benefit of said child;

(b) pay for said child's required/extraordinary medical and dental expenses (to the extent of his ability to do so).

(c) carry and maintain a policy of life insurance in the amount of $_______, and shall name as beneficiaries (Wife/Husband/said minor children).

V. PAYMENTS TO SPOUSE: (use A or B)

A. Waiver of Right to Support: In consideration of the other terms of this agreement, both parties waive all right or claim which they may now or may at any future time have to receive support or maintenance from the other. (See Chapter D regarding effect of waiver.)

B. In consideration of the other terms of this marital settlement agreement, _______________ agrees to pay _____________ the sum of $_____ per month, payable on the ____ day of each month, beginning 19__, and continuing until (the death of either party/remarriage of the recipient/(some date or condition)) whichever shall occur first. The parties intend that this amount (may/may not) be modified by court action in the future.

VI. PROPERTY TRANSFERRED TO WIFE: Husband transfers and quitclaims to Wife all his right, title, and interest in the following items: (list and indicate value of each item).

VII. PROPERTY TRANSFERRED TO HUSBAND: Wife transfers and quitclaims to Husband all her right, title, and interest in the following items: (list and indicate value of each item).

Note about Pension Plans: If there is a community interest in a pension plan, be sure to deal with it clearly in this agreement. If it is to be given entirely to the employee spouse, list it in item VI or VII. If there is to be a waiver, put it in here, using the language suggested in Chapter B3c as your guide. If the matter is to be reserved for the future, put that in here like this: VIII. PENSION PLAN. The parties intend that the community interest in the pension plan of (Husband/Wife), (full identification of plan), will be valued and divided when the employee-spouse first becomes eligible to receive payments under said plan. To this end, the parties agree to keep each other notified of changes in address and of any changes in pension plan provisions. (Employee spouse) specifically agrees not to apply for or accept benefits under said plan without prior written notice to (other spouse) and application to a court for determination and division of community property rights in said plan.

Note about separate property: If there is separate property or obligations that you want clearly confirmed as such, put that in like this: VIII. SEPARATE PROPERTY. The parties agree that the assets and obligations listed below are the separate property of (Husband/Wife) and are hereby confirmed as such: (list).

Alternative Method to Divide Property
(for cases with little or no significant property)

Husband and Wife agree that they have already divided their property to their mutual satisfaction, and each hereby transfers and quitclaims to the other any and all interest in any property in the possession of the other, and agrees that whatever property the other may possess is now the sole and separate property of the other.

VIII. DEBTS:

Husband shall pay the following debts, and indemnify and hold Wife harmless therefrom: (list).

Wife shall pay the following debts, and indemnify and hold Husband harmless therefrom: (list).

Husband and Wife each promise the other that they shall not incur any debt or obligation for which the other may be liable, and each agrees that if any cliam be brought seeking to hold one liable for the subsequent debts of the other, or for any act or omission of the other, then each will hold the other harmless, and defend such claim.

IX. TAXES:

A. Any tax refunds for the current fiscal year shall be distributed as follows: (specify).

B. Any deficiencies for the current year shall be paid as follows: (specify).

C. (Husband/Wife) may cliam the tax exemption for (name of children). Optional: ...for any year in which support payments for said child are not over two months in arrears.

X. EXECUTION OF INSTRUMENTS: Each agrees to execute and deliver any documents, make all endorsements, and do all acts which are necessary or convenient to carry out the terms of this agreement.

XI. PRESENTATION TO COURT: This agreement hsall be presented to the court for incorporation and merger into the Interlocutory Judgment in any dissolution proceeding between the parties.

XII. DISCLOSURES: Each party has made a full and honest disclosure to the other of all current finances and assets, and each enters into this agreement in reliance thereon.

XIII. BINDING EFFECT: This agreement, and each provision thereof, is expressly made binding upon the heirs, assigns, executors, administrators, representatives, and successors in interest of each party.

Dated: ______________________
Husband

Dated: ______________________
Wife

FOOTNOTES

[1]Reprinted with permission of the Northwest Mediation Service, Bellvue, Washington.

[2]Reprinted with permission of the Center for the Development of Mediation and the Law, Mill Valley, California.

[3]Reprinted with the permission of Harriet Whitman Lee as Family Law Counseling Services, Berkeley, California.

[4]From John M. Haynes, *Divorce Mediation*. Copyright 1981 by John M. Haynes. Published by Springer Publishing Company, Inc., New York. Used by permission.

[5]Reprinted with the permission of Art Bodin, Palo Alto, California.

[6]Charles E. Sherman, *How to Do Your Own Divorce in California* (Occidental, Calif.: Nolo Press, 1982).

ELEVEN

FINDING MEDIATORS AND TRAINING ORGANIZATIONS

Finding a mediator may take a bit more effort than simply looking in the yellow pages. If the yellow pages in your community do not yet have a listing for mediation, you might contact any of the following: the local court clerk or court-connected family unit, your local bar association, or the Marriage and Family Counselors Association or other mental health professionals organizations. Another possibility is to contact one of the national associations of mediators. Many of these organizations provide training, and maintain a list of members and professionals they have trained.

Academy of Family Mediators
111 4th Ave., Suite IV
New York, N.Y. 10003

American Arbitration Association
140 S. 51st St.
New York, N.Y. 10020

American Bar Association
Special Committee on Alternative Means of Dispute Resolution
1800 M Street, NW
Washington, D.C. 20036

Association of Family and Conciliation Courts
Nova University Law Center
3100 SW 9th Ave.
Ft. Lauderdale, Fla. 33315

Divorce Mediation Research Project
1720 Emerson Street
Denver, Colo. 80218

Family Mediation Association
5200 Wisconsin Ave. Suite 1250
Chevy Chase, Md. 20815

Society of Professionals in Dispute Resolution (SPIDR)
American Arbitration Association
1730 Rhode Island Ave. NW
Washington, D.C. 20036

PUBLICATIONS THAT LIST MEDIATION SERVICES

In May 1982 the Divorce Mediation Research Project published the Directory of Mediation Services, 1982. (Jessica Pearson, Ph.D., Director, 1982, Association of Family Conciliation Courts. To purchase a copy, send $10 to The Divorce Mediation Research Project, 1720 Emerson Street, Denver, Colo. 80218.) To date, it is the most complete source of information about divorce mediation services. (The American Bar Association also publishes a mediation directory, but it is not focused on divorce mediation.) The information it provides is derived from 1100 questionnaires sent to individuals and organizations during the summer and fall of 1981, primarily members of the Association of Family Conciliation Courts and the Family Mediation Association. Approximately 300 groups and individuals responded in time to be included in the first edition. One hundred and twenty-two of the directory's 138 pages are devoted to "service providers." An alphabetical, state-by-state synopsis lists the names, addresses, and phone numbers of mediators in addition to the following data:

1. Court-connected or private
2. Funding
3. Year mediation was first offered by the service
4. Other services offered to clients
5. Number of cases mediated in 1980
6. Type of mediation provided (for example, child custody)
7. Degrees and licenses held by staff
8. Mediation training received by staff
9. Format of mediation (for example, typical number and length of sessions, who drafts the agreement, use of attorney, conjoint or individual sessions)

Not every listing covers all these areas, because some questionnaires were not complete. There has been no verification of the information or evaluation of the quality of services listed. Providers have been listed as they describe themselves.

Many practices were only started in 1981 and therefore mediated no cases in 1980. A significant portion of the private mediators reported under five cases mediated in 1980. Public mediators typically reported caseloads ranging in the hundreds.

The second section briefly describes twelve organizations for laypeople and/or mediators interested in alternative dispute resolution. Contact information, an organizational summary, training, certification, and conference offerings are briefly mentioned.

The final section is devoted to mediation trainers and gives the names and addresses of seventy organizations or individuals who do mediation training.

The following chart provides an overview of the state-by-state response of mediators contacted. The first column refers to the number of court-connected mediation services that responded in any one state. Column two is a state-by-state list of the number of private mental health professional/mediators. Column three lists attorneys or cross-trained attorney/mental health professionals. Column four lists the number of separate private practices per state. (One might guess that a state that boasts a large number of mediators has many mediation practices. This is not necessarily an accurate indication of the number of operational practices because of the radical variance from sole practitioner to collective.)

Some practices have as many as twenty professionals associated with them. Column five indicates the number of private mediators that have received training in structured mediation. This is noted so that readers can gain an idea of the influence structured mediation has had in some states.

STATE	C.C.	MHPS	ATYS	SPP	SMED
Alabama	0	2	0	2	1
Alaska	1	0	0	0	0
Arizona	3	13	3	7	13
California	82	104	27	45	11
Colorado	1	21	7	7	12
Connecticut	2	20	3	11	7
Delaware	1	0	0	0	0
District of Columbia	0	3	1	4	3
Florida	1	34	0	11	11
Georgia	0	8	2	5	0
Hawaii	1	5	0	2	0
Idaho	0	1	0	1	1
Illinois	1	23	0	8	12
Indiana	1	22	4	8	6
Iowa	0	13	0	5	2
Kentucky	1	1	1	2	1
Louisiana	0	1	1	2	1
Maine	1	5	4	6	0
Maryland	0	47	10	26	50
Massachusetts	2	21	7	9	1
Michigan	2	21	7	9	1
Minnesota	2	7	1	4	8
Missouri	1	6	0	1	0
Montana	2	0	0	0	0
Nebraska	1	0	0	0	0
Nevada	0	8	0	3	3
New Hampshire	0	5	1	2	1
New Jersey	0	51	1	11	5

STATE	C.C.	MHPS	ATYS	SPP	SMED
New Mexico	0	1	0	1	0
New York	0	35	3	24	12
North Carolina	0	2	0	1	2
Ohio	2	21	9	9	7
Oklahoma	1	0	1	1	0
Oregon	3	24	11	4	14
Pennsylvania	0	18	4	10	12
Rhode Island	0	1	0	1	1
South Carolina	0	4	0	2	2
South Dakota	0	1	0	1	0
Tennessee	0	1	0	1	0
Texas	1	25	2	11	2
Vermont	0	5	0	3	0
Virginia	3	14	7	10	15
Washington	2	10	4	6	0
Wisconsin	3	5	0	2	5

This is by no means a complete list of available mediators. The directory reports that mediation services are already offered in forty-four states; many of those opened in 1981. In 1982 and 1983 mediation services have continued to multiply rapidly. Local and national professional associations should be able to provide the most current possible information.

TWELVE

TRAINING MATERIALS

The following descriptions of the stages of mediation, patterns underlying conflict, principles for resolution, and techniques for resolution were created by Gary Friedman and associates at the Center for the Development of Mediation in the Law. They are used for training attorneys in the theory and practice of mediation.

THE STAGES OF MEDIATION

The following five stages, in our experience, generally characterize the development of a mediation. While the first and last stages -- "contracting" and "concluding" -- clearly occur at the beginning and end, the intermediate stages tend to intersect and to repeat.

I. CONTRACTING

In this stage, the mediator has three principal goals: determining the suitability of mediation, setting tone and structure, and contracting with the parties.

Initially, the mediator elicits general information about the background of the dispute. The mediator then ascertains the parties' understanding of mediation and explains the mediation process. Once preliminary information has been determined and there is some general underestanding of the mediation process, a determination is made by both mediator and parties as to the suitability of mediation, both to the particular dispute and for the parties.

If an initial determination to go forward is reached, the mediator and parties then enter into an agreement about their working relationship and allocation of responsibility during the mediation process. It should be borne in mind that usually many of the ground rules which are established during this stage of the process need either to be reexplained or reestablished as a later phase of the mediation. At this early point, the parties are lacking in familiarity with the process, or are so focused on their own nervousness that it is difficult to reach real agreement regarding the working relationship. (For further details regarding the specifics of the contract, see memorandum on ELEMENTS OF THE MEDIATOR-PARTIES' CONTRACT.)

In addition to explaining the elements of the process, the mediator needs to set the tone of the process: to create informality, directness, receptivity, and to work toward establishing contact between the parties and between him/herself and the parties. As part of establishing the structure of the process, the mediator seeks to set the stage for movement toward common principles for the work of mediation. Part of the mediator's role at this point is to begin to help the parties open to the possibility that an agreement might be reached which would meet all of their needs, one which would not represent a compromise or tradeoff wherein each party can only seek to have his/her needs met at the expense of the other.

II. DEVELOPING THE ISSUES

In this stage, the goal of the mediator and parties is to get out all of the information necessary in order to identify the particular issues needing resolution and the dimension of those issues. This involves identifying all relevant facts including economic and emotional factors involved in each party's view of any particular issue. It also means clarifying the factual agreements, as well as the factual disputes, that exist between the parties, so that there is some understanding as to what has already been resolved, and what needs to be resolved as part of the mediation process.

During this informational stage, it is particularly important that the mediator allow the parties' room to explain the significance of any particular issue to them fully. The mediator can begin to notice the patterns between the parties in talking about these issues, such as blame or accommodation, and to begin to hold the parties to the agreements made in the contracting stage about the way in which they will approach the issues. This means that the mediator is continually focusing on both what the parties describe as the content of the issues and how the parties talk about these issues. The information the mediator obtains about how the parties are dealing with these issues with each other is an indication of what might need to happen on an emotional level between the parties, as well as what factual and legal content would need to be addressed in resolving a particular issue.

This stage can be facilitated by the parties each making outlines in writing outside the mediation sessions covering such details as assets, income, living costs, etc., and to bring them to the mediation. It can also be important at this point for many individuals to more fully understand the legal dimensions of issues, and parties may feel a need to consult a lawyer during this part of the process. The need to understand the details about information on any particular issue may also involve working with appraisers, accountants, or real estate brokers.

It is critical at this stage that no option be dismissed as unworkable. There is a tendency on the part of parties to dismiss certain kinds of resolutions or to refuse to explore certain kinds of issues because they feel that the resolutions they have in mind would be unacceptable to the other person. At this point, it is important that options are explored without judgment as to which options are going to be most workable in the situation. It is similarly important that no one fixed position by either party be established or determined to be immutable. By continually focusing on the importance of any ultimate resolution meeting the needs of both parties, overly rigid positions that either party might take can be defused and deferred pending an understanding by everyone of the larger context.

III. RESOLVING CONFLICT

The major work of this stage is for the mediator to help the parties to move past unproductive patterns of conflict that exist between them, and to work toward collaborative and productive ways of exploring the issues. The most essential aspect of this process is the identification by each party of their respective needs underlying specific concrete issues and moving toward resolution based on a mutual sense of fairness.

Through identification of underlying needs which are usually less narrowly concrete than any particular object, a multiplicity of options arises. A useful way of identifying underlying needs is for the parties to explore assumptions or feelings which have not been explored around a particular issue. By recognizing those needs that the parties have that are not in conflict, the mediator may uncover existing areas of agreement which can then form a basis for dealing with further issues.

Here, the mediator and parties begin to develop concrete options to explore and to play out the effects and consequences of each option without closing off any particular option. In helping each party identify and assert their own needs, the mediator needs to attend to the level of communication between the parties in order to determine exactly what differences do exist. It is also important that the mediator help the parties begin to recognize and appreciate the reality of the other person, including their needs. As the mediator works with the parties in this way, s/he is beginning to create cooperative patterns between the two of them, helping each to listen to the other and understand the importance of the other's needs while continuing to identify and assert their own.

This is also the place where common principles between the parties, both in terms of their motivation to use the mediation process and what is important to them in the content of the issues they are dealing with, can begin to be brought into play by the mediator as a way of helping parties focus on meeting both their own and each other's needs.

A useful shorthand for viewing the process of conflict resolution appears in the memorandum on PATTERNS, PRINCIPLES and TECHNIQUES. The mediator helps identify non-productive patterns of conflict and, based on the underlying principles of autonomy and mutuality, create a collaborative context for conflict resolution. Various techniques are outlined therein which can be employed in service of that end.

IV. REACHING AGREEMENT

During this stage, specific choices are made by the parties regarding not only their needs, but the concrete resolution of particular issues. It is important that any agreement reached on any particular issue be viewed as tentative, subject to review upon the resolution of all issues, so that neither party feels that an agreement which has been reached is immutable. This keeps the parties more fluid and open and allows them to reality test any particular solution over time. The tendency of the parties toward premature closure needs to be counteracted by the mediator, even when it appears that a particular agreement is in sight.

This is the time for the mediator to be giving feedback to the parties regarding whether any particular agreement is realistic and to be doing this in a way that does not assert the mediator's view, but asks the questions of the parties that need to be asked to determine whether the parties have fully understood the implications of any particular issue. As part of that process, it can be valuable for the parties to look at the impact of any of the alternatives which they are exploring on other people, such as children, and to examine the issue in relationship to a period of time over which the agreement will be working.

This is also the time for the mediator to include the legal context in a way that neither disregards law as irrelevant nor has it control the parties and keep them from using their own sense of fairness as the most important resting point for making choices among the alternatives. Here, the mediator's job is to work creatively with the parties to fashion possible resolutions that honor the persons and relationship of the particular parties, as well as the circumstances of their lives. To do so, both the mediator and parties may have to look beyond the norms of legal rules or customs to the deeper principles and concerns at stake.

V. CONCLUDING

Once the concrete agreement has been reached, the mediator enters into the task of drafting the agreement. It is important to use the words in drafting the agreement which are both understandable to the parties and reflect as accurately as possible both their intentions as to what the agreement is and how it will take effect. It is also useful to be clear about any areas which remain unresolved, and to articulate a process for resolving these issues.

This is also the stage where the parties can have their agreement reviewed by accountants, lawyers and others to determine whether any input from any of these "experts" affects the parties' view of both the fairness and the practicalities of the agreement. Particularly critical at this juncture is for the parties to orchestrate both the timing and consultation with these experts and to be using them as consultants rather than as "professionals" who take over with their view of what the parties should be doing, or who inject their views of how the parties should be looking at their lives. The parties need to determine both how they wish to use the expert and what weight to give the expert's view. Mediator contact with reviewing attorneys and others should also be done with care, mindful of the tendency of both mediator and experts to decide what the parties should do.

Similarly, the mediator should not become attached to the specific agreement reached as the best result of the parties, or as the result which should be adhered to regardless of its impact on the parties. Flexibility on the part of the mediator and a willingness to continue to explore with the parties can be helpful to the parties in determining whether or not the agreement needs to be modified or altered in any way.

Finally, once the agreement has been fully reviewed and modified if necessary, then the agreement is executed (signed) by the parties, and the decision is made as to whether or not the agreement shall be entered in court. The parties can take responsibility for preparation and/or filing of the papers in court if they wish, which can represent both a reaffirmation of their responsibility and control over the process and a real recognition of the degree to which they have been empowered. This kind of affirmation of the significance of the mediation process can also be achieved in other ways.

* PATTERNS, PRINCIPLES & TECHNIQUES *

We have found certain repetitive patterns within and between parties in conflict. Through awareness of the patterns, it is possible to draw upon principles underlying mediation to reach resolution. Individual mediators must be alert to recognize new patterns, principles and techniques, or to clarify or reconceptualize these patterns to make these models responsive to the individual situation. The following lists are not meant to be exhaustive.

* PATTERNS UNDERLYING CONFLICT

The mediator's ability to recognize patterns underlying conflict and, where appropriate, to make those observations explicit to the parties, can be crucial to effective mediation. Although these behaviors cross a wide range of categories, it can be useful to think of them in relation to the groupings of avoidance of process (refusal to enter in), attempting to control (the process or other party), or attempting to accommodate to the other party or standards of the law. Examples follow.

Avoidance:
- overwhelmed by complexity
- avoidance of feelings
- avoiding differences
- overwhelmed by emotional charge
- wanting it over with
- indecision
- withdrawal

Control:
- threatening
- blame
- seeing only one's own interest
- emphasis on disagreements
- rigidity of positions
- dominating other party or process

Accommodation:
- giving in
- deference to law or mediator
- emphasis on personal inadequacy
- failure to assert own needs

* PRINCIPLES FOR RESOLUTION

Certain principles underlying the mediation process can be helpful as referrent points for the mediator and parties in working through the conflict. These principles represent a balance of autonomy and mutuality or being willing to be fair to oneself and fair to the other person. Some of these principles:

- honoring each party's needs
- assumption of responsibility
- parties' sense of fairness
- mutuality - working together

* TECHNIQUES FOR RESOLUTION

In order to facilitate the mediation process, both in dealing with the patterns and honoring the principles, a variety of techniques can be helpful. These techniques are most effective when linked to the underlying principles. Again, the goal is to create a context where both parties' needs can be identified, honored and met.

- Simplicity, specification and categorization:
  - separate issues
  - identify steps to be taken
- Tapping motivation for being in mediation:
  - ask why parties want mediation
- Identification of all needs and interests:
  - articulate need underlying position
  - making positive assertions
- Appreciation of others' reality and limitation of own view:
  - role reversal
- Orienting to the present and future:
  - turning focus from past to future relevance
- Recognizing mutuality of problem:
  - identify consequences and parameters of problems
  - focus on problems, not people
- Fluidity:
  - inventing new options, keeping them open
  - recognizing multiplicity of answers
- Defuse pressure:
  - allow time
  - humor
  - ventiliation of negativity
- Expanding the pie:
  - pointing out overlapping or shared interests

INDEX